Matters Gray and White

ALSO BY RUSSELL MARTIN

Cowboy: The Enduring Myth of the Wild West
Entering Space: An Astronaut's Odyssey (with Joseph P. Allen)
Writers of the Purple Sage (coeditor)

Matters
Gray and
White

A NEUROLOGIST, HIS PATIENTS, AND
THE MYSTERIES OF THE BRAIN

Russell Martin

Henry Holt and Company | New York

All the names in *Matters Gray and White* are pseudonyms. Biographical details have been changed in several instances to protect the privacy of both patients and physicians.

Library of Congress Cataloging in Publication Data
Martin, Russell.
Matters gray and white.
Includes index.
1. Neurology—Popular works.   I. Title.
RC351.M36 1987   612.8   86–4725
ISBN: 0-8050-0087-9

FIRST EDITION
Designed by Susan Hood
Printed in the United States of America
10 9 8 7 6 5 4 3 2 1

ISBN 0-8050-0087-9

FOR FERRIER,
WHO MADE THIS BOOK POSSIBLE

Contents

First, the lower belly, nasty, yet recompensed by admirable variety. Second, the parlour (or thorax), and third, the divine banquet of the brayne.

> —William Harvey, outlining the curriculum of his three Lumleian Lectures at Physician's College, London, 1615

Matters Gray and White

Prologue

The cheerful pathologist carried the brain in a plastic bucket. Scrawled on its lid was the name of the deceased patient and a note: DON'T CUT W/OUT DR. FERRIER. John Ferrier and I followed the pathologist down the stairway to the basement of the hospital, then through the bright and barren hallway to the morgue. The pathologist tucked the tails of his tie into his shirt, then put on a paper gown and rubber surgical gloves. He lifted the brain and the spinal cord, which hung from the brain like a tail, out of the formaldehyde solution and laid them on a small stainless steel dissecting tray whose legs stood on the long and narrow autopsy table, plumbed like a kitchen sink, its surface stained by blood. With a delicate scalpel that nearly disappeared inside his hand, the pathologist severed the cord from the brain, then cut away the *cauda equina*, the horse's tail—the fan of nerve roots at the base of the spinal cord. He placed the brain on a scale and weighed it: 1,392 grams (about three pounds). It remained on the scale while Ferrier and the pathologist turned their attention to the spinal cord.

Beginning at the base of the cord, the pathologist made cross-sectional cuts at one-centimeter intervals, carefully laying each pale and spongy piece in a row in the order in which it was cut. "There. That's tumor there, isn't it?" Ferrier asked. "Yes, definitely," said the pathologist, as he cut away a small piece of the growth that had pinched much of the cord's white matter and the butterfly-shaped gray matter inside it. He placed the piece in a tiny plastic box to save it for microscopic examination. Ferrier put on a pair of gloves and held the section close to my eyes. "See how it had squeezed the cord completely out of shape? Mike had

1

lost motor function in both his legs. This may have been what did it."

Mike. This spinal cord and the firm gray brain from which it had been severed belonged to someone named Mike. They *were* Mike, weren't they? They shaped and controlled every aspect of the person that he was. Yet it was hard to imagine. Here in this cluttered and sour-smelling hospital morgue, his brain was just a wrinkled mass of aging cheese, some sort of science project—a strange and unsettling lump of tissue that seemed to me to bear no resemblance to a vital human being. Two days ago, although invaded by carcinomas that looked like little chanterelles, this brain, this person, was speaking, reasoning, speculating, and was probably more than a little filled with fear. This brain, during the three decades that it lived, was amazingly complex—an arrangement of a hundred billion cells forming a structure nearly incomprehensible in its sophistication. But now, removed from the body that housed it, pickled, and about to be cross-sectioned, it was a brain only in the same sense that a cadaver is a person; it was a remnant of life, a kind of scientific souvenir.

I watched while the pathologist separated the cerebrum from the cerebellum with a gentle cut and a twist of his wrists. Following each thin serial cut, he laid the flat and oval sections of the cerebellum in a series of rows, then picked up a camera with a 200-millimeter lens and photographed the sections. The large cerebrum was next. Ferrier poked with a scalpel—looking for tumors and the source of some significant hemorrhaging—and gave me a quick anatomy lesson while the pathologist laid each large section on the tray like a butcher slicing lunch meat. While more photographs followed, the two doctors speculated about why they had been unable to find an obvious source of the bleeding.

"I usually cut these all by myself," the pathologist told me as he wrote identifying notes on each of the small boxes into which he had placed bits of tissue. "Most of these guys just want the reports. They don't want, or don't have time, to come see for themselves. It's nice to have the company."

"The reason you watch autopsies," Ferrier said as we walked down the hall to the stairwell, "is to keep you honest. You can treat a patient for months or years thinking you know exactly where the tumors or lesions are. You can see lots of them on a

CAT scan. You may know why the patient has tremors, or can't speak, or has memory loss, but some symptoms remain unexplained. If you actually see the brain of a patient you've lost, it's right there. And if it doesn't look a whole lot like you expected it to look, it's pretty damn humbling, but at least you learn. Hey, how about a baloney sandwich?"

"You're a sick man," I said.

He laughed. "Did it bother you?"

"No, not really. But it was hard to believe that it was actually a human brain, that you knew who that fellow was."

"Before Hippocrates, people guessed that the brain was the marrow that filled up the inside of the skull, that its job was just to take up space. Looking at one that's pickled, it's an understandable assumption, isn't it? Listen, I have to look in on one patient," he said, "and then we can get out of here."

We walked through wide swinging doors and into the ward. He stopped at the nurse's station to get the patient's chart—the history of her condition and the medical responses to it scratched down, virtually indecipherably, on sheets in an aluminum folder—then went to the patient's room.

"Mrs. Bambridge," the doctor said, "how are you this afternoon?" I stood near the door while Ferrier sat on the edge of the elderly patient's bed and spoke softly, attentively. He examined her eyes, compared the movement and strength of her limbs, and asked her to name the day and the year and who the current president was. Her answers showed her obvious disorientation. He held her hand while they discussed how much longer her hospital stay would last, and joked with her about why she was in such a hurry, telling her she couldn't jog anyway while the ground was covered with snow. "You're looking great," he said, "I'll see you in the morning."

I pestered him with questions about Mrs. Bambridge and about the causes of her confusion as we left the hospital and walked toward his car. The new snow was packed hard on the steep sidewalk.

John Ferrier and I met on the summer day that Neil Armstrong and Buzz Aldrin first walked on the moon. There is no symbolism in that coincidence, and I remember it only because the two of us

3

took such adolescent pride in being bored by all the jingoistic fascination with that event, convinced that if it were really something important it would have surely captured our shrewd, seventeen-year-old attention. We met as counselors at a summer camp in the Rocky Mountains; he came from Denver, I came from a town in the southwest corner of Colorado, and we were both captivated by the complex prospects of coming of age. That summer was full of the heady discoveries of brash friendship and shared perspectives, of the euphoria of independence, and of the innocent resolve of that era's light-hearted, happy rebellion. After we left the camp, we climbed mountains and skied the snowfields that persisted in the shadows of craggy ridges; we camped in the bare and baking desert, drove long, lazy miles through the alternately harsh and hopeful terrain of the West, and forged an unspoken pact that has survived the ensuing decades.

Ferrier journeyed east to the Ivy League the following summer, acquired an art history degree in two years, then entered medical school at the University of Edinburgh, much of a continent and all of an ocean away from the place in the Rockies where I was trying to learn to write. Although he was passionately interested in art and music and architecture, there had never been any question in his mind that it could only be science, medicine in particular, out of which he could shape a career. I had seen the photograph, framed on a stairway landing in his parents' house, of Ferrier, aged five or six, examining his grandmother with a toy stethoscope, the ear pieces left neglectfully around his neck. He never said so directly, but I presumed that only medicine could combine for him the seductive lure of empirical science with an opportunity to express compassion. Intrigued by the work of Scottish psychiatrist R. D. Laing, he began his medical studies assuming that psychiatry would be his specialty. But it wasn't long before he discovered he was less interested in the subtle, and too often imprecise, investigations of the psyche than in studying, probing, the palpable brain itself.

He spent much of his final year in Britain studying neurology at Oxford, then went to a residency in medicine in Vancouver, then a neurological residency in Denver, and from there to visiting fellowships at Columbia and Cornell in New York City. He had often speculated he would finish his first decade in medicine by taking a research position in a teaching hospital. Yet the work of the clinician—the one job in which a doctor works directly for the patients he treats—was intriguing as well, and when an offer came to join another neurologist in private practice in a university town that was folded into the foothills of the Rockies, he surprised himself by accepting it.

It was great to be living within a few hours of John again, and our frequent visits always seemed charged with an energy I otherwise seldom encountered. I still lived in the country and worked alone in a quiet and bucolic backwater. The daily events and professional demands of our lives were starkly different. There were virtually no arenas in which we were forced to compete or to compare our successes and failures. Laughter, it seemed, was the main enterprise of each encounter. When I first called John to ask if I could come and watch him at work, he was puzzled, then interested, then quickly willing.

"It would be fun to have you," he said, "and probably good for me to have someone point out my miserable failures as a clinician. But if this is just some twisted fantasy of yours about being able to ask female patients to take off their clothes, you'd better forget it. We seldom have a real excuse in neurology."

I wanted to watch John Ferrier at work because I knew that he must be a fine physician and because I was envious of a job that afforded him the daily luxury of abandoning the suffocating self-absorption a writer knows too well in favor of direct, and intimate, undivided attention to the lives and concerns of others. John was no saint—I felt I had sufficient evidence to be sure of that—and I suffered no strange urge to build a literary pedestal for him or for any other member of his profession. But there was, nonetheless, the undeniable, nearly magical, lure of the healer, the shaman, the medicine man. What must it be like to meet strangers who immediately confess to you their bodies' most brutal secrets, who come to you openly acknowledging their need for help? What must it feel like to be able to help, to cure them on occasion, to touch them reassuringly on the shoulder, to put their minds at ease? How would it feel to fail?

Since my first months at college, I had consciously (and somewhat smugly, I have to admit) avoided contact with the world of science. I steered a careful path away from the science buildings and the severe professors in ties and short-sleeved shirts, away from even the most rudimentary knowledge of the foundations of the cosmos, the evolution of the earth, or the exquisite construction of the human body. I was interested in human lives, to be sure, but I had the strange, mistaken notion that little of life was to be found in the scientific search for truth. As the years passed, I slowly became aware of the gaping deficiencies of my academic background. I wished I knew something about the geological underpinnings of the earth; I certainly needed to know much more about the complexities of the biosphere; and with each unaccountable ache or the unsettling arrival of an unwelcome lump, I was made more aware of how silly it was that I knew nothing about my body. I had no desire to rush back to school to enroll in the courses that could ultimately make me a chemist or a geologist or a general surgeon, but at least I wanted to begin to pay attention to those disciplines, those ways of looking at the world, that I had so long ignored. And that, too, was why I wanted to watch Ferrier at work.

"Call me John," he said when we discussed whether the use of his real name would be a liability to him, or an impediment to me. "How about John Ferrier?" And so that has become his name— an immodest pseudonym suited to a British-trained neurologist, one borrowed from two important figures in the field: John Hughlings Jackson, a nineteenth-century Yorkshireman, was a clinician and a pioneer in the study of epilepsy. Sir David Ferrier (the name rhymes with *terrier*), a Grampian Scot, was a researcher and a colleague of Jackson's who helped establish the concept of localization of function in the cerebrum.

This John Ferrier, then, is tall and consumes just enough beer and burritos to avoid being thin. His bright eyes are blue and animated; his thick shock of dark hair is forever unruly, and for fifteen years he has worn a dense and disguising beard—beards being at least as common among neurologists and psychiatrists, I have discovered, as among mountaineers. I have seen him wear tweed sport coats or wool suits for so many years that it is hard to imagine him dressed less formally—although he occasionally does pull on a pair of jeans, and he has even threatened to wear a pair of cowboy boots. But the threat seems to be a tame one: Each morning he simply chooses one of three identical pairs of heavy brown shoes made for him at intervals by an English shoemaker in Oxford who keeps Ferrier's name and shoe size filed away on a card. The doctor carries a battered brown leather attaché case inside which he keeps a stethoscope, two tuning forks, rubber reflex hammers, a skin-prick wheel and needles, an ophthalmoscope, a blood pressure cuff, and, tucked behind a divider, an array of reports, brochures, and letters whose value has probably become merely historical. He drives between home, clinic, and the two local hospitals where he is on staff in a cluttered dark-green Saab, which is equipped with a radar detector because patrolmen never seem to believe that being a doctor entitles him to drive everywhere as fast as he possibly can.

During the year that I observed Ferrier, following him like a harried man Friday, I was continually astounded at the hurry he was in. From a predawn shower—dressing with facetious élan to the title song from *Oklahoma*—he was off to a ritual breakfast of french toast or scrambled eggs and decaffeinated coffee, then on to rounds at two hospitals before the first of a rapid-fire series of patients was due at the clinic. By noon he was inevitably behind schedule, and in the minutes between the last of his morning patients and the first patients of the afternoon, there were always several phone calls to return. He normally saw patients until five, then had more calls to make, dictation to complete, and items to discuss with the office staff before he was off to the hospitals again to read EEGs and make final rounds. By 7:30 or so we were free to go to dinner, his beeper clipped to his belt in case there were evening calls, usually accompanied by the woman who, for that month, at least, he was sure he was falling in love with. He seldom went to bed before one or two, staying up in a loosened tie and stocking feet, reading the *New England Journal of Medicine*, or *Annals of Neurology*, or perhaps with a bit more enthusiasm, watching "Barney Miller" and "Taxi" reruns on television, firing the set's remote control unit like a nervous gunfighter until exhaustion overtook him and he slept.

"You get this impression from people, from friends, sometimes amazingly from physicians in other subspecialties, that neurology must be a grim business," Ferrier told me as he rubbed his eyes at his office desk at the end of a frantic day. "They seem to think you see nothing but terminal cases, or untreatable dysfunctions that

7

put people in chairs. That happens. But I get to do a lot of hopeful work as well. Epilepsy used to be a killer. Now most epileptics lead normal lives. Migraine and cluster headaches we can successfully treat and often prevent. Great new things in research into Parkinson's disease; surgery's getting very sophisticated; tumors, benign and many malignant, can be dealt with. And there is incredible neuropharmacological work going on—very exciting. That said though, this isn't a party. Nobody goes to see a neurologist because they're wondering why everything is so great."

During the months that I watched anxious and apprehensive patients walk into Ferrier's office, then listened while they explained that an arm had gone strangely numb or described how a dull and frightening dizziness would overtake them without warning, I was intrigued by how answers to their questions—an explanation of what this mysterious malady was—often seemed more important than an assurance that something could be done to help. *What is this?*, each patient wanted to know. And even when the doctor's response brought the confirmation of their cold and nagging fears, many patients would visibly show relief. "Okay," they would say in soft voices. Then some would say: "That settles that, I guess." Others: "I kind of knew when I came in." When the news was good, on the other hand, when Ferrier was full of optimism, when the culprit was something simple, the patients took the words themselves like a tonic. Their faces would brighten; some would laugh. "Really? Is that all it is?" And even when drugs or therapy or surgery would be required, they got up from their chairs as if the cure were already complete.

"That guy could have kissed you," I said to Ferrier on a dark and snowy afternoon when a middle-aged electrician left his office. "He was afraid he had a brain tumor or something, wasn't he?"

"When something strange happens, some strange thing is wrong but it's not accompanied by pain, it can be very scary. Everybody knows they have a brain up there somewhere, but the damn thing's never betrayed them before. It's easy to suspect the worst."

"How do you feel when somebody's face lights up like that," I asked, "when you tell them it's not the worst?"

He thought for a moment. "Fortunate, I guess . . . I mean, that I'm the one who gets to say it."

8

1 An Agent from Cold Climates

Mark Sanders had symptoms that I knew by now were telltale: a tingling sensation across his chest for a few weeks sixteen years ago; a sudden, unexplained speech impairment in 1975; numbness on his right side at Christmas, 1978; and now, at age thirty-seven, slurred speech, a slight tremor in his right hand, and a lack of balance that would be frightening to anyone, but to a professional mime like Mark was especially so. He had made an appointment with Doctor Ferrier on the recommendation of a chiropractor who recognized that he likely was suffering from something more significant than spinal misalignment. Mark said he had known since that first episode that he was not in perfect health. Because he was a mime, he said, he had been able to pay close attention over the years to his body's strange and subtle deficits. Astonishingly, however, today was the first time in a decade and a half that he had discussed his condition with a physician.

Mark Sanders moved carefully, delicately, as he sat down in the black leather Eames chair that faced Ferrier's desk; he spoke slowly, his voice calm and quiet. His long dark hair hung straight down from a stocking cap, his thick moustache concealed his lips, and his small eyes were bright behind rimless glasses. I noticed that a Multiple Sclerosis Society brochure, one of dozens stacked beside months-old magazines in the waiting room, was tucked in his jacket pocket. He carried a yellow legal pad on which he had noted everything he wanted to mention. "The subjective view of it," he said after Ferrier had taken his history, questioning each suspicious symptom, probing each episode, "is that this time I looked drunk, I *felt* drunk; I was scared to death, and I guess I still have a great deal of inner fear and confusion." Mark walked ahead of us as we went across the hall to the examining room. I caught Ferrier's eye; he saw my unspoken question, then pursed his lips and nodded.

Five Decembers before—in the same hectic preholiday period during which Mark came to the office—Ferrier was finishing his neurology residency in Denver, and keeping crazy hours in a chaotic public hospital. I was on the road, researching a feature story for a magazine. I finally caught him at home one night at midnight. I was calling from a motel in Yuma, Arizona, desperate to explain that my right arm had gone numb, terrified that such a thing could happen, anxious to have him share my concern and to hear him say it was nothing to be alarmed about. "How soon are you coming up?" he asked. I told him I would be there in four days and he said he would examine me then. "But don't worry," he added, "you don't have MS."

"Why do you think I'm worried about MS?"

"Because everybody does," he said.

Despite his assurance, four days alone on empty desert roads—my arm the object of thought every idle moment—was plenty of time to convince myself that Ferrier was wrong and that I had better accept my fate. By the time I met him in the hospital's outpatient clinic at the end of the week, I knew he would finally confirm my fears. He wore a white coat with the name of the hospital stenciled on the pocket and a plastic name tag pinned to its lapel. He examined me at length—relishing, I think, that for the first time he was able to show me that he had indeed become a doctor—then delivered his diagnosis: "It looks to me like it's something that's called students' elbow—an irritation of the ulnar nerve, the 'funny bone'; it happens to lots of people who sit with their arms bent over desks for long periods, which you probably do, so it's all your fault. You see it in truckers, and people who rest on their elbows a lot. But otherwise, your exam is completely normal; I'm really sure it's nothing more serious than that. Try to keep your arm straight as much as you can; it should go away before too long. If not, we can always do major brain surgery or something."

"That's it? Students' elbow?" I suddenly felt very foolish.

"That's it. You're going to live—but now you owe me dinner. They'd take away my white coat if they thought I was doing free consults."

As I recall, the numbness took its time to disappear, but it finally did so, and five years later I sat on a stool and watched Ferrier examine Mark, remembering the silent, stunning fear I had felt in that similar situation, then feeling a disquieting guilt—wondering why I was lucky enough that my week of worry about multiple sclerosis had been a simple case of hypochondria, why Mark's frightened concerns had sadly been correct.

In his office again, Ferrier ignored his buzzing intercom and asked Mark what his own sense of the problem was. "Well, I'm not sure," he said. "When I asked the chiropractor, I kind of had to wrench it out of her, but she said she thought it might be something relating to MS."

Ferrier waited before he spoke. "Part of my job is to have to confirm these things sometimes. And I think that there's about a 99 percent chance that she's right, that you do have MS. You have so many classical symptoms—the different areas of paresthesias, the numbness, the problems with gait and speech, the fact that this last time your symptoms got much worse when you took a hot bath, all of them appearing over a period of years. Multiple sclerosis is, by definition, multiple in space, it affects different areas of the brain, and multiple in time, meaning the patient has more than one episode over a period of time. There are a couple of other specific tests we could do if you'd like, but with your history and your exam, I personally don't think we need them now, unless you'd really just like to have them to confirm things. In one we use a series of flashing lights, little clicks in the ears, and minor, painless shocks to the arms or legs to measure evoked potentials, to see if we can confirm slowing in the brain pathways that could be caused by MS lesions. A lumbar puncture, or spinal tap, is a test for a change in the immunoglobulins in the spinal fluid, something very common in MS patients. And an MRI, a new kind of scanner that uses magnetic fields instead of X rays, can help us see the areas involved."

"I've made it a point to steer clear of spinal taps," Mark said, a grin curling out from beneath his moustache. "You know, I panicked a couple of weeks ago when Dr. Ryan suggested I come see you. I've had time since then to pretty well adjust to the strong possibility of MS. I guess I don't feel any real need to do the tests either. What I probably ought to do is just figure out a few things for the future, shouldn't I?"

The fortieth parallel is an imaginary line that girdles the earth nearly halfway between the equator and the North Pole. It forms the border between Kansas and Nebraska as it slices across the short-grass plains, and it runs, undetected, a few blocks south of Ferrier's office before it cuts into the piedmont and the mountains. For reasons that remain mysterious, multiple sclerosis occurs much more often above the fortieth parallel than below it. Cities like Minneapolis or Billings, Montana, report ten times more cases per capita than does New Orleans, and *fifty* times more cases than Mexico City. MS is common in the temperate regions of North America, Europe, Australia, and New Zealand, but is rare in the tropical and subtropical zones that span the equator. The disease is most prevalent among Caucasians, and its incidence is highest in middle- and upper-income groups. It is the most common neurological disease that strikes people between the ages of twenty and fifty. It strikes women twice as often as men.

Neurologists and immunologists assume that certain genetic factors may play a part in the prevalence of multiple sclerosis among Caucasians and females, and its geographic distribution can possibly be partly explained by the fact that Caucasians comprise the majority of the population in the world's high-risk regions. But environmental factors may play a part as well: A boy who spends the first fourteen years of his life in Scotland, then moves to Singapore, remains as much at risk throughout his life as if he had stayed in Britain. Conversely, a girl who is born in Panama remains at low risk following a move, at age fifteen, to Pennsylvania. Does exposure at an early age to some environmental agent that is present only in colder climates make one susceptible to contracting MS later in life? It appears so, but scientists remain uncertain.

12

In the United States, for instance, roughly half the population lives in the higher risk zone. Of the more than 100 million people who could presumably be exposed to a cold-climate agent—a virus perhaps—only 1 to 2 percent contract MS. Why would most people be able to ward off an infectious agent while a few were not? Again, there are no answers.

Researchers do know that the disease sometimes exhibits a familial predisposition. Perhaps the increased familial incidence of MS exists because there is a genetically transmitted factor that is responsible for rare malfunctions in the immune systems of related individuals, causing normal disease-fighting antibodies, perhaps activated by a virus, to become "autoimmune"—to begin to destroy their bodies' own tissues. This much is known with certainty: Multiple sclerosis *is* an autoimmune disease, one in which the patient's immune system selectively destroys the insulating myelin sheath that surrounds axons, the nerve fibers, in the central nervous system. At the sites where myelin is destroyed, called lesions, absence of the insulating material can slow or prevent the passage of electrical impulses along the fibers. In late stages of the disease, hard "sclerotic" tissue forms at the lesions, creating permanent damage to the axons. The patient's brain sends out the electrical "message" that causes muscles in his or her leg to move, but the message is delayed by the MS lesion, and the coordinated movements involved in walking become awkward, the muscles ineffective. If sclerotic lesions completely block specific impulses, normal functions can fail entirely. A patient becomes unable to walk, or to grasp, or to see.

In an era in which celebrity surgeons routinely exchange healthy hearts for failing ones, and in which a sophisticated pharmacopoeia can successfully combat many of the cancers, it is discouraging to acknowledge that applied medical science remains nearly helpless in the face of dozens of the diseases and dysfunctions that routinely trouble humankind. A host of viral infections, their microbial culprits as elusive as leprechauns, must simply "run their course," as the physicians say, battled only by the body's own antibodies. The autoimmune diseases, to which virtually all the organs can fall prey, and the neurochemical diseases of the brain and nervous system are particularly puzzling, and many are only marginally treatable. In the case of multiple sclerosis—a malady in which one of the least understood of all disease mechanisms, autoimmunity, attacks the body's most complex and mysterious system—the likelihood of a "cure" or effective treatment still seems distant.

The assumption that medical science can actually cure or prevent *any* disease is relatively recent. Only a century and a half have passed since British physician Edward Jenner discovered that "vaccination" with the virus *vaccinia*, which is responsible for cowpox, can protect against the human disease smallpox. Vaccines and immunizations—for diphtheria, tetanus, rabies, and poliomyelitis—did not follow for a hundred years. All of the antibacterial drugs now in use are also products of the current century: Streptomycin, which at last brought an end to the widespread scourge of tuberculosis, was not proven effective until 1944. Penicillin, discovered in 1928, was not available in its pure, effective form until 1941. Sulfanilamide was first used to treat blood poisoning in 1933, and was followed by several related sulfa drugs used to combat gonorrhea, staphylococcus, and other infections. Acetylsalicylic acid, aspirin—a derivative of the substance salicin that is found in many plants, still the most commonly used drug in the world and one of the most efficacious— only became available in 1899. Medical science has come to grips with so many diseases and discomforts in this century that we— biochemists, physicians, and patients alike   tend to assume we ought to be able to cure or prevent *all* disease. It is an assumption that derives from the remarkable advances made in recent decades, but it obscures the fact that the business of healing, of understanding and thereby *curing* illness, is new to medical science.

During the medieval period, because of prohibitions against dissection, medical practitioners had very little notion of the body's components or its role in limiting disease. Since most of the insidious illnesses they observed seemed inevitably to lead to death, physicians risked very little when they tried any number of brutal and dangerous treatments on the chance that one of them *might* keep the patient alive. Administrations of mercury and toxic metals were popular. Vile potions that induced ceaseless vomiting were often prescribed. It was sometimes considered therapeutic to apply ointments that blistered the skin above areas of internal pain. Some physicians prescribed gluttonous consumption of food; others demanded total fasting. A practice called trephining, in which a small hole was bored into the patient's skull, was widely recommended for an array of psychotic disorders that were often considered the result of demonic possession; the hole's purpose was to allow the demon to escape. And as late as the first half of the nineteenth century, bleeding was considered an effective treatment for a variety of disorders that were presumed to be caused by "plethora," an excess of blood that congested the body's organs. Patients who were bled often died from hemorrhagic shock, but when they did it was not infrequently presumed that the treatments had come too late to save the patient from an illness that, to begin with, was doubtless very grave.

By the end of the nineteenth century, a substantial change in medical practice had taken place. Little by little, and certainly not without skepticism, most doctors had come round to the notion that the body could overcome many diseases *without treatment of any kind*. Furthermore, many noted clinical physicians had published their convictions that, in the cases of several specific maladies, survival rates were significantly higher for those patients who were not treated than for those who were. Medical science at long last began to acknowledge that, for the most part, there was little that it could cure.

Over the succeeding decades, the invasive therapies of earlier eras were replaced by a kind of simple, supportive care. Patients with serious illnesses were treated with bed rest and sensible diets; they were kept clean and warm and were given encouragement: they most likely would get better. Instead of assuming the role of an experimental and largely ineffective "healer," the doctor became an adviser, a reliever of anxieties, a comforter. And instead of continuing the centuries-old scattershot approach to illness and its treatment, the medical community began simply to *observe* the natures and courses of the many diseases that relentlessly troubled the human body.

Ironically, it was that willingness to watch, to do little other than study the processes of sickness, that ultimately gave rise to the advances of the twentieth century. Before truly effective treatments could be found, disease had to be examined empirically. Late in the nineteenth century, the work of researchers like Louis Pasteur proved that unhygienic conditions were responsible for the infections that often accompanied wounds and surgical incisions, and the role of pathogenic bacteria and viruses in hundreds of illnesses was becoming firmly established. As the twentieth century opened, the new science of epidemiology was able to trace the causes of several bacterial epidemics. And as more and more infectious agents were identified, biochemists began slowly to discover organic and synthetic substances that could kill invading agents without severely harming the host patient. The syphilis spirochete was isolated, and an effective treatment for the disease was found; the pneumococcus was identified and, following exhaustive laboratory efforts, most pneumonias were finally treatable. By the time vaccines for measles and poliomyelitis were perfected midway through the twentieth century, it was clear that medicine had a new mission. Clinicians were still expected to offer sound diagnoses, compassion, and comfort, but—with the help of thousands of dedicated biomedical researchers—they were also expected to *cure* the diseases they encountered. Medical science had proven its ability to understand and treat some diseases. If it only tried a bit harder—if there were more money, more scientists, more clinical studies—couldn't all illness be conquered?

Today, the medical community gives a qualified "maybe" in answer to that question. The prevention or successful treatment of disease is certainly medicine's goal; doctors are no longer content just to provide diagnoses and moral support. In only a few decades, medical science has made an enormous leap in its knowledge of the body and its burden of disease, and there is no reason to assume that similar strides will not continue in the future. Diabetes, arthritis, and many degenerative cardiovascular ailments may well be contained by the close of the century—or soon thereafter. The problem of cancer, the disease that now affects one in four of us, will indeed be solved, say the biomedical scientists. Brain research is yielding astonishing information, and there is real hope that many neurological and psychiatric illnesses now only minimally treatable may be effectively battled before long.

But the great sadness is that patience remains the only weapon for people attacked by the more intractable illnesses, as well as for the physicians who monitor them. The knowledge that his or her profession is in the midst of an era of great advancement is of little daily assistance to a neurologist treating dozens of patients with a disease like multiple sclerosis. It is of little comfort to a patient made immobile by the disease to hear that *someday* its cause may be found and conquered.

Elaine Peters was seeking a second opinion, and she did not mention that another neurologist had already given her a diagnosis until she had been with Ferrier for almost an hour. She certainly was not going to tip him off. If he was going to arrive at the same cruel conclusion, at least it would be doubly confirmed by the fact that he had reached it independently. She was reserved, almost remote, when she spoke, and something in her inscrutable expression made her appear older than twenty-seven by several years. Three months ago, she said, she began to experience frequent episodes of imbalance, sometimes accompanied by numbness in her left leg and buttock. Her family physician had suspected that some chronic low-back pain could be the cause. He recommended physical therapy, but although the pain subsided with therapy, the imbalance and numbness did not.

When Ferrier questioned Elaine about whether she could remember other unusual occurrences over the years, she said that two years earlier, for a period of weeks, her right leg seemed to drag when she walked, and during that time she often became dizzy when she turned her head quickly. Six months before, she said—this time without prodding—she began to see white dots out of her left eye. Later, vision in that eye became blurred and she noticed that when she looked solely through it, colors seemed flat, washed out, as if she had been staring into the sun. And finally, almost as if this were the clue that would give it all away, she said she had recently noticed that her speech had become somewhat slurred, words refusing to form in her mouth.

The doctor inquired about her family's medical history: her parents and sisters were alive and well. He asked about her social life: she lived with her boyfriend, with whom she had a good relationship; she did not use drugs and drank alcohol only on occasion; she had a secretarial job with a utilities company. When he asked about any other medical problems that seemed to her to be unrelated, she mentioned a skiing accident a year before that had resulted in a slight concussion, and a series of recent bladder infections.

When he examined Elaine, Ferrier found that her left pupil was slow to constrict to light and that a bright red square appeared pale to her when observed out of that eye. Strength in all four limbs was full and symmetric, her reflexes brisk. She had difficulty rhythmically tapping her left foot, and she was awkward when asked to move her left heel up and down her right shin. She felt pinpricks and vibration, and without watching could name the direction in which Ferrier moved her fingers and toes, but when asked to walk, her gait seemed unusually widebased, her steps unsteady.

"Another neurologist has actually done some testing," she said when we returned to the office. "They did one of those evoked potential tests on my eyes, and the left was abnormal. Then a spinal tap, and I think that report said they found 'greater than two bands,' or something like that."

"I'm glad you mentioned that," Ferrier said. "I'd like to see those results sometime, but from what you say they would confirm the sorts of things I saw when I examined you. Did that other fellow give you a diagnosis?"

"He didn't want to. When he sent me to get the tests, the slip of paper said something about checking for demyelinating disease. He was in a big hurry the next time I saw him, and when I asked him what 'demyelinating disease' was, he just said, 'oh, multiple sclerosis,' as he walked out the door."

Ferrier turned to me, rolling his eyes, sighing. "Sounds like a brilliant bedside manner," he said, then turned back toward Elaine. "Well, I apologize for the way you heard it, but unfortunately I think that's what we're facing here. With a positive lumbar puncture, positive visual evoked responses, and what you present with clinically, I'd be remiss to try to sugarcoat it. I think you have multiple sclerosis."

"Okay," she said, her expression still unchanged. "Well, that's why I came."

Before Elaine left the office, she asked Ferrier about a variety of diets that are sometimes touted as being beneficial for MS patients; he told her he was skeptical, but that he had no objections to any special diet as long as it was nourishing. They discussed how hot weather or hot baths can make symptoms worse, and how short courses of steroid drugs can often reduce the duration of symptoms during periods when the disease "exacerbates." Ferrier told her how important it would become to avoid physical and emotional stress whenever possible, and how valuable it would be to be cognizant of the ways in which the disease would limit her as she made career and family plans. When he asked whether her boyfriend was being supportive, Elaine at last let her face betray her feelings. She began to cry, wiping her tears with the back of her hand, then nodding. "He's been great. I know it's hard on him, but he's been great." Ferrier held both Elaine's hands when she stood, telling her he would be glad to see her again, but they did not need to schedule a subsequent visit. Elaine nodded again, and she was still crying softly as she left.

We drove through alfalfa-stubbled fields that were scattered with snow, the radar detector ever vigilant. Eating hamburgers as we went, we passed small farms and low, flat-roofed computer-chip factories, en route to the office in a nearby town where Ferrier spent one afternoon a week. "What do you think the chances are that Elaine will end up in a wheelchair?" I asked.

"By what age?"

"Fifty."

"Real good. Yeah . . . they're real good."

"I wonder what will happen with her boyfriend."

"He'll leave her," Ferrier said matter-of-factly. "Maybe not for a while, but even if they were married, he'd leave. By the time he goes, he'll probably convince himself that that's not the reason, so he doesn't go crazy with guilt, but he'll go. You know, there really is a difference between men and women, isn't there? If Moira and I were still together and I got MS, I think she would be right there for me. I don't think she'd leave." Moira McTaggart, an internist and violist from the Scottish Borders, is a friend and companion since medical school who came to this country when Ferrier returned. She practices medicine in a public health clinic and plays in a chamber orchestra in a nearby city. Following five years together in Scotland, Canada, and the United States, the two have now spent three years living apart. They see each other frequently, painfully keeping each other abreast of their current love lives, but a clear separation is now a pivotal aspect of their relationship. "But who knows what I would do if the situation were reversed—I can't pretend to be the person she is. Men really are bastards, aren't they?"

That afternoon, John Ferrier saw a teacher with migraine headaches, a homemaker with migraine headaches, an overweight, self-conscious college student who complained of muscle fatigue and headaches, a hardware salesman who had suffered a small stroke that affected his vision, and a severely retarded twenty-six-year-old who had begun to have grand mal seizures. At the hospital, he saw a patient who would have his left carotid artery scraped clean on the following morning in hopes of preventing further blood clots from lodging in his brain. In his hospital mailbox, Ferrier found an administrative note telling him he had failed to dictate a discharge summary on a patient who went home a week ago, the photocopied form threatening to suspend his staff privileges if he didn't get the job done. He got the job done, then I followed a few steps behind him as we left, past the waiting room where people with frightened faces sat on bright vinyl couches, past the little shop that sold candy and flowers and magazines, Ferrier hollering, "Hey, let's pick up the pace a little," as he pushed his way through the plate-glass door.

"Well, unlike the majority of neurological diseases that affect the gray matter, MS is a disease of the white matter," Ferrier said during the drive home in the darkness. "White matter basically comprises the tracks, the wires in other words, that interconnect the various parts of the brain and conduct impulses up and down the spinal cord. And it's strictly a central nervous system disease—meaning the brain and the spinal cord. MS plaques tend to concentrate, not surprisingly, in areas where there is lots of white matter, lots of myelin—along the cord, the brain stem, the cerebral hemispheres surrounding the ventricles, and the optic nerves, which are called nerves only because they look like nerves; they're actually part of the brain. The demyelination tends to concentrate on axons that deal with sight, sensation, and movement of the limbs, so we get the symptoms you've seen: the vision problems, sometimes periods of blindness, lack of coordination, numbness. During the latter course, permanent motor neuron damage in the brain and spinal cord causes increased muscle tone; you see very brisk reflexes. Some patients have bad, painful muscle spasms, most often in the legs. Sometimes, in the worst cases, they end up with permanently spastic muscles, their knees up at their chins. It's no fun. Occasionally, the only option is to destroy nerves or tendons to give the patient some relief."

"Can you predict what's in store for a given patient?"

"Nothing's completely predictable with MS; you never know. But generally, the earlier you contract the disease, the nastier the situation. If you get it as a teenager, you're usually in for a long haul. If you're forty or more, its course is often pretty mild. And one thing that's very interesting is that autopsies of elderly people who never showed any MS symptoms sometimes reveal brains with lots of MS plaques. We're just beginning to understand that this disease can occasionally be so mild that people don't even know they have it."

"I've noticed that whenever you've told someone that it looks like they have it, you always mention something that's a good sign—like saying that the later someone acquires MS, the more mild it probably will be."

"Jesus, what do you expect? The last thing I'm going to do after I blurt out the bad news is to tell somebody there's no hope. Because for one thing, there is often lots to be optimistic about. MS isn't a death sentence; it can be tragically disabling, but that doesn't happen to everybody, and you live a long time with it. At a given point, the disease seems to burn itself out; when patients reach their fifties or so they seldom have much further degeneration."

"Do you usually end up doing the evoked potentials and the spinal tap test?"

"Not always. With most people, there are good reasons at some point to do them, especially with patients whose clinical findings are subtle or a little mysterious. But with people like Mark, who look like they walked out of a textbook, sometimes you never need to. MS is a disease that we can only diagnose clinically. There is no specific test or battery of tests we can use to prove someone has it. The tests are helpful, but it's the clinical work, the history and the exam, that are always most important. It's just a question of looking for clues, and it's amazing, the really great clinicians can just watch a patient walk down the hall to their office, and from that they pretty well learn the whole story."

A neurologist conducting an examination is a little like an auto mechanic who listens to the idling engine and looks at the exhaust before he lifts the hood, a little like a police detective whose casual series of questions seems to have nothing to do with the crime, and a lot like a nosy neighbor who shamelessly peeks through gaps in the backyard fence and coyly glances through uncurtained windows. In the midst of an examination, a neurologist like Ferrier is an investigator, a scientist, a snoop—but the vital objects of his attention are not visible. Except for the optic nerves, two thin extensions of the brain itself that can dimly be viewed through a patient's pupils, the brain, the spinal cord, and the miles of peripheral nerves cannot clinically be seen, listened to, or touched. But because the nervous system mediates virtually all human activity, its function or dysfunction can be noted by observing that activity: thinking, speaking, feeling, hearing, seeing, moving. The neurological exam is designed to isolate specific physiological functions and the areas of the brain, spinal cord, or individual nerves that control them, to offer in under an hour a kind of complete checklist of a patient's neurological condition.

As is surely the case with every physician, Ferrier begins an exam as soon as he greets the patient, taking subtle but often unrecorded note of his or her handshake, hygiene, and deportment—the way in which the patient moves, listens, speaks—and, always important, the patient's "affect"—his or her mood or disposition. "Let's see, I guess Dr. Smith-or-Jones sent you in," Ferrier invariably says as a new patient sits down. When I am on hand, sitting beside a back-wall bookcase, facing the patient and flanking Ferrier, he explains who I am and why I am observing and asks whether the patient objects. "What can I do for you?" he adds, using the words a shopkeeper at a counter would choose; then he listens.

The history is the patient's story—what has happened, how it feels, when the symptoms began and whether they've worsened, whether they seem related to stress or personal problems, whether this has happened before. After he hears about the present complaint, the doctor quickly shifts the conversation to the problem's onset to the related episode that occurred longest ago, to the time it all began. Were you bothered by it as a child? he wants to know. How much time passed before you had another episode? The patient in turn explains each detail, moving from past to present, interrupted whenever the answer is too brief or convoluted or when something needs clarification. Is it a dull pain or a sharp one? Is it throbbing or steady?

When a patient says, "I experienced right leg paresthesia for about two weeks," or, "Then I had a bout of syncope," Ferrier inevitably interrupts, a tinge of just-which-one-of-us-is-the-doctor in his voice, and says, "Since different people mean different things with medical terms, it will help me if you can give me the simplest explanation you can." Before the history is finished, he asks about the patient's birth and general health, about related familial problems and current medications, about drinking and smoking and jobs, about friends and children and marriages. If a patient responds that a marriage is "perfect," Ferrier presses, unbelieving. "Oh, well, you know, we have our little problems like everyone else," the patient usually offers the second time, and that is enough to get off the hook. But if a patient continues to insist that a relationship is "just marvelous," free of problems, perfect, Ferrier scratches down that certainty on a white tablet. "Marvelous" marriages are always suspect.

The physical exam is conducted across the hall, in a small windowless room with bright fluorescent lights. It holds one footstool, a narrow counter where Ferrier's briefcase is always propped open—as if constantly at the ready—and a long, high examining table that is padded and covered with black vinyl and the requisite roll of crinkly, cumbersome sanitary paper. Patients seldom need to fully undress, but Ferrier normally asks them to remove their shoes and socks. He begins his examination of the twelve pairs of cranial nerves, the nerves of the head and neck, with an ophthalmoscope, viewing the optic nerves and the pupils' ability to contract. He moves a small silver disk across the patient's field of vision, observing the eyes' ability to follow it in synchrony. Then, with a litany of rapid requests to the patient, he notes the function of the nerves that move the eyes, the mouth and tongue, the jaws and the head itself, that control tasting, smelling, facial expression, and sensation: "Okay, hold your head steady and look to your left, your right, look down, look up, raise your eyebrows as high as you can. Up, up, way up high. Good. Close your eyes tight, tight, tight. Good. Show me your teeth like this. Stick out your tongue, move it to the left, the right, back in your mouth. Good." Ferrier uses a small tuning fork to test whether the patient's hearing is symmetric, and, if he is suspicious about the patient's ability to move his or her neck, he asks the patient to touch each shoulder with his or her chin.

The peripheral nerves are examined primarily by observing the symmetry of reflexes and of muscle tone and strength. By asking the patient to pull against him in a series of exercises that isolate separate muscles, he compares strength and tone in the patient's shoulders, upper arms, forearms, wrists, hands, and fingers, as well as in the patient's thighs, calves, and feet. Then, with the aid of a small reflex hammer, he compares the symmetry of the muscle-stretch reflexes in the arms, legs, and feet, noting whether any are increased, decreased, or absent.

He checks sensory nerves by using a stickpin to test for response to superficial pain, and a cold tuning fork to test for temperature appreciation on the skin and vibration sense in the toes, elbows, ankles, and other so-called bony protrusions. He manipulates the patient's fingers and toes—asking the patient to name the direction of movement without looking—to check the "joint-position" sense that is an indicator of the function of a variety of sensory systems. He normally uses one or more of the many tests that examine coordination: touching the outstretched finger to the nose with eyes closed, patting the knee alternately with the palm and the back of the hand, tapping the tip of the index finger on the first joint of the thumb, tapping the ball of the foot on the floor. Before he finishes the exam, Ferrier often does a variety of specific tests that provide more information about abnormal findings: color-vision tests, tests that attempt to isolate the source of pain in the arms and lower limbs, tests for speech deficits, memory loss, and problems with abstract thought. He often asks the patient to walk down the hall for him, to walk heel-to-toe, to stand still with his or her eyes closed, to walk on heels or toes, before he and the patient return to his office to talk.

"There's really no such thing as a complete neurological exam," Ferrier told me when I pressed him for details about the procedures I had watched him perform a hundred times. "There are literally dozens and dozens of tests you can do—simple clinical tests with very dependable findings—but there's no reason to do them all unless some signs point you in those directions. You tailor the exam to the history, and one test leads you to another based on what you're finding.

"If I'm seeing a patient whose history is suspicious for MS— let's say patchy numbness, vertigo, double vision, imbalance— then there are certain tests that have to be done, and others that don't have much bearing. With that patient, I'll want to know about any urinary incontinence or bladder infections, since those are so common in MS. I spend a lot of time on the optic nerves and the muscles of the eye for the same reason, looking to see if the nerves themselves are pale, looking for nystagmus—a rapid oscillation of the eyeball—loss of synchronization of eye movements, with one eye moving slower than the other and causing blurred vision, also a sign called a Marcus Gunn pupil in which a pupil doesn't contract to light properly because of an optic nerve lesion. I test for color desaturization, to see if a red square looks redder out of one eye than the other. You do very thorough skin sensation tests to see if the paresthesias follow specific nerve distributions, which might mean a more straightforward nerve impingement, or whether they follow less classical patterns as happens with MS. Increased reflexes, especially if they are unilateral, always add to the picture, and if you get a Babinski response, where the big toe goes up rather than down when the outside of the sole of the foot is scraped, that's an unmistakable sign of an upper motor neuron problem, and, given these other hypothetical signs and symptoms, it would likely be MS.

"A single foot reflex is that conclusive?"

"Newborns have a Babinski sign, and it's a pretty good thing to have. They reflexively pull away from stimuli to the soles of their foot, to sharp objects, hot objects, and so forth. But as their brains continue to myelinate during their first year, they lose the Babinski, which has to happen so they can learn to walk—otherwise they would reflexively pull their foot away from the pressure of the floor. So when you see a Babinski sign in an older child or an adult, it's always abnormal; and in the case of an MS patient, what's happening is that his brain, which myelinated so normally decades ago, is now demyelinating. You obviously don't like to see Babinskis in twenty-two-year-olds."

Richard Randolph's brain began to demyelinate in 1968, when he was a 22-year-old enlistee in the Air Force. Now, at age 38, suffering from a difficult form of multiple sclerosis that neurologists identify as chronic progressive spastic paraparesis— grossly, often painfully contracted muscles and loss of use of the limbs—he is confined to a wheelchair. He is barely able to feed himself; his speech is labored and nearly unintelligible; his bladder is emptied by a catheter, his bowels are embarrassingly unpredictable; his disposition is warm and jovial. He likes to laugh.

Richard came to Ferrier's office on a bright December day accompanied by Bill, a young man who lived with Richard and his wife, Julie. Bill was taking a year's break before medical school, and he was Richard's constant companion. The purpose of Richard's visit that day was to say good-bye to Ferrier. Julie and Ferrier had had a falling out, and she had found another neurologist she thought they would be happy with. "If it was up to me, I would stay with you," Richard said. He said it twice so Ferrier could understand. "But I have to *live* with her." His smile was broad and constant. His big glasses and bushy beard seemed to conceal the rest of his face.

I had met Richard and Julie a few months before, just after they had come to town. With the help of Air Force disability income, they were about to move into a new house that had been designed and built specifically for them; its ramps and doorways and bathrooms were wheelchair compatible; it had an indoor therapeutic pool and a whole room housing Richard's film collection—his avocation, his only recreation besides daily, solitary pot smoking. When he outlined his condition to Ferrier on that first visit, Richard said he had not tried to walk in more than two years. He said he was losing function in his arms and it was becoming increasingly hard to feed himself. With a new type of catheter, he had been free of bladder infections for four weeks, but both he and Julie were hopeful that something could be done to make his bowels function more dependably. "Sometimes he doesn't go for five or six days," Julie said, obviously exasperated by the situation. "And we decide against doing things, going out, because you never know when he'll have an accident." Richard smiled while she spoke.

During the following weeks, Richard adjusted his diet, began a bowel program in the rehabilitation department at St. Luke's Hospital, and succeeded in becoming more or less regular, emptying his bowels every other day. But Julie remained dissatisfied, and she was especially aggravated by Richard's lighthearted attitude toward the problem. Ferrier suggested that joint counseling might be helpful, pointing out to Julie that taking constant care of Richard understandably placed her under enormous stress—stress that was not eased by his euphoric personality, a typical feature of late-stage multiple sclerosis.

"Listen," she told the doctor, "I've got three degrees in counseling, and I know enough to realize that we don't need it. What we need is for Richard to take some responsibility for his own bowel movements. If he needs counseling to do that, well, fine. But I don't see what purpose joint counseling would serve."

Everyone agreed that the situation greatly improved when Bill moved in the following month. For a salary of $650 a month, he became available for Richard twenty-four hours a day, relieving Julie of some of the draining responsibility she had already borne for so long, and giving her the opportunity to get out on occasion, to begin to rediscover a life of her own. But she remained adamant that Ferrier was not sensitive to the gravity of Richard's problems, adamant that he did not understand her own.

"Richard really doesn't want to make the change," Bill said, as we spoke in Ferrier's office. "But I think he's right that it's important for Julie to feel as good as possible about everything."

"And please," Ferrier said, "don't worry about how I feel about this. I have every confidence in Dr. Bracken. He's a very nice guy, and he'll give you good care. You'll like him. I'm just going to be sorry not to see you any more."

Richard beamed and he nodded his head. "That's right," he said, "that's how I feel."

The sky was still clear the following morning and it was warm inside the car. We were late as usual, and Ferrier simply slowed and eased his way through the stop signs as we drove from one hospital to the next. But two blocks from St. Luke's, I pointed out Mark Sanders, who was carefully climbing the steps of his basement apartment, and Ferrier suddenly pulled the car to the curb, stopping a hundred feet behind him. We watched Mark move unsteadily along the sidewalk, his cap pulled low on his head, his old Levi jacket torn in the back, exposing its red lining. It took him a long time to take the key to his old beige Volkswagen hatchback out of his pocket, and he was slow and awkward as he maneuvered into the seat.

"Doesn't look like he's getting along too well," I said.

"No, it doesn't. I got a call last week from a social worker, somebody who processes disability claims. Mark's flat broke and he's applying for a full medical disability, but she was concerned that he might be faking."

"Faking MS?"

"I guess I sort of see why it concerned her. He's very earnest; he knows all the lingo; seems to be handling it so well. If he's much of a mime, it wouldn't be hard for him to get the ataxic gait down. And he really doesn't have a dime. I had to loan him the money to fill a prednisone prescription. Some people in his shoes are pretty attracted by the idea of a medical disability."

"How's he paying you?"

"He's not. I won't start charging him until he gets some disability income—which he really is going to have to have. He's in for some major expenses."

"Is he going to get it?"

"Oh, I'm sure he will. I assured her he wasn't malingering. He's got MS. I mean, look at him. Do you think he's doing that for the neighbors' benefit? Besides, the findings are just too strong. He's got bilateral Babinskis. You can't fake a Babinski."

There had been something arresting about seeing Mark struggling clumsily with his disease, but I did not realize until later that the impact I felt came less from what I saw, which was after all brief and uneventful, than from the fact I was, for the first time, seeing one of Ferrier's patients outside either the clinic or hospital—and, for the first time, it hit home that the patients whom I had met had lives that encompassed more than their illnesses. I had known them only as the mime who had MS, or the jovial Hispanic man whose left side had been disabled by stroke, or the meek young woman who was recovering from meningitis. They were defined for me—and for Ferrier as well, I discovered—by their diseases and dysfunctions, and it was surprising to realize, as I began to that morning, that the sicknesses besetting them, serious as they were in many cases, were not the only or perhaps even the central factors in their lives. They were people who also had jobs to go to, who had house payments to make, who worried about their pubescent children and the prospect of nuclear war, whose spirits rose and fell with the fortunes of the football team, who were in love with their husbands or wives, or perhaps with the best friends of their husbands or wives.

It was easy to assume that in hearing a patient's medical secrets—learning the man across the room had difficulty speaking, or had lost bladder and sexual function, or was plagued with persistent headaches—Ferrier truly got to know him. But that was seldom the case. The relationships between Ferrier and the majority of his patients were intimate and intense but they were necessarily limited. They seldom encompassed the complete spectrum of conditions and concerns, attitudes and interests, vocations and obligations that formed and defined each person who walked into his office. Ferrier always knew something about each patient's job and home life and the sources of daily stress, but he seldom knew, for instance, how a patient spent the weekends. He would sometimes know that a woman had been abused by her father and was now abused by her husband, but he might not know that she was in love with a woman she worked with. A man would tell him he had always been plagued by nightmares, dreams in which his co-workers conspired to eat him, but he would not tell Ferrier that he was homesick for Mississippi. The doctor would always know the details about how his MS patients managed their uncooperative bowels, but he would probably not know whether they had once been avid gardeners or whether they still attended church. In only the rarest instances did one of Ferrier's patients know anything at all about him.

"It's strange," Ferrier once told me, "how much I know about some patients—how much I really need to find out to get at what the problem is. But with that same person, I never find out if they are Reaganites, or if they play softball in the summer, or what kind of music they listen to. With some cases—serious strokes, or tumors that require surgery, or seizures that take a long time to control—I feel I have a very close relationship with my patients and their families, but then, especially if things go well, I won't see them again for six months or a year, maybe never. When I see someone on the street, I always remember faces, and I can kind of know whether I liked that person or felt warm toward them, but I'll have no idea what their name is, and sometimes I won't be able to remember whether they were once a headache patient or maybe their mother had Alzheimer's disease."

Ferrier has a notoriously poor memory for names and dates and incidental details, yet his medicine-related recall is always acute. When an internist who has asked him to do a consultation stops him in the hospital corridor to inquire about his thoughts on the patient's condition, Ferrier often needs prompting. "Now, refresh my memory about Mr. McAfee. . . ."

"He's my febrile twenty-two-year-old at County—lethargic, a little dysphasic," the internist will say, and Ferrier's eyes will brighten with recognition.

"Oh, sure, I saw him early this morning," he'll say, then go on at length about the specifics of the young man's case.

The problem with modern medicine, according to some critics, is that it deals with symptoms instead of systems, that it treats disease instead of the person suffering from the disease—and Ferrier's selective memory can certainly support their argument. Most subspecialists like Ferrier are in partial agreement: they do not come to know or attempt to perfect the "whole person"; they do not feel qualified to attempt to do so. What they know in intricate detail, and what they endeavor to treat, is simply one of the body's systems—the gastrointestinal tract, the heart and circulatory system, the brain and its awesome network of nerves. They are not country physicians, much less parish priests, they argue, and they cannot be their patients' sole support. They care about their patients, of course, and they sometimes spend sleepless nights wondering whether they are doing the very best thing to help the patient survive, but as subspecialists, their talents and expertise are limited, as are their responsibilities. It is certainly too much to assume that any doctor, however capable, can take charge of a patient's whole health or well-being. That, surely, is the patient's own job—one in which he or she can only be assisted by the physicians, all of them sometimes fallible, who specialize in the strange shortcomings of human hearts or stomachs or brains.

The Billitson boys were obviously afraid when Ferrier ushered them into the large examining room at the university's health center, where he spends one afternoon a week seeing students and school employees. He had already seen the boys' parents at his office the day before, and the three of them had decided that, since the health center was nearer the boys' school, Ferrier should speak to the two teenagers there. They were old enough now to be able to understand why multiple sclerosis had made their mother bedridden, and perhaps they would pay attention if Ferrier was to tell them how much their support mattered to their mother's health and state of mind. Rickey, fifteen, had recently run away, and both he and his sixteen-year-old brother, Tommy, had begun to resent and openly rebel against the ways in which their mother's disease placed special demands on their time and activities. When Joan and Ted Billitson returned from Ferrier's office, they had told the boys only that the doctor had asked to see them, but they had offered no explanation.

The boys caught a bus after school the following day, then waited on a couch in the hall while Ferrier saw his last patient. From the looks on their faces when at last he asked them to come in, they must have assumed that he was going to tell them their mother was about to die. They sat in stiff metal chairs, their jackets still on, their shoulders hunched, and their eyes trained to the floor.

Their mother had contracted multiple sclerosis before Rickey's first birthday. Its course quickly required a cane, then Canadian crutches, then Joan could no longer walk. She had been wheelchair-bound for ten years, and now, because of the extreme spasticity in her legs, she spent much of the day in bed. She was cared for by her husband and by the boys; a woman came in regularly to clean the house, and a Meals-On-Wheels lunch was delivered every weekday. A physical therapist came to the house three times a week to massage her spastic muscles, and a circle of friends stopped by often to visit, but except for doctor's appointments and occasional summer camping trips in the family's van, Joan's mobility was drastically limited. She was soft-spoken, warm, and friendly, and like Richard Randolph, she had become rather euphoric. She smiled easily. Her speech was very clear, though she spoke little. Ted, on the other hand, was talkative, opinionated; he was plainly patronizing toward Joan, but he was also patient and concerned, and he had defied Ferrier's rule: he had not left his wife.

"I thought it was time the three of us had a talk," Ferrier told the boys, "and I appreciate your coming in. Your mom hasn't gotten worse or anything, but I thought it might be helpful to everyone if you heard from me what things will probably be like for her in the future. I guess you know that MS affects people in many different ways and that some people are more disabled by it than others. Well, obviously, your mom has been severely disabled. She won't ever get better than she is now, but if there's any good news, it is that she probably won't get much worse. For reasons we don't understand, the disease kind of plays itself out in people her age. She won't ever be able to take care of herself better than she can now, and she won't walk, of course, but her mental status—her personality and thought processes, the things that make her *her*—shouldn't change much. I think you should feel fairly certain that she'll always be able to talk with you and to joke around at the dinner table and that sort of thing. She'll always be a good mom." Tommy's glasses were low on his nose. He pulled at his long dark hair and he nodded, but he didn't look up. Rickey, taller and twenty pounds heavier than his older brother, stared straight at Ferrier now, his mouth barely open, his eyes hardly daring to blink.

"What kind of jobs or responsibilities do you guys have with your mom?" Ferrier wanted to know. He leaned back in his chair, flipping a pencil end over end in his hands.

"Oh, well . . . we help get dinner ready, then we do the dishes and stuff," said Rickey. "One of us is always supposed to get her ready for bed, empty her bag and brush her teeth and stuff."

"Do you ever get out of doing it?"

"Well, that's part of the trouble," Tommy said, his eyes still averted. "Like if it's Friday night or something and you want to go out with your friends, I can't go until I've put my mom to bed, and by then sometimes everybody's already gone. It's no big deal taking care of her, but sometimes just doing it screws everything else up."

"Do you think your folks are too strict, that they ask too much of you two?"

"No. No, I wouldn't say too strict really. We never have to clean the house or nothing," Tommy said. "It's just—"

"Just that my dad has a big mouth," said Rickey. "I get along with my mom great. She's real nice, always pretty happy. But my dad, I don't know, I guess he just doesn't like young people. Him and my mom get along great, but he's always riding me."

"Is your dad the reason you ran away?"

"Yeah, I guess so. Just the whole deal was getting me down."

"How have things been since you've been back?"

"Oh, I have my bad days," Rickey said, still staring straight at the doctor, "but things are getting better. School's better, and my dad has kind of laid off a little."

"The thing that I'm concerned about," said Ferrier, "is whether your mom senses that sometimes you guys resent having to help her. Since she's my patient, she's the one I'm most concerned about. There's no question that your mom's MS is a very big deal for the whole family. It places lots of demands on all of you. I know that sometimes it's very hard on you guys. But just think of the demands it puts on your mom—*those* are big demands. And if she sometimes hears the two of you arguing, say, over who has to go get her ready for bed, well, you can imagine how that would make someone feel."

"Yeah," Tommy said, twisting his hair around his index finger.

"Yeah, I know," Rickey said, "but we don't argue much about it. Just sometimes we'll flip to see who does the dishes and who does Mom."

"What does the winner usually choose?"

"The dishes," they said in unison. Tommy at last looked up, and the three of them smiled. "But that's only because we can listen to our music when we do the dishes," he said. "Mom doesn't like it, so we can't listen to it in with her."

"You know, I'm not saying any of this is fair to you guys. Things like this shouldn't have to happen to people like your mom, and they shouldn't have to happen to you. But, I guess I just want you to remember that, in spite of it, your mom's quite a remarkable person. She really is."

"Yeah," said Rickey, the single word meant to convey his comprehension.

"Yeah," said Tommy, "yeah, okay. We know."

Enough had been said, it seemed, and Ferrier offered to drive the boys home. They sat in the backseat and we drove away from the university, beneath the freeway and south to the suburbs, past the restaurant where Tommy worked on the weekends, past the shopping center that flanked the supermarket, and into the new subdivision where leafless trees barely rose above the roofs of the houses. The boys were almost at ease now; they were openly enamored with Ferrier's car, impressed by the audacity of the radar detector, and Rickey was so bold as to point out the house where Tommy's girlfriend lived. "That's where *he* hangs out," Rickey said, "the lucky dude." I turned in my seat and asked if their father ever went out alone.

"No, I don't think so," Tommy said. "They pretty much stay home, you know, and watch the tube and read and stuff."

"About the only thing they still do is go camping," Rickey said. "Not very often, because Mom just kind of has to sit there, and sleeping in the van is pretty hard for her. It's no big thrill for us anymore, but they still get a charge out of it, I guess."

The van was parked in the driveway at their house, and a long concrete ramp led from it to the front door. Each of the boys thanked Ferrier for the ride, and he asked them to say hello to their mom for him. "She's going to want to know what we talked about," Rickey said.

"Tell her as much as you want to," Ferrier said.

"I'll tell her you basically said to be cool," Rickey said, smiling. His brother was peering into the mailbox.

"Their dad breaks your rule, you know," I said as we drove back toward St. Luke's Hospital, where Ferrier had to see one patient and read two EEGs before the day was finished.

"So you think I'm full of shit, do you?" He glanced at me as he waited impatiently for a light to turn.

"That's been obvious for some time," I said. "This is just further proof, which I couldn't resist pointing out. But, maybe he's the exception that proves the rule."

"Well, luckily, not every male is as depraved as we are. Lucky for Joan. Can you imagine life for her without her family? I'm sure Ted gets a little weird sometimes, but God, he hangs in there. That's quite a load for anybody."

"Will she just get more spastic?"

"We've begun to discuss doing a nerve block, injecting a drug epidurally that would anesthetize the nerves in her legs, and then the muscles would go flaccid like they do with lower motor neuron damage. Sometimes it's pretty successful. The incredible discomfort is gone, and it makes transfers a lot easier."

"Transfers?"

"Going from bed to chair, or chair to car or whatever. I try to leave tendon cutting as a very last resort."

"But the disease itself . . . I guess there aren't any hopeful prospects, are there?"

"We can at least make life a lot easier for people who have it—with a few drugs, but principally with therapies. The physical and occupational therapists, speech therapists, too, are the people who really help the patients."

"Does it look like it will always be pretty impossible to prevent?"

"You never know, but nobody expects any sudden breakthroughs. And if one ever comes, my hunch is that it won't be because we finally isolate that cold-climate agent and come up with a drug that zaps it. The breakthrough will come via autoimmune research. Every specialty deals with different autoimmune diseases, but they're all related, all of them involve the immune system mistaking the body's own tissue for foreign antigens. Once we make real progress with any one specific autoimmune disease, we ought to be able to translate it to the others. And maybe MS will be where the first progress is made; that could happen. Here, Canada, Britain, and other European countries, they're all doing lots of MS research. They have to; that's where the disease is."

"You've always been in places where the incidence is pretty high, haven't you?"

"Yeah. By the time I'm through, I'm afraid I'll know this disease pretty goddamn well. Whatever that's worth."

I sat in the waiting room in X-Ray while Ferrier read the EEGs, browsing through an MS brochure I had tucked away in my briefcase. Its cover called multiple sclerosis "the great crippler of young adults." That familiar phrase had been around a long time. Inside, it pointed out that for every person who suffers muscular dystrophy, ten people contract MS. The brochure said research had reached a critical stage, and it quoted Dr. Jonas Salk, the discoverer of the polio vaccine, who pronounced MS as "a disease whose time has come." But that evening in the empty room, a cure for the disease did not seem close at hand. Joan and Richard and Elaine and Mark the Mime would not be well when I saw them again in a month or two.

What kind of sense did it make for an MS society to feel it had to point out to potential donors that there are ten times as many multiple sclerosis sufferers as "Jerry's Kids"? In a wealthy society like this one, why does one research foundation have to compete with another for private charitable contributions? Can we really do no better than to fight these diseases with brochures and coin boxes and telethons? When he came to find me, I told Ferrier it all seemed crazy. His tie was loose, his eyes were red, and we both were ready for a drink, ready at the end of the day to forget about sick people for a few hours, anxious to do nothing more than laugh our way through a long dinner, to ponder weighty issues like skiing, football, sex, to ignore as long as we could the cruel constancy of illness. "Of course it's crazy," he said. "But forget it. There's nothing you can do about it tonight. Welcome to modern medicine."

The winter had descended with a vengeance by the next time I came to town. Snow lay deep on the lawns and was piled in mounds at the sides of the streets, and more spilled out of the sky. The first three patients that morning held parkas and topcoats under their arms when they walked into Ferrier's office, putting them on before they left, each one assuring us it was miserable outside. The fourth patient called to cancel because the canyon road had been closed, so Sarah Mayer was the last patient before lunch.

Her big blue parka covered a cotton turtleneck, and she wore sweat pants and red running shoes. Her dark hair was pulled back; her lovely face was flushed by the cold. She had made the appointment, she said, because she needed to know whether the birth control pill would increase the frequency or severity of MS exacerbations, and Ferrier told her he knew of two separate studies that had concluded it did not. "The consensus seems to be that the emotional and physical stress of pregnancy, or of worrying about whether you are pregnant, is probably a greater risk."

Sarah's fingers and toes had begun to tingle two-and-a-half years before. Then her right leg became weak and she suffered a loss of balance. Not long thereafter, the vision in her right eye became blurry, and five months before her twenty-fourth birthday, she was told she had multiple sclerosis. "I had just moved out here from Ohio," she said, "and I thought 'what on earth do I do now?' My mom, of course, thought the first thing to do was to get right back to Ohio where they had good doctors." She smiled at Ferrier.

"Probably pretty good advice," he said, returning the smile.

"I have an uncle who's had MS since 1950, so everybody in the family was already fairly familiar with it. Oh, and I guess I should tell you: Since I was here last, my older sister was diagnosed with MS."

"How old is she?" Ferrier asked.

"Thirty-seven. She lives in Miami."

"How did your mom handle that news?"

"Well, she didn't. She hasn't. My sister and I talked and we decided not to hit her with it right now. We probably should, but I've been hard enough on her. And she feels so far away."

"How have you been?"

"Oh, pretty good, really. I'm being very careful about my diet—no sugar, no alcohol, no MSG or any other additive stuff. I'm still seeing that chiropractor, and I really like him. He helps me a lot with the muscle spasms. I'm really trying to pay attention to my body, and I think that's helping too. I guess the biggest problem is just being tired. I'm always just so exhausted. I come home from work and I just collapse. My boyfriend ends up asking if I mind him going by himself over to friends or to a concert or something. I say 'sure, I want you to,' because I just can't manage it. I know sometimes he thinks I ought to push myself to do things more, but I don't think he realizes how draining this is."

"Are things basically good between the two of you?" Ferrier asked.

"He's frustrated, I know he is," she said. Tears welled in her eyes and she held her breath for a moment. "Now I'm not going to start crying. . . ." She waited before she spoke again. "One problem is that I'm getting really numb sort of from the waist down. I hardly feel anything when we have sex, so it's real strange. And that makes it hard on him. But he's real supportive, he really is, and the people at work have been great. I had to quit waiting tables about two months ago—MS is not a good disease for waitresses to get—and they moved me back to the office and I do books and other stuff. The manager told me I'd always have a job, which was real sweet of him." She stopped again; the tears returned. "Damn it, I told myself I wasn't going to cry today."

Ferrier told Sarah he would send a letter to her gynecologist outlining his opinion about the pill; he helped her put on her parka, then gave her a hug. "You're doing great," he said, then he sat down to dictate the letter. I walked to the waiting room with Sarah, trying desperately to think of something valuable, something supportive, to say. I wanted to tell her how much I liked and admired her in the twenty minutes since we had met, but all I was able to do was to wish her the best of luck. Courage she already had plenty of, but luck she could surely use.

We shook hands, and I turned to go back to the office, but I stopped and asked, "By the way, what have the doctors been like during the course of this?"

She was quick to answer and her eyes brightened as she started to speak. "Most of them have been very good, very concerned, they really have. One guy was a total jerk. Awful. But the others have been great. You know, whenever I have an appointment, I end up feeling sort of sorry for Dr. Ferrier. He's so nice and everything, but there's just nothing he can do."

2 Fire at Brief Moments

Doctor Ferrier sat in the corner of a cramped County Hospital nurses' station at six-thirty in the morning, dictating an admission note into a smudged white telephone. A tired obstetrics technician, her all-night shift now almost over, leaned against a counter and listened to him speak, his voice an impatient slur of words: "Paragraph. Impression, underlined. This twenty-year-old right-handed woman is being admitted after having presented post-ictally in the ER following a grand mal seizure. She had a second, two-minute seizure in the ER before she was brought up to Four North. She is thirty-three weeks pregnant with her first child, unwed, and has a long seizure history. Prior to her pregnancy, her seizures were well controlled on Dilantin, but with the pregnancy, she has developed a rash on both arms that Dermatology attributes to Dilantin and she has begun to have frequent seizures. We will now begin to withdraw the Dilantin, administer phenobarbital IV, and will slowly begin a course of Tegretol. The patient has had labor contractions following her last several seizures, all of which have been resolved, but OB tells me that the fetal movements have slowed significantly. I have ordered a complete blood workup, and the nursing staff will monitor her very closely. In summary, the admission diagnosis on Wendy Stetham is seizure disorder with an IU pregnancy, patient number 300–102. This is Dr. John Ferrier dictating on January 6."

"That's going to be one tough kid," said the technician when Ferrier hung up the phone.

"You're telling me. At least it's still growing."

"Heartbeat's stayed strong. I don't know."

"Long night, huh? You look beat."

The technician turned to me. "He's such a charmer, this guy." She gave us a weary wave, then walked away.

Ferrier smiled, looked at his watch, then jumped to his feet. "Jesus, we've got to get moving. Can you settle for doughnuts again?"

"I can settle for doughnuts," I said from a few steps behind him, seeing him lunge at a closing elevator door. He held the door for me in mild exasperation, as if I had certainly taken my time.

"This might be your chance to see a seizure in progress," Ferrier had said earlier that morning as we drove to the emergency room in the waning darkness. "The first time you see one, you're amazed. They really are fascinating." I had heard him express his interest in seizures on other occasions, and I knew the visiting fellowship he had done at Columbia Presbyterian was in electroencephalography—a brain-wave study that is the principal confirmatory test used in the diagnosis of epilepsy—but I was nonetheless surprised to find him so spirited, so *enthusiastic*, about this most dramatic of brain dysfunctions at a time of the day when I still had difficulty forming simple sentences. Still, the drama was unmistakable, and I was suddenly wide awake in the emergency room when Wendy Stetham had her second seizure— her eyes white and staring blankly, saliva pouring from her contorted mouth, her limbs shaking wildly, tearing at the sheets, with Ferrier, an ER physician, and two nurses surrounding her, watching, waiting, doing what little they could to protect her big and shiny belly.

Two hours later, following rounds at St. Luke's Hospital and an eight o'clock meeting with its rehabilitation staff concerning a stroke patient's progress, we were gobbling glazed doughnuts in Ferrier's office, scattering crumbs on his rosewood desk, when he took a call from Wendy's nurse. "How long?" he asked, taking a sip of coffee. "Okay, give her two hundred milligrams orally as soon as she's conscious, keep her on the IV, and let me know how things go. Yeah. Very good. Okay. Thanks." He hung up the phone and scraped the crumbs into his hand. "Goddamn it," he said, "she had another one."

Ferrier's frustration, his aggravation, at his inability to stop Wendy Stetham's seizures that morning was ironic evidence of how confident he and his neurological colleagues have become of their abilities to limit epileptic activity in the brains of patients whose lives would otherwise be badly scarred by what are very literally electrical fires rising suddenly in the cerebral cortex. The contemporary treatment of epilepsy is, for the most part, the brightest story in neurological medicine; the disease is only a shadow of the scourge it once was, and the rare patient whose seizures cannot be harnessed is as perplexing and troubling to the doctor as the occasional patient who comes in with symptoms he has never seen.

Seizures have long fascinated the physicians and scientists who study the brain, in part because they can be undeniably exciting to observe—the patient's brain seeming to shut down, to malfunction bizarrely during the course of the seizure. But there are other reasons for their interest. Unlike the majority of the brain's diseases and dysfunctions, to which only a small percentage of the population is susceptible, every person, given sufficiently stressful conditions, is capable of having a seizure. Moreover, the several types of seizures that affect only one portion of the brain give researchers invaluable information about the localization of brain functions; and the study of the wild, abnormal storms of epilepsy leads to fundamental questions about the normal physiology of the brain—one neuron signaling another in an astoundingly complex electrochemical chain reaction that ultimately results in a blinking eye, a tightened fist, a thought. How does the exceedingly intricate circuitry in nonepileptic brains avoid the periodic "power surges" to which seizures are analogous? And in brains that are prone to epileptic activity, how do seizures stop? What quells the fire once it has started?

It surely has to be assumed that seizures also hold special fascination for Ferrier and his fellow neurologists simply because they can do something about them. Unlike multiple sclerosis, whose treatment is still very limited, or degenerative dementias, such as Alzheimer's disease, which essentially cannot be treated at all, epilepsy has been pharmaceutically controllable, with at least partial success, for a hundred and thirty years—ever since Sir Charles Locock first used bromide in 1857 to prevent his patients' seizures. Today, the epilepsy pharmacopoeia includes more than a dozen different anticonvulsant drugs, a few of them limited to treatment of a particular type of seizure, many of whose chemical mechanisms in the brain are only slightly understood, but which

41

somehow control misfiring neurons and limit the spread of the seizures. Instead of being able to do no more than diagnose the disorder and observe its calamitous progress, the clinicians can, in this case, actively alter its course.

Four-year-old Elliott sat on his father's knee in the neurologist's office on a day when the dark sky bore wearily down on the foothills and covered the plains like a gray blanket. He wore new blue jeans and red high-topped tennis shoes; his blond hair curled around his ears, and he seemed only a little bored by another visit with the doctor. He answered John Ferrier's questions without coaxing from his parents, telling him he felt fine, saying yes, he had just had a birthday, and explaining that his favorite television program was "Sesame Street." His father and mother wore slight, adoring smiles as they listened to him, and his mother kissed his cheek when Ferrier suggested that Elliott might like to go play with Bonnie, the receptionist he had met on his first visit.

"I still tell myself he can't have epilepsy," Elliott's mother said when the door had closed behind him. "He seems so normal except for the seizures. It's hard for me to believe he isn't just my perfect, precious little boy."

"It's funny," his father said, "it's been a real adjustment for us, but it doesn't seem to bother him a bit. He even tells the babysitter that if he has a seizure to turn him on his side because he might throw up—as though it's not a big deal at all to him."

"That's great," Ferrier said. "That's exactly the way he should feel. As I've said before, you two should just treat him as an absolutely normal child."

"Except that he isn't absolutely normal," his mother said. "I still cringe at the word *epilepsy*. I think the only way I'm coping with this thing is to hope he may grow out of the seizures."

Ferrier leaned forward, resting his arms on his desk, the long fingers of his hands entwined. "Don't use the word *epilepsy* if it bothers you," he said. "Tell his teachers, or his friends' parents when he's old enough to go stay the night, that he has a seizure disorder, a disorder that's completely under control, and that it's quite unlikely that he'll have one."

"I'm going to be terrified to let him go. The seizures are so frightening," his mother said. Her husband pursed his lips, nodded his head. "If he ever has to have them, I want to be with him," she said.

Seven months before this day's follow-up consultation with Ferrier, Elliott and his parents were driving home from a baseball game when Elliott suddenly seemed to become very drowsy, then slumped backward in his car-seat. His eyes rolled back and his body began to quiver, but he did not drop an ice cream cone that he held in his hand. "We knew something was definitely wrong," his father said. "He was pale as could be and wouldn't respond to us; then he just kind of stared at his mother but wouldn't speak." When Elliott regained consciousness, he was drowsy and his speech was slurred. He fell asleep as his parents continued the drive, then woke crying.

Ferrier examined Elliott the following week. In his write-up of the consultation Ferrier noted that there was no history of seizure disorders in the family; Elliott's mother recalled that Elliott's heart-rate dropped slightly as he was being delivered, but that he began to breathe immediately. On examination, Elliott was normal except for weak ankle reflexes and less ability to jump off his left foot than his right. The electroencephalograph, or EEG, was slightly abnormal, showing unusual electrical activity in the right frontal region of his brain in the minutes of the test during which he had fallen asleep.

Four weeks later, Elliott had another episode; presumably coincidentally, he was again riding in the car, again eating ice cream. His mother, who was alone with him, noticed Elliott's head flopping back and heard gurgling noises. When she was able to stop the car and get out to check on him, Elliott's body was stiff, his left leg jerking involuntarily. Following the second episode, Ferrier ordered a brain CAT scan—a sophisticated, computer-aided X ray—as a precaution; it was normal. At the doctor's urging, Elliott's parents reluctantly agreed to begin treatment with phenobarbital, a long-acting barbiturate and the drug most commonly used for seizure control in children. Two months passed before Elliott next had a seizure, at which time his phenobarbital dosage was slightly increased. He had remained seizure-free during the four months since.

"I think we're where we want to be with the phenobarb," the doctor told his parents. "We're in good shape now. But I do wish you two felt better."

"It'll just take some getting used to," his father said. He straightened his tie. "We're happy, of course, that he hasn't had any more seizures. And who knows . . . maybe this isn't forever." Elliott's mother smiled as she stood, but it was a smile shaped by resignation.

"Good to see you both," said Ferrier. "And really, he's doing great." He walked them down the hall to the waiting room, and I could hear him reassure them again as their voices grew faint.

"Oh, this is one of the easy ones," Ferrier said as we sat at a wooden table burnished with cattle brands at the Wrangler, a restaurant surrounded by medical offices and a block from County Hospital. "Elliott will lead a totally normal life, and his parents will eventually be comfortable with it. It's understandable. It's a frightening thing to see your child having any kind of seizure. There's nothing you can do and it looks like he's being destroyed. You wonder whether he'll ever come out of it."

What would have been in store for him, or for other epileptics, without anticonvulsants, I wanted to know.

"There's a condition known as *status epilepticus*, which used to be defined as twenty-four hours of unrelieved seizures. Nowadays, of course, we try not to let anyone have seizures for that long, so we define it as three seizures in a row uninterrupted by a return to normal consciousness. Before anticonvulsants, many epileptics were prone to go into *status epilepticus* at one time or another, and could die—from inhaling vomit, contracting pneumonias, simply not regaining consciousness. Seizure victims were accident prone; they'd have seizures in the middle of roads or in the water or on the edge of a cliff—to say nothing of how outcast they were. Think of the word we use to describe it. We thought people were being *seized* by something, and it looked like something evil."

Epilepsy is rooted in the Greek word *epilambanein*, which means to seize upon, or to be seized, and it is the latter meaning that first described the sudden way in which people appeared to be overtaken by forces outside themselves. One moment they were perfectly normal, and the next they had fallen to the ground unconscious, foaming at the mouth, their bodies convulsing violently. Seizures seemed to be the work of demons, and the hapless people who were under the spell or curse of epilepsy where shunned and always suspect.

The first investigation of epilepsy as a medical, rather than supernatural, phenomenon began as early as the fourth century B.C. with the Greek physician Hippocrates, the first to assert that "the brain is the most powerful organ of the human body . . . the interpreter of consciousness." Hippocrates wrote at length about his clinical observations of epilepsy, which he called the "sacred disease," noting his assumptions that seizures were related to the brain.

Yet while Hippocrates and his contemporaries recognized the brain's involvement, they presumed that seizures resulted from "vapors" or from some pneumatic substance passing from the limbs and trunk into the head. They referred to the variety of premonitory sensations that patients experience prior to a seizure as *auras* (the Greek word for breezes), assuming that an aura was simply the sensation of a rising vapor or epileptic mist. By the sixteenth century, having progressed little beyond the work of the ancient Greeks, most physicians still presumed that auras, such as nausea, a tingling in the hand, or a bad taste, were proof that seizures were afflictions that arose outside the brain and traveled to it.

Attempts at treating epilepsy varied from religious rites to superstitious potions, from confining epileptics in asylums to a barbaric series of surgical procedures in which the patient's head was squeezed or beaten or pierced. As recently as the eighteenth century, the array of popular epilepsy remedies included mistletoe, elk's foot, and peony root.

During the course of the next century, physicians increasingly noted the association of major head trauma, brain tumors, and lesions with the onset of seizures. The clinical evidence strongly supported the notion that epilepsy had its genesis solely in the brain. In a series of experiments in the early 1870s, two German researchers, Gustav Theodor Fritsch and Eduard Hitzig, and a British neurophysiologist, Sir David Ferrier, confirmed that localized areas of the cerebral cortex governed specific sensory and motor functions. By applying small electrical shocks to various regions of the cortices of laboratory animals, they were able to produce a variety of movements in the animals' bodies. And quite intriguingly, electrical stimulation that was only slightly stronger could induce convulsions in those same motor areas, convulsions that appeared identical to epileptic seizures. The experiments provided convincing ballast for the hypotheses of English neurologist John Hughlings Jackson, who had devoted much of his clinical attention to epilepsy and who was already certain that seizures were initiated by abnormal electrical activity in one or more parts of the brain. "A convulsion is but a symptom," he wrote in the same year that Fritsch and Hitzig's landmark experiments were published, "and implies only that there is an occasional, an excessive, and a disorderly [electrical] discharge . . . it is a local discharge." In other words, seizures are the visible effects of electrical storms that rise unpredictably in areas of the brain where nerve cells have suffered minute damage or have minor structural abnormalities—storms that can limit themselves to a local area or that can spread suddenly, like a lightning chain, throughout the brain.

"It was Hughlings Jackson who really initiated the modern era of epilepsy research," Ferrier said as we walked back to his office. A cold wind curled down out of the mountains and whipped through the streets of the town. He wore a parka over his sports jacket, his hands stuffed in its downy pockets. "Jackson's wife had seizures, and presumably that's why epilepsy was such a concern of his. There is a type of focal motor seizure—one that, say, causes only a left leg to jerk, or a right arm—that we still call a Jacksonian seizure. And he did great work in the study of seizures that spread or "march" across the cortex, causing convulsions to march to different parts of the body. It's amazing that we've been quite certain for well over a hundred years now that all epilepsies result from a minor scarring of neurons, scarring that in many cases would not be detected at autopsy. But we still don't know why a group of neurons that are prone to spike in synchrony, in other words, prone to seize, don't do so all the time, constantly. And once a seizure has started, how is the brain able to stop it? Those are the really exciting questions that may not be answered for a long time."

We waited at a crosswalk for the light to change. Cars with empty ski racks sped by on the icy street. "Are epileptics ever able to drive?" I asked.

"Oh, sure. It's only the cases where patients have grand mal seizures that are never well controlled or aren't predictably preceded by auras that let them know they're about to have a seizure, that make driving really impossible. Most states have laws saying you can't drive for so long after you've had a seizure, a year or so. Here, the state leaves that decision up to the doctor. But I'm supposed to alert the motor vehicle people if I'm aware that a patient is driving against my wishes."

"Is driving the only limitation?"

"I tell people not to work in high places, or with heavy machinery; and not to fly planes, and you know—not to rob or murder or abuse young children."

"You're strict."

"Did I ever tell you about the guy who was referred to me because he supposedly had these strange stealing seizures? He had no other seizure history—and he didn't remember these episodes, of course—but he had a 'seizure' one Saturday during which he drove his car to the place where he worked, which was closed, and filled his trunk with copper wire. Two weeks later, another seizure; he went to the plant and put more copper wire in his trunk. And then he told me, 'And when I came out of the third seizure, I was in my garage and the police were arresting me because I guess I'd been selling the wire.' "

"What did you tell him?"

"Well, this guy was a giant and a little scary, so I said I wasn't sure what he had, but that it didn't sound like epilepsy. The guy was just a crook, of course, although he definitely could have blanked those episodes out of his memory. But there are a lot of interesting pseudoseizures. All kinds of things that look like seizures but that actually have some sort of psychiatric cause. It's very possible that Wendy—the girl you saw at County who's pregnant—has pseudoseizures, at least part of the time. Some of them begin awfully suspiciously—just as someone walks into her room. And I've got another patient, an eighteen-year-old who's really pretty insightful, who has both a genuine seizure disorder and these things she refers to as 'tension seizures.' When she was small, she probably began subconsciously to mimic her real seizures to help break up fights between her parents. She still has the pseudoseizures, usually in stressful situations, and I think it's intriguing that she models them after her epilepsy."

Melanie Brubaker unbuttoned her coat but did not take it off. She wore a fashionable silk print dress and charcoal-colored stockings; her eyes were heavily made up, and her face bore an implacably sad and serious expression that masked the fact that she was still a teenager. She listened intently as Ferrier spoke, and her responses seemed measured and thoughtful, yet quietly detached, as though at times she was speaking about someone else. Her hands remained motionless, cupped in her lap.

During the past three months, Melanie had experienced unusual episodes on five different days, sometimes recurring throughout the day, each one lasting from fifteen to forty-five minutes. At the onset of each, her vision would become blurred, then tunnel-like. She would feel hazy and unfocused, she said, and invariably experience a metallic taste in her mouth, a feeling of weakness, and a queasiness in her stomach. Since childhood, she had taken medication for seizures that had been diagnosed by another physician as "petit mal"—the so-called *absence* seizures common in children, which are characterized by brief periods of vacant staring—a sudden and relatively innocuous loss of consciousness that is followed by an immediate return to normal function. Petit mal seizures tend to disappear by adulthood, and, on daily anticonvulsant medication, Melanie had—until the recent episodes—remained free for more than a year of the seizures that her several physicians characterized as "epileptic."

Melanie also had "tension seizures." These had first surfaced when she was in grade school and continued to recur periodically. She had told Ferrier on her first visit, a month before this day's follow-up, that when she was quite young she would rock back and forth and start to scream when she got angry or tense, eventually falling asleep. As she grew older, the start of the tension seizures made her feel she was about to faint. If someone was with her, she could let him catch her. If she were alone, she said, she could force herself to stay up.

48

"Have you had any more of the tension seizures since I saw you last?" Ferrier now asked.

"No. I know I can get both kinds from stress, so I've tried to avoid it. Since I moved in with my dad, everything has been much smoother. Whenever things went bad at home, I could feel myself going into a seizure. And when the anger was directed at me, I'd almost always have one. I couldn't handle anger."

"Well, as we discussed last time, I think the tension seizures are totally stress-related. You used the word 'psychological' to describe them, and I think that's right. You're fully aware that they happen when you are in intense emotional situations and then they serve as a release for you, just as in the past they were a way to break the tension in your family. I think the best way to treat them is to do as you're doing—to try to work on the things in your life that create the problems. You seem much more relaxed today than when you first came in. The move to your dad's seems to have worked out; you look happier."

Melanie nodded; she pulled absently at the hem of her dress and smoothed the fabric against her thighs.

"But as for those other seizures," Ferrier said, "I think there's no question that you do have a true seizure disorder, that you probably won't have any more of the petit mal seizures you had when you were young, but that you will have to remain on medication indefinitely to control these new episodes. They are a type of seizure we call 'temporal lobe' because they involve a disturbance in the temporal lobes of the brain." He touched his fingers to his temples, "—areas on both sides of the brain that are involved with memory and the senses, like tasting and smelling, and which also play a major part in emotion. You experience the blurring and tunnel vision and the bad taste because the parts of your brain that deal with sight and smell and taste malfunction for brief periods. You don't fall down, lose consciousness, and go into convulsions the way people with grand mal seizures do. But you do have something very intense, very unexpected and unpleasant happen to you. Something unacceptable. And you may be pleased to know that we can prevent it." He smiled broadly, his eyes flashing in hopes of some sort of response. Melanie betrayed the hint of a grin.

Ferrier thumbed through Melanie's records and found his note from her last visit. She had been on three anticonvulsant drugs

49

when she first came to see him—Phenurone, Diamox, and Tegretol—several drugs sometimes used in concert to obtain good seizure control. Ferrier had raised the daily dosage of Tegretol slightly, and Melanie had had only one episode in the two weeks since her first visit. He discussed with her the possibility of raising the dosage levels again slightly, but they agreed that the current levels should be tried a while longer. "And stress will play a role with your true seizures as well," he said. "Emotional stress, lack of sleep, alcohol, hormonal changes, all can make you more seizure prone, even when you're taking your medication properly."

Before Melanie got up from her chair, Ferrier asked if there was anything else she thought he ought to know. "No. No, I feel good about it, everything. I think I can more and more avoid the tension seizures. And if the drugs are helping with the others. . . ." She got up from her chair.

Ferrier stood. "Tell Bonnie one month then," he said as he handed her the billing form. "Take care of yourself." Melanie put out her hand and at last she surrendered a smile.

With a miniature tape recorder that he held pressed to his lips, Ferrier dictated a note on Melanie's visit that would later be typed, then scanned and initialed by him, and added to her records. When he clicked off the recorder, I asked him how he distinguished between epileptic seizures and ones that are psychosomatic.

"Several ways. Most people don't respond to pain during an epileptic seizure, so if you're with a patient during a seizure you can test for that. Also, the history you get from a patient really does tell you an awful lot; it's the most useful way of differentiating. And there's a nice new video monitoring technique with which you can watch a seizure in progress while the patient is hooked up to the EEG machine, and you can compare the seizure with the simultaneous electrical activity in the brain. One of these methods can almost always give you enough information to know whether anticonvulsants are called for."

"Are drugs always going to be the primary means of treating epilepsy?"

"Oh, I think so. There'll be newer, better drugs. A huge percentage of the neuropharmacological work going on now is di-

50

rected at epilepsy. I think there's a likelihood that if we ever find a perfect anticonvulsant it will be one similar to chemicals that already exist in the brain, compounds that prevent most of us from having bizarre neuronal discharges, and hence seizures, and which stop seizures naturally once they start."

"It's amazing to me that we've come up with such an array of chemicals that we can consume beneficially," I said.

"Why? Why does that amaze you?"

"Well, that our bodies can benefit, or be cured or whatever, by things that are foreign to us."

"Food is foreign. An apple is as foreign as phenobarbital. Anything that we ingest can be either beneficial or detrimental—or benign." He called the receptionist, and asked whether his next patient had arrived. "Okay, buzz me when he gets here. That," he said, "is why I just can't deal with people who're so vehemently antidrug. Food is simply a collection of elements and molecules. But some people still can't accept the idea that man is capable of inventing a molecule that can produce good effects and that doesn't come from the bosom of Mother Earth."

"But you have to admit that some doctors deserve their reputations for being all too eager to prescribe drugs."

"Some. Sure, there are a few, but that's not the point. Some people tend to lump thalidomide and penicillin in the same group, and that's absurd. There are lots and lots of wonderful, valuable drugs—Tegretol, L-dopa, *aspirin*—that are very important to us. Have you heard of Paul Ehrlich, the German bacteriologist who came up with the term 'magic bullet'? He said it's easy to understand the concept of a bullet that enters your body and kills you, but the concept of a bullet that enters your body and kills only your disease is a bit more complex. He found a magic bullet for the treatment of syphilis, a drug called salvarsan, which probably saved thousands of lives. And for God's sake, if you have magic bullets for syphilis or seizures or what have you, you *use* them."

"So are we eventually going to find magic bullets for everything? Magic bullets that will keep us alive indefinitely?"

"I suppose the true goal of medicine is to see that people live good, long, healthy lives, and then that they die as quickly and as painlessly as possible. We're never going to be able to keep people alive forever."

"But the average life expectancy keeps getting longer."

"That's because of better diets, better hygiene and sanitation. Also because of better medicine. But there's a ceiling. Maybe someday virtually everybody can live to the limits of human capability, but there is a limit. A few people make it to a hundred; you hear of the odd case of some guy in South America who claims to be a hundred and fifteen or whatever; but I think the genetic age ceiling for the general population is probably about ninety to ninety-five—a long time, plenty of time to have a great life. There's that Chinese saying that a moth lives but a few hours and has time enough." Ferrier smiled at me. "Well, I've only got one response to that. Thank God I'm not a moth."

The next patient never arrived. Ferrier and I sat in his office and waited; he was happy to have the break. I asked him if it was common for patients simply not to show up.

"Oh, it doesn't happen every day, but it happens," he said. "People decide they are feeling better and don't bother to call and cancel. Nobody loves doctor visits. Have you heard the joke about the woman who goes to see the doctor? He examines her and tells her she has a very serious problem with her liver. The woman looks shocked and says, 'Liver? But the pain is in my back. Doctor, I'm afraid I'm going to need a second opinion.' So the doctor says, 'Okay. Kidneys?' "

I groaned, then changed the subject, asking about the auras and strange sensations that accompany many types of seizures. Ferrier turned in his high-back chair and scanned the wall of books behind his desk. "The vast majority of things people report are unpleasant—bad tastes, bad smells, nausea; sensations of fear or anxiety are also common. But let me see if I can find something. Yes, this is great. Here." Ferrier found the book he wanted and turned back to face me. "Dostoyevski was an epileptic. Have you heard that? He claimed his seizures were wonderful experiences, and his main character in *The Idiot* has the same kind of sensations. Listen:

> *There was a moment or two in his epileptic condition, almost before the fit itself, when his brain seemed to catch fire at brief moments. . . . His sensation of being alive and his awareness increased tenfold at those moments, which flashed by like*

lightning. His mind and heart were flooded by a dazzling light. All his agitation, all his doubts and worries seemed composed in a twinkling, culminating in a great calm, full of serene and harmonious joy and hope, full of understanding.

Ferrier looked up as he closed the book. "The lucky bastard."

I laughed. "But that's rare, huh?"

"Extremely rare. But you do encounter them, the so-called orgasmic seizures—people report religious or cosmic experiences, intense sexual sensations, or unbelievable euphoria."

"Do people report sensations of pain?"

"Pain as a symptom of a seizure is almost nonexistent, probably because perception of pain is a deep brain function. The feeling of pain is localized in the thalamus, two tiny bits of brain tissue that are tucked under the big cerebrum, which comprises most of the brain. Seizures usually take place in the cortex, the bark, the thin layer of gray matter that covers the cerebrum. So the manifestations of seizures are all related to cerebral functions—sensations, movement, thought, emotions, memory—all of which are at least partly cortical. That's why so-called focal, limited, seizures are so fascinating. Grand mal seizures, which affect the whole cortex, look pretty much alike: people lose consciousness, fall down, they foam at the mouth and can become incontinent, and have tonic-clonic style convulsions—their arms and legs and trunk become stiff and then jerk and flail. But with focal seizures, the manifestations always depend on the part of the cortex that's affected. So you get one arm jerking, or you smell rotten eggs, or you have an intense *déjà vu* experience. Of course, with some patients, their seizures have a focal onset, a sudden bad taste, say, that then spreads to the rest of the cortex, at which point they have a grand mal seizure."

"Didn't you say that things, certain conditions, can bring on seizures?"

"Sure, absolutely—lack of sleep, too much alcohol, drug ODs. But there are types of seizures that have actual triggers, that are precipitated, in effect, by some specific stimulus. They aren't common, but they're amazing. Flashing or blinking lights are probably the most common. Then there are seizures called 'kinesogenic' that are caused by only a particular movement. If the patient gets up out of a chair with his left leg first, he never has a seizure. But if he gets up in a certain fashion, with the *right* leg first, he *always* has one. And with 'musicogenic' epilepsy, a certain tune or melody does it. Let's say it's the first notes of the first movement of Beethoven's Fifth Symphony. When you hear the 'ta, ta, ta, tum,' you have a seizure—but *only* when you hear those notes in that order."

"Meaning that those notes have some sort of drastic psychological effect?"

"No. That's what is so intriguing. They seem to be true physiological seizures."

"Do you have any patients like that right now?"

"I do have a patient who came in saying that for several months she had been experiencing these strange, spacey, detached feelings, lasting a few seconds or a few minutes, always at work, always associated with looking at a computer monitor. She didn't report any sensations of fear or bad taste or smells and had no other history of seizures herself or in her family. She said that although she was separated from her husband, things between them were amicable—he lived next door—and I didn't detect any pronounced recent stress. Her examination was entirely normal. I scheduled an EEG, during which we rolled in the office Apple and tried to evoke an episode, but no luck, and the EEG was normal. But for focal seizures the first EEG is positive less than 25 percent of the time, so I thought her situation warranted a trial of Tegretol—she was having up to twenty of these episodes a day at the office. Three months later the episodes still hadn't slackened in frequency, and on the weekends she said she was still 100 percent free of them. It would have been really very interesting if she had had a true seizure disorder, but it just didn't stack up. Her EEGs were all normal and the medication made no difference. I had to believe it was psychosomatic, and I sent her to Tom Tea, a psychiatrist. When he probed the whole issue of her husband, she responded quite emotionally, I guess, and Tom got the impression that she regarded the husband, or ex-husband or whatever, as almost mysteriously powerful. Then, unfortunately, she canceled her second appointment with him. And isn't it interesting that she has the episodes at work and not at home, next door to the guy? She's really a very intriguing patient, but wouldn't it have been great if she had an epilepsy that was triggered by a computer terminal?"

"Great for you."

"Well, sure. That's what I mean," he said.

The electroencephalogram (EEG) is a series of amplifiers that are able to enhance minute oscillating currents being produced by groups of brain cells. The electrical waves are detected by electrodes placed symmetrically around the scalp and are transmitted as continuous ink traces—one for any combination of the twenty or more electrodes—on a long paper strip. The EEG is an invaluable tool for the diagnosis of epilepsy, but it is not an electronic litmus test, and neurologists must remind themselves to treat the patient, not the EEG. Regardless of what an EEG shows—even if it is grossly abnormal epileptiform activity—if a person does not have seizures, he or she does not have epilepsy. And conversely, a person who, without obvious precipitating factors, has had two or more seizures, has epilepsy—even if the EEG is normal. Like many other neurological disorders, the diagnosis of epilepsy is ultimately a clinical one, meaning it must be based on the patient's history and the physician's examination, not on a battery of laboratory tests or electronic investigations.

Physicians lump seizure diagnoses into two basic categories. Symptomatic seizures are those for which there is an obvious cause—severe head trauma, encephalitis, tumor, stroke. Idiopathic seizures are those that have no obvious genesis, but they, too, are most likely caused by injury—by subtle trauma at birth that results in the minute scarring of cortical gray matter, too insignificant to be detected on a CAT scan—or even at autopsy—but pronounced enough to cause groups of neurons to misfire on occasion.

The actual cause of a given seizure disorder is of less importance than is the seizure variety and its focus in the brain—which ultimately dictate the drugs that are prescribed. Petit mal is usually best controlled by ethosuximide or valproic acid, for example; Tegretol is often most effective for temporal lobe seizures. But a seizure patient's regime of daily medication also depends on which drugs he or she can most easily tolerate. Rare but documented side effects to the array of anticonvulsants now in use include drowsiness, insomnia, rashes, headaches, and anorexia. Dilantin, a versatile, nonsedative anticonvulsant in use since 1938—and the world's most widely prescribed drug for the treatment of epilepsy—can commonly and rather inexplicably cause gingival hyperplasia, that is, excessive growth of the gums.

The beneficial mechanisms of the anticonvulsants remain somewhat mysterious. Since early in this century, when phenobarbital was first used with success, physicians and scientists have known that anticonvulsants somehow slow or quiet electrochemical activity within and between nerve cells, but a detailed understanding of how they do so is only now in its formative stages.

Virtually all drugs that affect brain function do so by interacting with one or more of the brain's neurotransmitters—endogenous chemicals that either facilitate or inhibit electrical "communication" between one neuron and another. Although scientists do not know how many neurotransmitters are active in the brain, they have so far been able to identify more than twenty, and some speculate that there may actually be hundreds, each acting to enhance or block transmissions between discrete groups of neurons—nerve cells.

The transmission of information between neurons is a process that involves both electrical and chemical actions. A nerve impulse travels the length of a neuron's fiber, called its axon, by means of altered electrical potentials. The interior of a resting or unstimulated neuron is negatively charged; when it is stimulated, the permeability of its membrane briefly allows positively charged sodium ions to flood into it, reversing the electrical charge down the length of the axon. As the positive charge reaches the end of the axon, it causes the release of the particular neurotransmitter that that neuron releases into the "synapse," the small space that separates that neuron's axon from the branching fibers of its neighboring neuron. If the neurotransmitter encounters "receptors" on the branching fibers (the "dendrites") of a second neuron to which it can chemically connect in a kind of lock-and-key fashion, the resulting connection charges the second neuron positively and the impulse is in turn conducted down its length, the whole process finished in no more than one thousandth of a second.

Drugs are basically able to affect the transmission of electrochemical information by influencing neurotransmitters. Some, for example, lock onto receptor sites and block neurotransmitters that would otherwise stimulate an electrical charge. Conversely, others mimic a specific neurotransmitter, thereby charging neurons that, without the drug, would tend to remain at rest. In the case of the anticonvulsants, it seems likely that most act on *both* inhibitory and excitatory neurotransmitters. Recent studies have found, for example, that phenobarbital and Dilantin facilitate the action of the amino acid GABA, a major inhibitory neurotransmitter, as well as block glutamic acid, an excitatory neurotransmitter that is plentiful throughout the brain. Do the small brain lesions that give rise to seizures do so by causing groups of neurons to produce too much glutamic acid or too little GABA— leading on occasion to the chaotic, uncontrolled firing of millions of minute neurons? Are other as yet undiscovered neurotransmitters involved with them in the complex seizure process? Or are seizures the result of some still unknown mechanism whose action is halted by the anticonvulsants, their effects on these two neurotransmitters only a coincidence?

We had not gotten beyond the guacamole on a clear January evening and I had just ordered my second Corona Extra when Ferrier's beeper summoned him to the health center at the university. We made a quick deal with the waitress and were off. The patient was a freshman named Sandra Fischer, whose friends had brought her in because she had recently begun to have frequent "staring" spells, each lasting ten or fifteen seconds. At first, her boyfriend said, they assumed she was just "spacing out," but beginning today the short spells had begun to occur every five minutes or so, sometimes accompanied by slight jerking in her arms or legs.

Ferrier spoke briefly with Sandra's friends, who waited nervously near the reception desk, then went into an examining room and introduced himself to her. She was pale and looked tired; she was obviously afraid, but otherwise seemed normal. When he asked her what brought her to the health center, she said she wasn't sure, but that her friends said she had been blanking out, going into a kind of sudden trance.

"Are you at all aware of the times when you've had a spell?" he asked.

"No. If it wasn't for them, I wouldn't know I've had them. They say that when I come out of them I go right on with what I was doing or saying when it started. Somebody'll say, 'Do you know what you just did?' or something, and then I'll go, 'Oh, I guess I did it again, huh?' "

Sandra sat on an examining table; the paper stretched across it tore as she turned to remove her shoes, and, as he began his examination, the doctor asked if she had recently noticed unusual tastes or smells or stomach discomforts. Then, as Sandra was answering his questions about whether she had had a difficult delivery, rheumatic fever, or encephalitis as a child, saying, "I don't think I've ever heard—" She suddenly stopped speaking. Her eyes rolled slightly back, her face was blank and uncomprehending, and her left leg quivered steadily. Ferrier quickly held her head in his hands, shouting her name, slapping her cheek, blowing into her eyes. Her expression did not change, the quivering continued, and her eyelids did not blink until a few seconds later, when she was just as suddenly alert again, saying, "my mom talking about any of those."

He asked if anyone in her family had epilepsy, if she had had a head injury of any kind in the last year or so, if she had recently been aware of any strange thoughts or sensations. She answered no to the first two questions, then paused before she said, "The one thing I can think of is that I've had lots of *déjà vu*. You know? Lots of things have happened that seem like they're repeating."

"Well," Ferrier said as he looked at his notes, scratched down on a prescription pad. "Several things. I think we're going to have you spend the night in the hospital. You're going to be fine, but it looks quite likely that you're beginning to have what are called temporal lobe seizures—the episodes of blanking out—caused by some occasional misfiring in the temporal lobes on the sides of your brain. I'm going to start you on some medicine that should begin to limit them rather quickly, but as long as you're having them so often it's important that you be where you can get plenty of attention. Tomorrow we'll do some testing, a brain wave test and a CAT scan, that should make us quite certain of where we stand and how to proceed."

"So I'll get over them?" Sandra asked.

"You may well have to stay on medication a long time to avoid having them, but I'll be able to give you better answers tomorrow after I see the tests. In the meantime, though I know this is a bit frightening, I promise you you're going to be fine. Ever ridden in an ambulance before?"

Sandra shook her head. Ferrier told her he would speak to her friends again, and that they could meet her at the hospital. "By the way," he asked, "this isn't just a rather drastic means of avoiding an exam tomorrow, is it?" Sandra grinned, and Ferrier said goodnight.

We drove through the brightly lit campus streets, then down the hill to the restaurant; a pall of wood-smoke was suspended in the air. Ferrier punched in a tape—Ian Tyson singing cowboy songs. "So those are seizures, huh?" I asked.

"Definitely," he said. "I'll need to see her EEG, but yeah . . . those are seizures. Hers look a lot like petit mal, like the *absence* seizures you see in children. But you don't get petit mal all of a sudden at age—what?—nineteen. Most temporal lobe seizures involve certain automatic movements—chewing, eye blinking, retching; some people in the midst of their seizures can very carefully take their clothes off, then very carefully put them back on. In her case, it seems to be just the *absence* and that minor tremor in her leg. I'll show you her EEG tomorrow. I imagine we'll see some spiking in her temporal lobes. The CAT scan will be normal, but with seizure onset at her age, she's already old enough that it's a good idea to be sure that these aren't the result of a tumor. This certainly doesn't look like it involves a tumor, but you've got to rule that out."

"I'm beginning to get the impression that epilepsy, one type or another, is very common."

"Oh, sure, seizures are real common. I think the statistics are something like 2 or 3 percent of the population for all the seizure disorders combined. That's similar to the incidence of diabetes, for instance. Have you looked at the brochures that the epilepsy organizations put out? All of them have sections listing the great people in history who had epilepsy. Julius Caesar, Socrates, Dostoyevski, Tchaikovsky, Handel . . . Van Gogh, Martin Luther, Dante—all the truly groovy guys had seizures."

Wendy Stetham was sitting up in bed when we walked into her room. She looked up, letting her Harold Robbins novel rest on her round stomach. The rash that had covered her arms a few days before was almost gone. She gave Ferrier a nod when he said, "Hey, there," but she didn't speak. "So I hear you're still not cooperating," he said. "Another one last night?"

"Another one."

"How's the baby?"

"It wants out."

"I don't blame him. If I was him I'd be ready to run away from home, I think. Have you had more contractions?"

"Yep. But they say I still haven't dilated. I'm getting so sick of this."

"I know you are. But your Tegretol levels *are* looking better, and believe me, we're going to work through this. I guess Dr. Moore's going to decide about inducing labor after today's sonogram."

"Tell him we're both ready."

"We?"

"Me and the baby."

"I will. Is there anything else I can do for you?"

"You could get rid of these seizures."

"We're trying." Wendy said nothing more.

"God, I hope that kid's okay," Ferrier said to me as we hurried down the hall.

Sandra was watching a tiny television that hung on a slender arm above her bed when we entered her room; she waved hello as she turned off the set. Ferrier sat on the edge of her bed. "What are you watching?" he asked.

She blushed. " 'General Hospital.' "

"Great show," he said. "I actually didn't go to medical school. Everything I know came from 'General Hospital.' You're feeling better, I guess."

"Yeah, not quite so freaked out. And the nurses said I wasn't having nearly as many spells."

"That's what they told me, too. And your CAT scan was normal. The EEG, the test where they taped all the electrodes to your head, showed some unusual activity on the sides of your brain, in the areas we call the temporal lobes. What happens is that the nerve cells get overexcited at times and they fire abnormally, causing your seizures."

"Does this mean I'm not going to be able to drive and all that other stuff?"

"I'm not going to want you to drive for a while. But it probably won't be too long. Our first job is to get you on a medication you respond well to that will calm those nerve cells and prevent the seizure activity. The most important thing for you to do will be to take your medicine absolutely religiously. If you do, you'll be driving again, doing everything completely normally. It may take us a little while to get you on the right level of the medications you do best with, but once we get there we'll be in business. And I highly recommend soap operas. Be sure you see several a day."

"Gotcha," she said. Then in a quiet voice, "I am kind of scared about this."

"Sure. You're bound to be. But I don't think you will be for too long. Just between you and me, if I had to get a neurological disease, I'd probably pick this one. Epilepsy really gets a bigger billing than it deserves." Ferrier reached for her hand. "You're going to do real well." He stood. "I'll see you this evening. They'll come to take a little blood after a while so we can check the level of the Tegretol, but I'll tell them to go easy on you."

I followed Ferrier to the nurses' station and waited while he scribbled a note in Sandra's chart. He looked up and smiled at a tall nurse in a raspberry-colored uniform who had just come around the corner. "Oh, I like it," he said. She held her hands up to her short, curly hair and made a face. "No. I definitely like it," he said. Then to me: "Come on. If I don't get back to the office, Bonnie will kill me."

"I thought you were the boss," I said.

"Jesus, you haven't learned anything about this business, have you?" He marched toward the EXIT sign at the end of the long, quiet corridor, and I followed a few steps behind him. Most of the wide wooden doors that led to the patients' rooms were open and I glanced quickly, furtively, into each one as I walked—wondering who besides Sandra was captive in this cavernous place that smelled like alcohol and cleanser and clotting milk, wondering in a cold but inquisitive way if each one's condition were serious, wondering for only a moment what could be the matter.

3 The Involuntary Dance

There were times during my tenure as Ferrier's onlooker when I was lured by his life as a physician. The hours he spent at his job were oppressive; the dozens of conflicting daily demands could drive him to shrieking frustration; and the beeper he wore on his belt was a sort of time bomb, always threatening to shatter a quiet evening or a carefree Saturday afternoon. But there were real attractions nonetheless, aspects of his profession that offered him an enveloping sense of purpose, an opportunity to think, to search, to be challenged—an occasional chance to step outside himself, to lose himself in his own rapt attention to someone else's survival.

A healthy ego is no doubt a necessary prerequisite for any physician, and Ferrier's ego was most often in fine condition—an able assistant in deciding whether the faint shadow on a CAT scan film was "artifact" or a small but thriving tumor, in deciding whether to risk surgery or the side effects of medication, in assuring a grieving family that he and his colleagues had done all that they could. Too much self-doubt, too much indecision, could be crippling, it seemed to me, and I was intrigued by his ability to worry only up to a point—to stew, to pull at his brown beard—until a decision *had* to be made, then to make it and to forgo the second guessing. I was envious, at times, of the opportunity to be put under that kind of pressure.

There was an attraction to the sleuthing as well, to the detective work of diagnosis—determining whether a weak arm and lethargy in an eighteen-year-old meant a pinched thoracic nerve, a benign postviral complication, or the ominous first episode of demyelinating disease. I was attracted, too, by Ferrier's opportunity simply to provide some reassurance, a bit of hope, to be able to say to the pale, patient people standing outside the doors of an intensive care unit, "It looks like he's out of the woods; we think his chances are good." But perhaps most of all, I was lured by the palpable reminders that he mattered, that he and his talents were needed the full pages of the appointment book, the phone calls from ophthalmologists and internists and pediatricians in need of a consultation, the high-pitched beeps of his pager.

The practice of clinical medicine is ultimately a business, of course, a means of earning a living, regardless of its lures and liabilities. Ferrier and his fellow physicians—who are more than willing to talk about fee schedules and medicare copayments and collection agencies among themselves—tend to ignore the financial aspects of their profession in front of their patients, wanting, understandably I suppose, to appear to care more about the patient's malady than his money, saying, "Please give this to the people out front," when they hand the patient the billing form, never confessing, "Here, Mr. Cohen, is exactly what you owe me." Is it silly to assume that medical care is any different from car repair? Would everyone be better served if doctors admitted that they were simply in business to offer a service? Or is the care and treatment of the body fundamentally so different from other occupations that physicians will always seem a little separate from the rest of us—better paid, harder worked, and, for a complex mix of reasons, more often envied?

Ferrier's office is one of many medical clinics housed in an ugly beige-brick, two-story box—an architectural travesty whose ultimate insults are the strange, swirling, Gaudi-esque bars that block every window. The building, filled each weekday with more than forty physicians and dentists, hundreds of technicians, nurses, secretaries, and receptionists, and an endless exchange of patients, sits next door to an abortion clinic, where armed security guards keep a twenty-four-hour vigil, and across the street from County Hospital, the largest of the two hospitals in town, both staffed by a self-governing association of physicians and surgeons in private practice.

Inside Ferrier's clinic, beyond the dim waiting room that is furnished with six new sofas, a plastic child-size table and chairs, and a small aquarium that gurgles quietly in a corner, is the bright and busy clerical area where three secretaries keep the operation afloat, scheduling patients, greeting them when they arrive, processing their payments, typing mounds of dictated letters and record notes, filing charts, puzzling over obscure insurance forms, culling the daily mountain of mail, and playing the role of traffic cop in phone conversations with patients, other physicians, and the occasional insistent stockbroker, all of whom simply must speak to the doctor at once.

Ferrier's office sits at the far end of the suite of rooms—beyond the "conference room" where cardboard file boxes confer with an unused Apple computer, beyond his tiny examining room, and across the hall from the large room with exercise mats and massage tables where Leslie Sachs, the staff physical therapist, sees her patients. His office, dominated by a simple Scandinavian-style desk and the black leather chairs he has appropriated from his father, is decorated with rows of imposing thick-spined books standing in teak cabinets that fill one wall, another wall of diplomas and certificates calligraphed in Latin, and two white walls hung with black-framed posters of exhibitions of the work of Alfred Stieglitz, Giorgio Morandi, and Ruffin Cooper. Except for the fat bars that almost entirely block it, the view from the single window would be a lovely one of the rocky, now snow-draped, escarpment that slides into the upper streets of the city.

At the opposite end of the suite, around the corner from the coffee machine and the newly acquired microwave oven, adjacent to the room where EEGs are administered, is the office of Ferrier's partner, Wilson Putnam, a gentle and engaging man only a few years older than Ferrier, a Floridian now ensconced in the Rocky Mountains. He is the devoted father of two sons and he cannot be on call on Tuesdays because that is the evening the scout troop meets. He is an avid bicyclist and an admitted Italophile; he rarely takes vacations, but when he does, he invariably travels to Italy returning with tales of encounters with incredible pastas and spectacular days in the Dolomites.

Ferrier and Putnam seem suited to sharing a business, although neither one would be likely to use that term to describe their practice. They argue regularly about office decor and the fate of crates of abandoned files, but on issues like fee schedules and employee salaries they seem comfortably in sync. When one suggests that a new telephone system is needed, or an aquarium pump, or a replacement for the antiquated copying machine, the other normally assumes a ceremonial skepticism for a few days, then agrees that a check should be written.

The two neurologists spend their days sixty feet apart, but they see each other only at the odd thirty second rendezvous; they quickly solicit each other's opinions or share unusual cases or discuss some ominous new change in the Medicare "regs" as they cross paths in the parking lot, in the radiology department at County Hospital where CAT scan films are mounted on lighted boards, or at the private entrance to the clinic. On occasion, they schedule a bona fide office meeting, each one making the other swear he will be on time. At least once each week they agree that they really should get together for a drink, a meal, or a movie sometime. It is always a great idea, and they agree they will do it just as soon as they can.

I had spent many weeks with Ferrier, watching him and Putnam struggle to stay on schedule, before I realized that it isn't actually the business of seeing patients—taking their histories, examining them, providing direct consultation and care—that makes their days so frenetic and so long, making it a very bankable bet that a phone call from one of them saying he will be right over means he will try to be along within the hour, meaning that an appointment scheduled for two-thirty is not likely to begin before three. Instead, it is the business of *documenting* their daily activities that becomes the chief consumer of time. Following a fifteen-minute examination, each doctor often spends five minutes or more dictating a note that will be typed and added to the patient's file. And at the end of an hour-long evaluation, Ferrier often spends another ten minutes drafting the letter that will be sent to the physician who referred the patient. During rounds, a morning check on a patient can be as quick as a minute. The time it takes to scribble orders and progress notes into the patient's chart takes double or triple that time. Letters, charts, admission and discharge notes, insurance forms, legal depositions, EEG evaluations, and a ceaseless series of phone calls—these are the relentless demands of the doctor's day. At times, the surprisingly isolated and undivided attention he is able to give to his patients can appear merely peripheral.

65

At the end of a twelve-hour day, a day in which he has probably spent half his time writing up the medicine he has practiced during the other half, Ferrier's last task is to read and sign off on all the letters, all the notes on office visits and phone calls, all the forms and official folderol that he generated the previous day. He makes his way through the stack like a weary accountant at work on an endless audit, his quick signature just a half-circle followed by a short, loping line. Then, before he puts on his coat and closes his cluttered briefcase, he glances at the covers of the medical journals that wait at the bottom of the pile and circles the titles of the articles that he really needs to read—at home tonight, or maybe sometime next week.

"I'm not going to do this forever," Ferrier has told me. "Ten or fifteen years max." Like his father—an architect who designed scores of schools and hospitals, and who dreamed of a retirement when he would be able to do nothing but paint—Ferrier, too, imagines the day when he will be a painter who used to be a doctor. Ferrier knows I am skeptical—I think he is more addicted to medicine's mad pace than he knows; I think he is a whirling dervish who is buoyed by the frantic dance—but he maintains that he will simply quit, gladly and without regret, someday. "Of course, I like what I'm doing, sure I do. But I like lots of other things, too. Don't you think it would be crazy to keep this up forever?" Today, a decade into his retirement, Ferrier's father uses the studio he built at the edge of a mountain creek only as a guest house. He works as an architectural consultant and sits on design-review boards and planning commissions. He never has time to paint.

Professor Joseph Varga had been a friend of Ferrier's father since they met in the late 1940s and discovered that they were raised in nearby towns in the Carpathian piedmont, near the present-day Czechoslovakian-Ukrainian border. Neither man was the sort who enjoyed pining about the old country, but there were few people in the Rocky Mountains who spoke Czech, few who intimately understood what America meant to its postwar immigrants, and the two men had remained in touch throughout their careers' hectic decades.

Now a physics professor emeritus and suffering from Parkinson's disease, Dr. Varga had become the patient of his old friend's son. When Ferrier joined Putnam in practice two years before, Professor Varga—Dr. Putnam's patient at the time—explained the family friendship to Putnam during an office visit, hoping the doctor would not be offended if he switched physicians. Putnam happily endorsed the change, and the professor walked down the hall to Ferrier's office, announcing, in an accent Ferrier had known all his life, "I am in your hands, young man. Please take good care of me."

In the two years since Ferrier had become Professor Varga's neurologist, his office notes had begun to reflect a slight worsening of his patient's condition. The tremor in his left hand had increased perceptibly and he admitted that it was becoming more difficult to initiate movement. He had the drawn, blank, "masked" facial expression that is characteristic of the disease; his voice was weak and a little flat; he walked with a slow, shuffling gait, and his posture was stooped at the waist.

"I don't think you should write a book about Parkinson's disease," Professor Varga told me on the morning that I met him and his wife, Helen. "It would not have a happy ending." He did not smile, but it seemed as if he were trying to. Varga, his thick shock of white hair parted close to one ear and raked toward the other, nodded at Ferrier. "Am I his guinea pig, John?" he asked.

"Absolutely not," said Ferrier, "you're my guinea pig. You came to me first. How have you been?"

Professor Varga slowly turned in his chair to look at his wife, as if to confirm that he would say what they had agreed upon. "Up and down," he said. "Up and down. A good day is when I can speak clearly. Other days, I don't know what happens to my speech. My lower lip doesn't seem to move as easily as it should. On those days, I have difficulty to get up from the chair, and to turn over in the bed is a big transaction. Getting started can be very difficult. I have to think it through, to develop a strategy just to stand up."

Ferrier leaned across his desk to observe the professor's arms, both revealing a steady, rhythmic tremor, his wrists and palms rocking in the slow manner that is referred to as "pill-rolling." The tremor lessened when Ferrier asked him to touch his outstretched fingers to his nose and to pick up a paperweight on the doctor's desk.

"Joseph thinks the Parlodel is making him groggy. He says he has a hard time thinking clearly for an hour or two after he's taken it," Helen said. She glanced at her husband as she spoke.

"And you're taking the Parlodel when?"

"With breakfast. I had the same problem when I was on it before. It makes it hard to get anything accomplished, but you people have always pushed hard for it."

"Bromocriptine, or Parlodel, as I've mentioned, is relatively new and is showing some very impressive results with lots of patients. And if they move onto it slowly enough, many, many people seem to be able to tolerate it very well. I think we ought to try switching it to bedtime, so you can just sleep through that groggy phase, and depending on how that goes, we might try to slowly increase it. You know, I have some patients on ten to fifteen a day. And they do very well."

"Joseph has this thing about taking pills," Helen said.

"You and everyone else in this town. If it's a garlic tablet or smashed barley seed or something, they'll swallow dozens, but if a doctor prescribes it, it's got to be poison."

"No. I simply wonder if I might not explode if I take too many pills," the professor said.

"You mean that dreaded exploding patient syndrome," Ferrier said facetiously, smiling, leaning back in his chair. "I think people in your discipline refer to it as the big bang, don't they?"

The professor's rigid facial muscles shaped a thin smile. He turned to Helen as if to show it to her.

"If you promise him he won't explode, maybe we can get him to try the Parlodel at night," Helen said.

"I want you to tell me honestly, John," the professor said, his mind now set on something new. "Do you think I'm deteriorating?"

"Well, it's difficult to say, because Parkinson's changes so much from day to day. Some days, as you know, you hardly think you have it, you seem virtually normal. And on other days, well, you just told me what the other days are like. But to try to be honest, I think you are a little slower, definitely. But your speech, especially today, seems very good, and when you walked in, your posture looked a little better. So I think things in general look encouraging—and they'll look even better, I predict, when we get more of the Parlodel on board."

"I'm in your hands," he said, his own hands trembling slightly in his lap.

In the centuries before late-eighteenth-century British physician James Parkinson's name was attached to the disease that he was the first to identify, virtually all disorders of movement were called "chorea," the Greek and Latin word for dance—a word whose medical meaning began with a raucous medieval rite. In 1374 at Aix-la-Chapelle, townspeople celebrated the festival of Saint John the Baptist by forming circles hand in hand, singing "Saint John, so brisk and cheerful Saint John," and dancing in near delirium until they finally fell to the ground, writhing, their limbs flailing, their whole bodies sometimes shaking uncontrollably. This strange new phenomenon soon became a very popular one to induce on festive occasions, spreading throughout France and Germany, a "malady" that held excellent prospects for recovery and that came to be known as *Chorea Sancti Viti*, Saint John's dance, or Saint Vitus's dance. For the next hundred and fifty years, medical practitioners, such as they were, simply assumed that all the unexplained involuntary movements that they observed were variants of Saint Vitus's dance. It wasn't until a German physician, Bombastus von Hohenheim, asserted in the early 1500s that there was indeed a distinction between frenzy-produced *chorea lascivia* and what he called *chorea naturalis* that the possibility of truly physiological movement disorders was considered.

In a text published in 1686, pioneer British physician Thomas Sydenham still used the term *Saint Vitus's dance* to describe the childhood movement disorder that is now known as Sydenham's chorea, describing the "dance" as "a sort of convulsion which attacks boys and girls from the tenth year until they have done growing." He wrote:

> At first it shows itself by a halting, or rather an unsteady movement of one of the legs, which the patient drags. Then it is seen in the hand of the same side. The patient cannot keep it a moment in its place. . . . Do what he may, it will be jerked elsewhere convulsively . . . he will exhibit a thousand gesticulations like a mountebank.

Its ritualistic origins were largely forgotten by this time, but the term *chorea* had firmly established its place in the medical lexicon and had done so to such a degree that dozens of discrete disorders were confusingly called chorea until early in the nineteenth century. When Parkinson published his description of a hitherto unrecognized disorder in 1817, he used the term *paralysis agitans*, or shaking palsy, to help distinguish it from the better-known choreiform diseases, and indeed it was distinct. Unlike the arrhythmic and unpredictable jerking movements that were characteristic of the choreas, Parkinson observed a malady whose principal obstacle was difficulty in initiating movement , accompanied by a slow and rhythmic tremor of the limbs when the patient was at rest. It seemed likely that the choreas and the shaking palsy were somehow related, but they were very different diseases.

In France in the following decades, Jean Martin Charcot and Gilles de la Tourette used the term *tic* to describe small, repetitive twitches of the muscles of the head, neck, and limbs; they, too, seemed distinct from the movements produced by choreas. Tics often had a psychological origin, the researchers presumed, and could afflict patients for years, principally out of habit. Years later, however, Tourette made an exhaustive study of a disorder he called *tics convulsifs*, which was characterized by multiple, lifelong tics, often including violent grimaces and short, explosive vocalizations, a disease—now known as Tourette's syndrome—that he believed was not habitual and whose origin was certainly physiological.

At the end of the nineteenth century, at about the same time that Tourette was studying tics, another movement disease was isolated in North America, this one a rare, inherited, and invariably fatal disease that was popularly referred to as "the magrums," probably deriving from an old Dutch word synonymous with "fidgets." George Huntington, a New York physician, the son and grandson of physicians, was first introduced to the disease when he was eight years old, traveling with his father on remote Long Island:

I recall it as vividly as though it had occurred but yester-
day. . . . Driving with my father through a wooded road lead-

ing from East Hampton to Amagansett, we suddenly came upon two women, mother and daughter, both tall, thin, almost cadaverous, both bowing, twisting, grimacing. I stared in wonderment, almost in fear . . . my medical education had its inception. From this point on, my interest in this disease has never wholly ceased.

Huntington called the disease "hereditary chorea," and, while he was still in his twenties, he succinctly described its unique characteristics—the tragic familial incidence, onset in adulthood, and its eventual result in severe dementia and death. Patients suffering from the disease were referred to him throughout his career, yet he was never able to determine its pathology or to slow its sinister progress. Nearly a century later, the medical community still has no means of treating the disease. Huntington's chorea remains one of the most insidious, yet mercifully rare, diseases known. One of every two children of a Huntington's sufferer will develop the disease, and for now, the only means of combating it is to encourage the children of confirmed Huntington's patients not to have children of their own.

Medical scientists do know now that Huntington's disease destroys the brain's caudate nucleus, one of four small and contiguous nerve cell clusters that are known as the basal ganglia—a deep brain system, surrounded by the cerebrum, whose principal function is to facilitate smooth and coordinated movement. In fact, all diseases of movement—the choreiform disorders, parkinsonism, the multitude of tics, and a variety of other "dyskinetic" disorders—probably have their pathogenesis in the basal ganglia. Some are hereditary, and all have very different onsets, symptoms, and courses, yet what they are believed to share are abnormalities of one or more structural elements of the basal ganglia, resulting in overproduction or underproduction (or a combination of both) of essential chemical neurotransmitters, principally dopamine and acetylcholine, which seem to need to exist in a kind of balance in order to make normal movement possible. Dopamine and acetylcholine are abundant throughout the brain and are essential chemical catalysts for many functions; within the basal ganglia, if the two neurotransmitters are not present in precise quantities, the effects are profound. Relatively too little dopamine is presumed responsible for the "bradykinesia," or paralysis, that is the principal feature of parkinsonism; conversely, abnormally high dopamine or acetylcholine activity appears to produce sudden, unexpected movements, tremors, or hyperactivity.

Charcot, experimenting a century ago, was the first to treat movement disorders chemically when he prescribed a belladonna alkaloid that produced a beneficial anticholinergic (acetylcholine-blocking) effect, and the drug remained an accepted treatment until a number of synthetic acetylcholine-suppressing drugs were introduced during the years following World War II. It was not until the early 1960s, however, that Canadian neurobiologist André Barbeau and his colleagues were able to demonstrate that low dopaminergic activity could be increased by a drug called levodopa, or L-dopa, which the brain is able to convert into dopamine. And in recent years, a new "mimicking" drug, bromocriptine, which the brain responds to as if it were dopamine, has proven successful in many patients. Research into the treatment of Parkinson's disease, the choreas, and all the diseases of the basal ganglia remains focused on this neurochemical front. More than with any other class of neurological diseases, the clinical treatment of movement disorders is a slow, and often frustrating, trial-and-error process, the patient enduring the prescription of a changing series of drugs administered at changing levels in an effort to find the chemical balance that comes closest to producing normal movement, to slowing the ceaseless dance.

Ferrier leaned forward and spoke into the small tape recorder that I had set beside the napkin box on the restaurant's Formica tabletop. "This is Neurology Update," he said, imitating the announcer on a cassette tape of a conference, "coming to you today from Tom's Tavern. Participating in today's luncheon discussion of basal gangliar disease is John Ferrier, a barely adequate neurologist with significant training deficits. Dr. Ferrier is questioned by Russell Martin, who, as you shall hear, asks far too many questions.

The questions were quickly interrupted, however, by the arrival of the hamburgers, Ferrier's ordered so rare, as always, that it was simply shaped into a patty and seared. He told me while he ate that he probably has twenty-five patients with Parkinson's disease, perhaps that many more who have tics, choreas, and a variety of relatively rare dyskinesias. I asked him if he had ever had a patient with Huntington's disease.

"I saw it during my residency, but in private practice I've never actually made a diagnosis. I do have two patients right now, not related, who are the children of people who died of Huntington's. They know what the story is, of course, and tend to come in concerned about some strange twitch or moodiness that could be a signal of something. And given half a chance, both the patients and I can get very scared by some of these symptoms. But for now, we're certainly not going to diagnose either one of them."

"What is it that ultimately kills people with degenerative diseases like Huntington's?"

"Normally, respiratory arrest or pneumonia or what have you. As the brain atrophies, so does the part of the nervous system that regulates breathing, heartbeat, the gag reflex; then nutrition suffers . . . you know. When the patient loses his gag reflex, for instance, he can inhale food or vomit and die of pneumonia—that sort of thing. The sad thing about Huntington's is that we could, in effect, prevent the next generation from contracting it—it would simply disappear—if everyone who had a positive family history of Huntington's decided absolutely not to take the chance and have kids. The problem is that by the time a patient is diagnosed with the disease, at thirty or forty, most have already had children, and by then it's too late. And some people, although it seems strange to me, when presented with the facts and the risks still choose to have children."

"It would actually just vanish? Become extinct?"

"That genetically transmitted biochemical defect would no longer be transmitted. The defect would disappear with the death of the last Huntington's patient—assuming a weird spontaneous mutation didn't occur."

"With something like Parkinson's, there isn't even that kind of theoretical hope, is there?"

"Well, Parkinson's certainly doesn't appear to be inherited, so the two are not similar as far as that goes. Parkinson's is actually on the rise, just because when people live longer, the incidence of older-age diseases goes up. I think the incidence of Parkinson's is something like ten to fifteen people per ten thousand, but that means the whole population, all ages, so it's really fairly high for a serious, disabling disease."

"Is it always going to be a question of treating it by trying different drugs?"

"Let me figure out how to explain this. Dopamine is an essential neurotransmitter throughout the brain, not just in the basal ganglia. We believe, for instance, that people with schizophrenia are often overproducing dopamine—the high levels of dopamine are actually responsible for some of the psychotic effects. That's why you've heard some of my parkinsonian patients say 'well, yes, the Symmetrel really does seem to make movement a lot easier, but I have these strange nightmares, and sometimes I even see things.' The Symmetrel can cause so much dopamine to be released that the patient's perfectly normal cerebrum gets too much of it and the patient starts to hallucinate. And it happens in reverse. When you give dopamine-suppressing drugs to schizophrenics, you can have significant success, you can make their lives livable, but sometimes the side effect is that the patient will develop parkinsonoid features—the paralysis, the stooped posture, the so-called masked facies, which is that characteristic drawn facial expression. So the challenge is to develop drugs that stimulate dopamine production, or that act like dopamine, but that do so *only* in the basal ganglia. When that happens, when we can isolate and act on only the individual dopamine receptors in that area, we'll be able to avoid some very serious side effects, and that dopaminergic-cholinergic balance will be much easier to—"

He was about to say "maintain," I suppose, when his beeper sounded; he unclipped it from his belt and glanced at the numbers on its display. "I guess I'd better check on this. It's the ER at County." I turned off the recorder, paid the check, and met him at the phone booth in the foyer.

"Trouble?" I asked when he hung up.

He motioned toward the door, then spat out bits of information as we walked the block to the car, a cold wind keening through the narrow street. "Fifty-seven-year-old man, works for the city, shoveling this morning, some water main or something, lost most of the movement on his left side. Mental status okay, left leg is numb. They said he can raise his left arm, but can't use his fingers."

"Do you think it's a stroke?"

"Sounds like it. This may take thirty minutes or so. You'd better call the office from the ER. Tell them I would have been on time."

Mrs. Pembroke had invited us to tea and we arrived only fifteen minutes late. Ferrier had seen her in his office three days before and the home visit was principally social. "If you could come to tea one day, you'd see how this disease has shattered my life," she'd told me in the office while Ferrier took a phone call. "I used to love to entertain, and I fancied myself a fine conversationalist. My husband was a barrister and we often had important guests in our house. Now, the very thought of hosting a dinner party with this"—she lifted her arms from her lap to show me her tremor—"seems completely impossible."

Ferrier was reluctant to accept the invitation when she phoned the following day, probably in part because he thought it might be awkward—he virtually never visits a patient at home—in part because there would surely be something else he should be doing late on a Thursday afternoon. "Hey, you don't get paid for going to tea," he joked, but I pestered him for an hour or two, and he relented at last, and I returned her call to say yes, we could come.

Mrs. Pembroke had moved from London to live near her two daughters eight years ago—four years after her husband had been killed when their weekend cottage burned, two years after she had developed Parkinson's disease. The tremor that began in her left hand and arm had gradually spread to her right arm, and to her legs. Under the care of physicians in both Britain and the United States, she had had varying degrees of success with several drugs. Sinemet, a dopamine agonist—a stimulator of the dopamine receptor—lessened her symptoms but caused nausea and vomiting as well. Symmetrel, a similar drug, produced nightmares when she took it at therapeutic levels. Parsidol, an anticholinergic, proved effective in controlling her tremor, but also invariably caused an unusual hip pain. In the months before she became Ferrier's patient, she was placed on an experimental "drug holiday," and her condition worsened greatly during the four weeks she went without medication. Subsequently, Ferrier had initiated Parlodel, as well as a low dosage of Sinemet, and, for the time being at least, both she and Ferrier felt good about her control.

Mrs. Pembroke showed us into her sitting room. A small fire had been laid in the fireplace, and the silver tea service sat on a dark fruitwood table. "Would you be kind enough to pour, Doctor?" she asked. "I'm afraid I don't trust myself." Ferrier put two shortbread biscuits on his saucer after he had poured the tea, then followed us to the small painting of the brick row house that had been her London home. A Morris Minor was parked on the street in front.

"It's not a very fine painting, but it was a wonderful house, really," she said. "Splendid. I'm still a bit cross with myself for selling it."

"I had a Minor when I lived in Edinburgh," Ferrier said. "One of my favorite cars."

"Oh, they were marvelous, weren't they?" she said. "Yes. Please sit down." Her voice was little more than a whisper, but the disease had only begun to freeze the muscles of her pretty, placid face. Her eyes were animated and bright and she could shape a beatific sort of smile. She placed her teacup on a table beside her chair, as if she had no intention of drinking from it, then folded her trembling hands in her lap. "This disease simply steals away any quality you've got," she had told me earlier in the week in Ferrier's office. "Its strength matches your own. When you're strong, it is strong; when you're weak, it's weak as well. I don't mean to be morbid when I say this, but if it weren't for my daughters, I would love to be able to take a pill and simply go to sleep. I don't believe there is such a pill, but to be very frank, I find the thought appealing."

But today was a better day. She could move more easily, and the worst of her tremor was absent. She told us about the many friends she had made in her years in the United States, and about the circle of young people who had come to depend on her for advice and support. "They seem to think I'm wise, which flatters me. Of course, I'm merely old. And they are very kind to me, they and my daughters. They take me shopping, and to concerts when I feel up to it—I'm still very keen on opera. I'm never at a loss for assistance if I need it. Let me tell you the most wonderful thing. One of my daughters' friends said to me one day, she said, 'you know, most elderly people suffer from at least something.' She made me realize that the only unfortunate thing for me is that mine is manifest. It's there for the whole world to see. I'm sorry that people have to observe this. I know it makes them uncomfortable."

"I'm sure people have told you often that they don't even notice it, and they really don't," Ferrier said.

"Oh, I can't possibly believe that. When the tremor is at its worst, it simply makes conversation impossible. People assume I'm shaking so horribly that I can't hear what they are saying. I don't believe that anyone who doesn't suffer this actually understands its effects, even the doctors. Years ago, you know, one's general practitioner became one's friend, really. He knew you well enough to understand everything a bit more subtly. Now, he is so busy that he simply directs you to the specialist, who is very well informed, but who is even busier. You are treated by a man—or by a woman, of course—who knows your disease very well indeed, but who doesn't know you."

"You're right," Ferrier said. He adjusted himself in his chair. "No. It's a real problem. I wish I could learn more about my patients, get to know them better. I'd like to have tea with them more often, as a matter of fact. But it's kind of a vicious circle. If you're a good, conscientious doctor, you tend to become popular. And if you're a specialist with a good reputation, you can't just say to the GPs, 'Listen, I really appreciate all the patients you've sent me in the past, but now I'd like you to cool it.' So you get very, very busy, and no one really wins."

Mrs. Pembroke nodded her head. "It is a problem, isn't it?" She nodded again. "But Doctor, I know this is a bit cheeky of me, but would you mind very much if I asked you a question about my condition?"

"Of course not," Ferrier said, smiling.

"Often, I find that when I have a very long sleep, my tremor is worse the following day. What do you make of that?"

"I don't know. I've never heard that from anyone before. You know, sometimes just in general, if we oversleep we feel kind of sluggish the next day. It may simply be that, but I suppose there could be something about oversleeping that affects your medication levels. I'll try to remember to look into it for you. Do you know, by the way, that parkinsonian tremors disappear when you sleep?" He glanced at me. "Most movement disorders do. Even people with really wild choreiform movements, or strange writhing, twisting dystonias, become steadily quieter as they are falling asleep, and then when they're soundly asleep, they're completely still. We don't know why."

"It's a mercy, isn't it?" said Mrs. Pembroke.

When Ferrier said he was due at the hospital, she asked us if we could take just a moment to look at something before we left. We followed her into the dining room where a row of framed photographs stood on the sideboard—two schoolgirl portraits of her daughters, a portrait of her husband in his black robe and long silver wig, and a large, hand-colored portrait of a young woman with a familiar smile, wearing a formal white-satin dress. "This was made on the occasion of my presentation at court, the court of King George V, ages ago. I'm hardly the same woman, am I?"

At the front door we thanked Mrs. Pembroke for her hospitality, both feeling guilty that we had to go so soon. "It was very kind of you to have us over," Ferrier said. "I hope we can both find the time again."

"Oh, I've masses of time," she said.

It is easy to assume that the mysterious brain is simply a single lump of tissue that somehow allows us to think and to speak, to move and to love, but in fact, a single brain is comprised of many intricate structures, each one separate from, yet interconnected with, the others. The great gray wrinkled walnut that is the cerebrum comprises about 70 percent of the entire brain and gives it its external shape. It is the 8 billion neurons in the cerebrum's thin gray-matter cortex—its outer quarter of an inch—and the insulated linking fibers of its interior white matter—roughly ten thousand miles of them per cubic inch—that allow us to perceive, to remember, to act. But without several small supporting structures cradled deep within the arching hemispheres of the cerebrum, we would perceive nothing, remember little, and action would be impossible.

The brain stem, jutting up from the spinal cord at the base of the cranium serves as a relay station for both sensory signals traveling to the cerebrum and for motor signals flowing out from the brain to the body's peripheral nerves and muscles. The point where the brain stem meets the spinal cord is a profound kind of junction where most of the million or so fibers in the incoming and outgoing nerve tracts cross over, giving each side of the brain input from, and control over, the *opposite* side of the body. The cerebellum, the "little brain," is the second-largest brain structure; tucked under the back of the cerebrum, it interprets information from the muscles, tendons, joints, and inner ear, controlling posture, balance, and basic muscle movements. The size of the cerebellum has trebled in the million years since the first humans began to walk upright and to use their arms for increasingly complex tasks.

Surrounded by the giant cerebrum are the several small structures that comprise the "forebrain." The two egg-shaped thalami integrate information from the sensory organs, then route it to the cerebral cortex; the hypothalamus, no larger than a thumb tip, regulates body temperature, controls thirst and appetite, and influences blood pressure, sexual behavior, aggression, fear, and sleep. The pituitary, or "slime" gland—it was once strangely thought to be the source of nasal secretions—yields hormones that affect growth, sexual development, and the conversion of food into energy; the little-understood pineal—"pinecone-shaped"—gland may affect sleep-wake cycles and sexual function. The limbic system, curling around the two thalami like a wishbone, triggers emotions that range from joy to misery, as well as helping to maintain memory. Also part of the forebrain are the four nerve-cell clusters of the basal ganglia—the lentiform nucleus, the caudate nucleus, the amygdala, and the substantia nigra—whose joint function is to integrate information between the cerebellum and the cerebral cortex, facilitating smooth, coordinated movement, helping a hand that is meant to reach for an apple to go gracefully, directly to its target.

In an era in which localized functions within the brain are understood only on a rather fundamental basis, it is surprising that physicians and medical scientists can report with certainty that the tremors, rigidity, and bradykinesia that are the debilitating symptoms of Parkinson's are caused by a drastic depletion of dopamine in the basal ganglia, a depletion that appears to be triggered by a degeneration of cells in the tiny substantia nigra. In numerous studies, researchers have found that the greater the degree of degeneration of the substantia nigra, the less dopamine there is certain to be found elsewhere in the basal ganglia. It is fascinating to note that the precipitating factor in Parkinson's disease is so specifically understood. But it is also sobering to realize that, at least for now, the medical community has no idea why some substantia nigras are selectively destroyed in the latter decades of life—a destruction of a bit of tissue no bigger than a button which makes it a struggle for Professor Varga to turn over in his bed, which makes Mrs. Pembroke reluctant to pick up a teapot.

On Friday morning, Ferrier was up at five. I took a groggy, somnambulist's shower, turned my bed back into a sofa, and joined him a half hour later for the trip to the hospital, almost falling asleep again in the car. He wanted to talk to a patient before she was sedated for surgery, to reassure her as best he could that things would go very well and that the tumor that had begun to affect her speech—a small tumor of the meninges, the brain's protective membranes, which was putting pressure on her left temporal lobe—would almost certainly be benign.

"I guess I'll be bald when you see me again," she said, "or half bald. They said they wouldn't shave it all."

"Oh, it's very new wave," Ferrier said. "You may decide to keep it that way."

"My kids'll freak out when they see me. But . . . here goes. When will you be back?"

"I'll see you this afternoon. You'll probably be able to deliver the Gettysburg Address by then. I think Ed Holly is one of the best neurosurgeons in the business; it's going to go real well," he said, squeezing her hand.

"Promises," she said, and she closed her eyes.

Ferrier saw four more patients on his rounds, then stopped in radiology to see the new CAT scan films of the laborer who had suffered the stroke. We ate scrambled eggs in the hospital cafeteria and arrived at the office thinking we were ahead of schedule. "Morning. Your first patient's here," said Bonnie.

"Jesus, I thought I was early."

"You told me yesterday I could schedule this guy in for fifteen minutes first thing."

"Oh. Yeah, yeah I did. Okay. Where's his chart? We better get going."

Ferrier saw two seizure patients, three patients with migraine, a college basketball player who had suffered a whiplash injury in an automobile accident, and a two-year-old who had not yet begun to walk, then had a break for lunch. Putnam had ordered a pizza, and we all shared it while the two doctors sat on the secretaries' desks, joking about whether one of them was allowed to date patients, briefly discussing a rash of scheduling mix-ups. Back at work, Ferrier started in on his stack of correspondence and record notes but gave it up when the buzzer announced his next patient, a seventy-three-year-old woman who, according to her daughter, had become very forgetful. He saw a ten-year-old boy who had awakened on two recent mornings with his tongue bitten and his bed wet, a twenty-three-year-old auto mechanic who had suffered an excruciating hour-long headache in the middle of the night every night for the last three weeks, and a lighthearted, boisterous boy with cerebral palsy. Then Harry Baxstrom arrived.

Mr. Baxstrom was well over six feet tall, and although he had just turned seventy-eight, he stood very straight. His face was gaunt, his cheekbones pushing against his pale skin. His shirt was buttoned at the neck; his tweed sport jacket with leather elbow patches once fit a far heavier man. He was accompanied by his wife, a small, smiling, silver-haired woman in a smart wool suit, and as Ferrier introduced me to them I could see that Mr. Baxstrom's mouth was plagued by a rapid, nearly chaotic series of movements, his jaw open wide, his lips constantly pursing into O's and ovals, his tongue darting in every direction. He eased himself into the chair that faced the doctor's desk; his wife sat in the chair beside him. Ferrier stared at him, observing the movements for a moment before he spoke.

"Well, I think I definitely see some slowing today," he said. "What do you think?"

"Oh, I think so," said Mrs. Baxstrom. "I think there's a marked improvement."

"How about you Mr. Baxstrom? Are we getting anywhere?" Ferrier invariably used surnames when he addressed patients who were more than a few years older than he was.

I could see Mr. Baxstrom struggle for a second to take control of his manic mouth so he could use it to shape his words. He spoke slowly, his lips refusing to close, his jaw still open. His voice was hollow, his words oddly inflected but intelligible. "It might be a little better," he said, "but from this side the change seems pretty small." His eyes brightened and the facial muscles below them moved as though they meant to induce a smile, but smiling was plainly impossible. "I've got a confession to make. We haven't yet gone out to a restaurant."

"What? I thought that was the deal we made. You two agreed to go out on occasion, and I agreed . . . to encourage you to go out. I have to tell you I disapprove. You'd really enjoy it, and it would be good for both of you. The embarrassment would be gone by about the second time you went to dinner."

"He's almost ready to give it a try," said Mrs. Baxstrom, "aren't you, Harry?"

"I'm devoting some attention to the idea, yes."

"What about eating at home? How are we doing there?"

"Still slow. Swallowing is better since I started seeing the speech therapist, but . . . eating can be a struggle."

"He's definitely eating a little more. I can vouch for that," Mrs. Baxstrom said.

"Well, then I think we should certainly continue the therapy. If both your speech and your swallowing have improved in only—what?—three or four sessions, then that's a very good sign. Getting a few pounds back on you has to be one of our primary goals."

"I would like you to know that I think Patty is the best therapist I've ever had."

"Oh, she's a marvel," Mrs. Baxstrom said.

Ferrier smiled. "That's great. So many people report good things about her. Now if you could only find a neurologist who could solve this thing for you."

"Oh, we think we're on the right track," said Mrs. Baxstrom, something in her voice attempting to assure him that they hadn't given up hope.

Ferrier turned to me. "Mr. Baxstrom has what's called an 'orofacial dyskinesia.' It's rather rare—but not extremely so—and like the other movement disorders, it's a basal ganglia problem. It responds to anticholinergics—when it responds—and we're trying a drug called Artane. He is on, let's see, twenty-five milligrams a day right now, with some improvement, as you've heard. Several articles maintain that the drug's full potential isn't reached until you get as much as forty milligrams on board. What we're trying to do now is to inch the dosage upward very slowly—grogginess and confusion can be a real problem if you increase it too quickly in hopes we can continue the improvement." Then he addressed himself to Mr. Baxstrom. "Is your patience wearing out?"

"This isn't brand new, you know. I've dealt with it for enough years that I don't really expect it to vanish." Then he looked at me. "I'm quite a specimen, aren't I?"

I didn't know what to say. I was flustered and on the spot, and I said something about how I was pleased to hear that the Artane had some effect. I wished I had said, "No, you're a nice man with a frenzied mouth, but you certainly aren't a freak," but I had let the opportunity pass. Ferrier could tell I was uncomfortable, and he intervened, asking Mr. Baxstrom if he would agree to increase the Artane by another five milligrams a day. They discussed the special denture he recently had fitted to assist him with chewing, and they agreed that the speech therapy would continue for the time being. "And I guess we should schedule our next appointment for the Greenbriar or someplace, shouldn't we?"

Mrs. Baxstrom laughed. "You might end up eating alone, Doctor." She glanced at her husband and took his hand.

"First, we had better see if I can handle any more Artane," Mr. Baxstrom said as Ferrier stood up from behind his desk.

Anthony Bodino was the last patient of the afternoon. He arrived on the heels of an hour-long evaluation of a stereo salesman whose recent car accident had left him without the sense of smell. Ferrier had seen Anthony for almost two years, and both men obviously enjoyed their infrequent encounters. Anthony was the plant engineer in a hospital in a nearby city, his wife was a nurse, and I could quickly tell that the medical mystique was one that he had long ago gotten over; he was willing to disagree with Ferrier, to kid him, to laugh and relax in a way that most patients found impossible. And although it was easy to tell that he trusted Ferrier's capabilities, he also seemed to test him, to make sure as best he could that the doctor knew what he was talking about.

Anthony was diagnosed with Tourette's syndrome only four

years before, but he said he could not remember a time when he was free from the maddening jerks and grimaces, snorts and grunts that characterize the disorder. "I was raised in Brooklyn, Italian immigrant family, and at first my parents thought it was just some bad habit, you know, the sort the nuns are always worried about. But my mother always wondered if it wasn't some sort of disease, and over the years I must have seen several doctors, even a psychiatrist. When I was about twelve, one doctor decided I should be taken out of school for extensive bed rest, but it didn't do any good, of course." He spoke quickly, his Brooklyn accent still with him, but I could see no sign of his tics. His face was tanned, his dark beard was trimmed short. He wore a striped tie and a cardigan sweater.

"I suppose that one of the most devastating things was that my father became totally convinced that it was a habit, something I could control. I remember him screaming at me to stop it; it must have driven him crazy. And at school, it was kind of tough. In addition to being small in stature, I had this, and I had to fight twice as hard as anyone else. I don't know what would have happened to me—I was beginning to get into a few scrapes with the law—if a teacher of mine hadn't taken me under his wing and really straightened me out. He really helped me gain some self-confidence and a sense of what I could do, and I thank God he did. I realized through him that this thing didn't have to defeat me.

"So I somehow grew up and got married, and we came out here, and all through this time I thought I was the only guy in the world who had this. Then one day at work, a guy who was a good friend of mine said he had something he thought I should read. He was a little uncomfortable about giving it to me, sure, but he knew me real well, and, of course, I was fascinated. It was an article in a Sunday magazine about this thing called Tourette's syndrome—multiple lifelong tics—facial jerks, sometimes jerks in the limbs, sniffs and vocal sounds, all things that the person can't control. I was astonished. I was damn near forty years old and here was someone claiming I really did have a disease. I went to see this neurologist down in the city and he heard me talk for about ten minutes and said, 'yeah, you have Tourette's syndrome.' I said, 'I've had this for thirty-seven years and you can listen to me for ten minutes and know I have it?' I thought that was ridiculous. But he said it was a pretty straightforward diagnosis. He could see my tics, hear them, and me telling him I'd always had them was all he needed to know."

Ferrier was smiling when he turned to me. "You should have heard Anthony when he first came to see me. I thought I was taking boards again. He grilled me for half an hour about what I knew about Tourette's and what the current therapy was and whether I was familiar with depression as a side effect of Haldol."

"That first neurologist had put me on Haldol, which I guess is still the most effective drug for most people, and I saw some real improvement but I was always drowsy, and after a month or two my wife was convinced that it had put me in a real depression. Well, I knew I was depressed, but this was the first time in my life anything had actually slowed these tics and things down, so I didn't want to give it up, but after four months we agreed, my wife and I, that I should stop it for a while, and sure enough, the depression lifted."

"In answer to his question," Ferrier said, "I told him that depression with Haldol, haloperidol, was well described, but that it might be worth a second try. I had had very good luck with it in controlling Tourette's, and we agreed to slowly put him back on the Haldol. If the depression returned, we would know pretty conclusively that the drug induced it, but if it didn't, well, great."

"What happened was that this guy was out to get me," Anthony said, and he winked at me. "The Haldol knocked me for an absolute loop this time, and I ended up in pretty bad shape. The Tourette's almost completely disappeared at one point, but the depression got kind of serious."

"Anthony came to the office one day in what I would have to characterize as an emergency depression. I had always known him like he is today, jovial, lively, but that day he looked terrible—drawn, vacant—and he cried at the drop of a hat. He said his problems at work and at home seemed really insurmountable. Well, we stopped the Haldol immediately, of course, and I briefly put him on an antidepressant and the situation resolved, but there we were. The Haldol was out of the question, but it had done a great job with the Tourette's, and we were back to where we started."

During the moments when Anthony was not speaking, his tics subtly seemed to come upon him. He would fiercely wrinkle his nose, his eyes squeezing shut for only a moment; then, a few seconds later, he would toss his head or twist his shoulder as if he had suddenly been hit. I saw him move his hand to his mouth, seemingly unconsciously, to shield or suppress the snorts and grunts that emerged as he stopped speaking. Yet whenever he spoke again, they would diminish. "So, now the Tourette's is back, which doesn't please me, but at least without the Haldol life appears to be worth living, and I am at this man's mercy again, God help me."

Ferrier shook his head, smiling, as he took a note pad out of his drawer. "Listen, maybe you could do better down the hall. . . ."

"No, no, I'll stick it out. I'm a gambling man."

"Well, in that case, the real question for us today is whether you want to try some other medications. There are a couple of drugs that I was familiar with in Britain, pimozide and tetra-benazine, that are used very successfully in Europe. I could check on those to see if they are available here yet. And we could also try a couple of other sedative-type drugs, but only if you want to. I need to know whether you want to try other drug therapies or whether you'd rather not take any chances and just live with the Tourette's, at least for now."

Anthony straightened himself in his chair, then spoke. "I can live with the Tourette's; I've done it a long time, haven't I? But before I got so down on the Haldol, I've got to tell you that it was really something to have this disappear. It was wonderful, as a matter of fact. So I guess what I'm saying is that I'm in no rush, but I don't want to give up. That would be good if you could look into those European drugs. Yeah, let's do."

Ferrier asked Anthony to make a return appointment in a week. He would make some calls, he said, and based on what he hoped to find out, they would decide how to proceed.

While I waited for Ferrier to finish his dictation and to return a string of phone calls, I thumbed through the new issue of the *New England Journal of Medicine* that was stacked with his mail, stopping by chance at a short article by a cardiologist who had contracted lung cancer in 1982. The cancer had gone into remission, then later metastasized, and he doubted he had long to live. His purpose in writing the piece was to encourage his fellow physicians not to presume they were personally immune from disease—a presumption that, at least subconsciously, must be very common. But he also said—and the point seemed to be so simple as to be hardly worth making—that doctors should be careful not to let their professions keep them from living their lives.

Does the contemporary practice of medicine necessarily make physicians one-dimensional people, their lives limited to medicine except for an annual week at the Las Vegas craps tables or golfing at Mauna Kea? Ferrier did not fit that stereotype—at least I did not want to think that he did—and an isolated look at a dozen other physicians would probably reveal twelve people whose interests ranged from ragtime piano to Shakespearean sonnets, and whose families and friends were always claimed as their first priorities. Yet the stereotype exists because it has some basis in truth; the people who become doctors tend to be obsessive personalities who can drive themselves till they drop; the number of physicians who admit to drug and alcohol dependency is alarming, and it has to be presumed that still more successfully hide their habits. Statistically, a doctor's marriage is twice as likely to fail as it is to succeed. If you care about your own life, the cardiologist wrote, you will do a better job of caring for the lives of your patients. It was a simplistic kind of statement, it seemed to me, but perhaps it needed to be made.

An hour and a half later, Ferrier had finished signing a stack of letters and record notes and he announced that we were ready to leave. The rest of the suite had long been deserted and he checked to see that the phone had been switched to the answering service, checked the locks on the doors, turned out the lights, then said goodnight to the disinterested fish that were still visible in the aquarium's aqua glow.

"I mean, the history of the medical profession is not particularly glorious," Ferrier said that night when we sat in his living room, listening to Yo-Yo Ma play Bach sonatas, drinking beer out of long-neck bottles. "It wasn't that long ago that surgeons were barbers, for God's sake. They'd give you a haircut for five shillings and bleed you for ten. And the physicians didn't even pretend to know how to treat disease. It was considered a big enough challenge just to figure out what something was, to give it a name. The idea that we can actually *do something* is basically brand new. And when it comes to the brain, trying to cure things can be a fairly iffy proposition. The tools, the drugs, that are available to us just aren't that sophisticated yet in lots of cases, so when we can't cure the brain, or stabilize it, for whatever reasons, there's a tendency to blame the psyche. Look at Anthony, for instance. When Tourette described the syndrome a hundred years ago, he made a strong case that it wasn't psychological. But sixty years later, Anthony's doctors were trying bed rest—they thought he just needed to calm down—and the psychiatrist probably thought it had to do with parental repression or some bullshit. The fact that he had a basal ganglia disease didn't cross their minds."

"But there's a much bigger likelihood that people will look for organic causes these days, isn't there?"

"Yeah, greater, but things haven't totally changed. There's a movement disorder, an organic movement disorder, called wry neck or 'spasmodic torticollis,' where the neck is chronically twisted and the head is turned toward one shoulder. Up until about five years ago, literally, the general consensus, the 'party line,' was that a patient with wry neck had a psychological problem that involved an unwillingness to face life head on, that the patient was turning away from life's problems and challenges. I'm serious. Five or ten years ago. So any time you hear how this is medicine's golden age—which, damn it, it is in some ways—you ought to remember what a brilliant job we've done with spasmodic torticollis."

The telephone rang sometime during the dead hours of the night. I heard Ferrier answer it and talk for a few minutes before he came into the living room, buttoning his shirt. "I've got to go to the hospital," he said. "But it's three-thirty. Stay and sleep."

"What is it?"

"Some guy had a seizure after doing cocaine all night long. He had another one in the ER, and the ER doc's afraid he may have more. He wants me to see him before we admit him."

"I'll go," I said. "I signed up for this, didn't I?"

"Wear your coat. He told me it's ten below."

At the hospital, Ferrier examined the twenty-nine-year-old man, took his history, assured him that no one would be making a police report, then a nurse took him up to the ward. Ferrier signed the requisite ER treatment form, dictated an admission note on his new patient, then—staying longer than he had to—drank a cup of hot chocolate and chatted with the physician before we left.

The car was cold again, the streets empty, the stoplights blinking yellow. The icy air stung my cheeks as we walked back into the house. Ferrier turned up the heat, hung his parka on the back of a chair, then went into his room and lay down on the bed, his clothes and shoes still on. "Please God," he moaned, loud enough for me to hear him from the bathroom, "get me another job!" I turned out the bathroom light and stopped at his door to say something clever, but Ferrier, motionless at last, was fast asleep.

4 Infant Hemispheres

Twenty-five days following conception, the human embryo, little more than a fertilized egg, just three millimeters long, has formed two paired structures at one end of its simple neural tube—two bulging, symmetrical pieces of tissue that soon will become a brain. At five weeks, the brain dominates the growing guppylike embryo, and two eye buds have formed as extensions of the forebrain. By the twelfth week of gestation, the cerebrum and cerebellum have taken shape, their size overwhelming other brain structures. The optic nerves are well developed at four months, as are other forebrain structures—the two thalami, hypothalami, and the basal ganglia. The cerebrum has begun to form the two lateral fissures that distinguish its temporal lobes. By eight months, the developed brain is tightly packed inside the soft bone of the cranium, and the cerebrum is becoming wrinkled with the sulci and gyri—fissures and ridges—that maximize its surface area, its gray cortex.

At birth, an infant's head is almost half its body length, the weight of its brain already one-quarter of its adult weight. Every one of the many *billions* of neurons the brain will ever have is already intact, already potentially functional. Except for the myelination of long nerve fibers and a doubling in weight, both of which will be accomplished during the first six months of infancy, the brain at birth lacks only the intricate synaptic interconnections between its neurons; it needs only, in other words, to be programmed, to be exposed to the world, to learn.

The brain of the newborn is, however, at least primitively programmed, enabling it to turn its nipple-seeking mouth toward a touch on the cheek—the rooting reflex—one that is obviously

90

invaluable for a hungry baby, a reflex which, in fact, is a rather sophisticated neuromuscular response. Newborns also reflexively grasp with their fingers, raise their arms as if to grab hold when suddenly lowered, and move their legs in walking motions when held upright. These primary reflexes slowly decline over the course of the first few months and are replaced by more complex, clearly protective secondary reflexes—the extending of legs to catch a fall when the infant is quickly lowered, arms similarly stretching out when it is tilted forward, one arm and hand reaching out to brace when the baby is turned sideways.

The development of the infant proceeds at a quick pace. At four months, the baby has acquired its full field of vision; it can walk if its hands are held, grasp and hold a small object, move its head toward a familiar sound, and it is able to produce the sounds of most vowels and several simple consonants. Eight months later, by the end of their first year, most babies have 20/20 vision; most are walking or are nearly ready to do so; they can pinch objects between thumb and forefinger, quickly locate subtle sounds, and—certainly most remarkably—most are beginning to speak their first words, making and monitoring sounds that *mean something* to them and to the people around them. They are beginning to learn language, to use an abstract system of symbols to communicate.

Language is the tool, the talent, the obsession, that propels each of us beyond "infancy"—a word rooted in the Latin *infantia* meaning "without speech." Perhaps more than any other skill we possess, language is the human hallmark; we are a speaking species, and those of us who cannot speak—whether we are six months old or sixty years—are literally in the mute midst of infancy.

Until the second half of the nineteenth century, little anatomical attention was paid to the nature of human speech. Just as the ability to see seemed to depend on the eyes, speech seemed to have its center in the mouth, the larynx, and the vocal cords, and the comprehension of speech obviously had much to do with the ears. A person's ability to express language vocally and to decode the spoken sounds of others seemed to have much more to do with peripheral organs than with the brain; perhaps the brain simply supplied those organs with the currents that allowed them to operate. Aphasia, the loss or impairment of language, was often ascribed to some strange paralysis of the throat, the tongue, the ears.

In Paris in 1861, however, Dr. Ernest Auburtin delivered a landmark paper to the Society of Anthropology and with it began a new era of language research. Auburtin argued that damage to the frontal lobes of the brain often resulted in impairment of speech, from which he inferred that "language" might be localized there. He discussed numerous cases in support of his claim. One of them was that of a young man who had tried to blow out his brain with a pistol, but who had only succeeded in tearing away the front of his skull, exposing his cerebral cortex. The patient could understand spoken speech and he could talk perfectly well himself—until his frontal lobes were compressed with a spatula, a moderately gruesome bit of experimentation that invariably caused an immediate, but temporary, loss of speech. It seemed obvious to Auburtin: Some part or parts of the frontal lobes governed the expressive aspect of language.

Among Auburtin's colleagues who listened that day was Paul Broca, secretary of the society, a surgeon whose real passion lay in the fledgling field of anthropology. Impressed by what he had heard, Broca invited Auburtin to visit one of his own patients, a man who was speechless and whose right arm and leg were chronically weak. It was the physicians' good fortune—as it was not the patient's—that the man died the day after their visit. At the autopsy, Broca found a superficial lesion on the third convolution of the left frontal lobe of his brain.

A month later, Broca heard of a similar speechless patient who also had died. A postmortem inspection of the brain of the second patient showed damage to much the same area of the left frontal lobe. In publishing findings from these and subsequent cases, Broca pointed out that lesions of what would become known as "Broca's convolution" or "Broca's area" seemed to affect only the articulation of speech. The aural comprehension of speech, and sometimes even the ability to *write*, remained intact. Most patients could still make sounds, and with great struggle many could sometimes pronounce an intelligible word, finally stammering words like "rain" or "rainy . . . day" to describe the weather.

A rather heated debate ensued. During the decade that followed, many French physicians, Broca and Auburtin among them, argued whether Broca's serendipitous discovery of a total of eight cases in which similar brain lesions resulted in similar aphasias was proof that there was a "language center" in the brain. Then, in 1874, Karl Wernicke, a German medical student, complicated the debate by demonstrating that damage to an area of the left temporal and left parietal (upper lateral) lobes of the cerebral cortex—damage that spared Broca's area in the front of the brain—could result in a very different kind of speech loss. Unlike patients with Broca's area lesions, who could usually comprehend normally, patient's with lesions in "Wernicke's area" often had great difficulty comprehending anything that was said to them. And in contrast to the slow, frustrating efforts to speak that were common with Broca's aphasics, Wernicke's aphasics spoke smooth, rapid, grammatical *gibberish*. Did these new findings mean that there were *two* language centers in the brain—one responsible for the efficient articulation of sounds, and another for the conveyance of meaning? Were these simply two of many centers? And what, in fact, was "language" after all? Was not language an integral element of thinking and memory, not just of speech? Was it possible to lose speech but to retain language? Was it possible to lose language and to remain conscious of oneself?

Over a century later, neuroscientists, psychologists, and linguists still struggle with the relation of language to the evolution, development, and function of the brain. Answers to questions such as whether the acquisition of language is genetic or behavioral or both, or whether thinking is necessarily a linguistic activity, were unavailable to Broca, Wernicke, and their peers— and they are unavailable today. The neuroscientific community is united in its belief that there is *not* a localized language center; it is simply too much a part of too many cerebral functions for that to be possible, and a variety of language functions are often located in different brain areas in different individuals. No one doubts the general localized roles of Broca's speech area or of Wernicke's area, but ironically, the legacy of the century-old knowledge of those speech centers has more to do with language *lateralization* than with localization.

Four years following his initial investigations, Paul Broca himself noted that only one thing was shared completely in common by

93

the several lesions affecting speech that he had observed: each was located in the *left* cerebral hemisphere. The huge cerebrum, shaped like an inverted bowl, is split front to back by a deep valley called the longitudinal fissure. Except for the *corpus callosum*—hard body—a kind of bridge containing a dense collection of millions of connecting fibers that unites the left and right hemispheres, the cerebrum is, in fact, two *cerebra*. To Broca and his fellow physicians, the two hemispheres appeared to be identical; they were mirror images of each other. But inexplicably, right-sided lesions very seldom affected speech; lesions of the left side almost always impaired it to some degree. The nineteenth-century scientists and clinicians were already well aware that each cerebral hemisphere controlled the sensory and motor functions of the opposite side of the body—a fact which was unexplained but whose symmetry seemed straightforward enough. The notion that a function like language could exist in one hemisphere and not the other was little short of mystifying, however, and its mystery gave rise to the investigations that continue today into the nature of hemispheric dominance—for speech as well as for a variety of other functions—now a confirmed aspect of brain physiology that is often called cerebral lateralization.

Much of the mystery derives from the anomalous nature of hemispheric dominance. In humans and in the vast majority of other animals, paired organs and body parts are commonplace—lungs, kidneys, legs, ears, eyes. Only in the brain does one organ serve a function that its matched organ does not, possibly *cannot*. The anomaly is partly, but incompletely, explained by the fact that the two cerebral hemispheres actually do not mirror each other as precisely as was thought in Broca's time. Subtle asymmetries are numerous: the sylvian fissure, which separates the temporal lobe from the parietal lobe on the side of the cerebrum; the upper surface of the temporal lobe, called the *planum temporale*, an extension of Wernicke's speech area; and—perhaps not surprisingly—Broca's area of the frontal lobe all tend to be asymmetric. Numerous studies have now shown that these areas in the left hemisphere are significantly larger than the homologous areas in the right hemisphere in the great majority of people. One obvious explanation for their comparative differences in size, weight, and the number and position of sulci is that perhaps they have different jobs to do; and although it seems too simplistic to be true, the total mass of the left hemisphere appears to be bigger because, in most of us, it is dominant. It has a *bigger* job to do.

Nine out of ten people are naturally right-handed, which means—since most right-sided nerve tracts cross over to the left side of the brain—that their left cerebral hemisphere is dominant for motor activity. Beginning at about one year of age, they choose their right hand to accomplish a variety of simple and complex tasks not because *it* is inherently more adept than their left hand, but because their left hemisphere is better programmed for fine motor control than their right. Curiously, speech is also dominant to the left hemisphere in virtually all right-handers— about 98 percent of them. On the surface of things, there seems to be little correlation between motor function and the complexities of language and speech; and if there were a vital correlation between them, it would seem reasonable that left-handers— whose *right* hemisphere is dominant for motor activity—would also reliably show right hemispheric dominance for speech. But it is not that simple. Roughly 40 percent of all left-handers do demonstrate a right-sided dominance for speech. But confoundingly, about 50 percent of left-handers are speech dominant in their *left* hemispheres; to complicate things even further, some left-handers seem to share speech functions in *both*.

In the great majority of us, the facility for, the possibility for, speech is located in the left cerebral hemisphere—that much is very clear. But those left-handers with right-sided dominance demonstrate that the right hemisphere is certainly capable of governing speech; the region of the right frontal lobe that is homologous with Broca's area can control articulation, and the right-sided region that mirrors Wernicke's area can successfully manage the encoding and decoding that are essential to comprehension. Speech can reside in either cerebral hemisphere, yet in more than nine out of ten of us, it "chooses" the left. Is it genetically programmed to do so? And when the right hemisphere is dominant, is it because the left hemisphere was damaged at some early stage of development? Does the left hemisphere normally tend to be larger because it houses speech, or does speech tend to "select" the left hemisphere because, by chance, it is larger?

There is mounting evidence that we are born predisposed to

locate speech in our left hemispheres, and that barring some sort of subtle trauma to that side, or a minute malformation, the left hemisphere will begin to program itself for most aspects of language as early as the first few days of life. Studies of fetal brains have shown that their cerebral hemispheres possess structural asymmetries that are similar to adult brains—the left-sided speech areas growing observably larger than the right even before birth. Separate studies have demonstrated that newborns lying on their backs have their heads turned to the right nearly 90 percent of the time, paying little attention to the world that lies to their left; they respond more quickly to food stimuli offered from the right than from the left, and the hearing in their right ear is demonstrably superior just a few weeks following birth—all correlative to a kind of predisposed left-hemispheric dominance. Perhaps most remarkably, sophisticated evoked electrical response tests of infants as young as twenty-four hours reliably record right-sided electrical activity in response to nonspeech sounds—bells, whistles, barking dogs—but *left-sided* activity in response to spoken words.

It does not appear to be by chance that the vast majority of us have dominant left hemispheres, no more coincidental than our opposable thumbs or the double arch of our feet. Beginning at birth, the left hemisphere seems somehow to be more attuned, *readier*, to comprehend the world, to take neuronal note of it, to respond to it with coos and cries and, finally, with words.

A warm chinook had swept south from Alberta and finally seemed to have broken winter's spirit on the March Saturday when Yoshi Kurumata lost his speech. He had gone swimming with friends at the university's sports center and had been swimming laps before a lifeguard noticed him struggling in shallow water and pulled him out of the pool. His right leg and arm were weak; he seemed dazed, lethargic, and he vomited as the lifeguard sat him in a chair. The lifeguard repeatedly asked him if he was okay, but Yoshi didn't respond. When his friends noticed that something was wrong, they came over to him and questioned him in Japanese. What had happened? Was he all right? Yoshi seemed confused by their questions, and when he tried to speak, he could not.

Ferrier was on call but so far it had been a quiet Saturday, and we were watching *Desperately Seeking Susan* at a theater downtown when he was paged from County Hospital's emergency room. He desperately did not want to leave Rosanna Arquette, but he simply had no choice. "We'll come back for the seven o'clock," he whispered, and I followed him up the carpeted aisle.

An ER physician named Sandy met us as the electronic door opened; he wore corduroy jeans and a polo shirt, and the stethoscope around his neck seemed to be there simply as a sort of symbol of credibility. "I'm afraid this is a little out of my league," he said. "Could be an intracranial bleed, but God, he's only twenty-two. He was swimming up at the university, but nobody saw him bash his head. No signs of head or neck trauma that I can discern."

"How long ago did it happen?"

"I guess at about five—thirty, forty minutes ago. His pressure and pulse are fine; pupils are sluggish and he's real out of it. Marked right-sided hemiparesis—leg, arm, right facial droop. And I just don't know about the asphasia; maybe his English isn't very good. I hope that's it, because he sure doesn't seem to be getting much."

Ferrier said hello when we went in to see him and Yoshi nodded his head. "How are you?" Ferrier asked, and he nodded again. "Can you tell me your name?" brought only another nod. Yoshi's short dark hair capped a round, pudgy face; he looked tired and more than a little confused; his eyes were red and puffy. As he examined him, Ferrier found that Yoshi's pupils were now responding normally to light, but the right side of his face was still weak. Ferrier used me to demonstrate to Yoshi how he wanted him to try to move his limbs, how to pull and push against the doctor's hold. Yoshi seemed to understand the visual cues without difficulty, and his subsequent efforts revealed that the strength in his right leg nearly matched his left, but coordination in the right leg was clumsy. His right arm remained flaccid. He could raise it slightly, awkwardly, but he had to concentrate and almost struggle to do so. Ferrier used the shaft of a pencil to apply pressure to the middle fingernail of Yoshi's right hand; he responded with a sudden grimace, but was unable to move his hand away from the pain. Ferrier tried to test skin sensation, but he could not make Yoshi understand that he wanted him to nod when he felt the point of a pin.

"They're ready to scan him," Sandy said from the doorway. "then we'll take him on to the ICU, I guess."

"Good. Let's get him down there. And we're going to have to find somebody who speaks Japanese."

"I got hold of a professor, a Dr. Fukuda, who supposedly knows him. He's on his way down."

While we waited for the results of the CAT scan, Ferrier sat on the desk behind the admitting counter, talking to no one, twisting his beard, pulling it up to his mouth. "I sure hope we can avoid doing an angiogram tonight," he said, turning to me, breaking the silence. An angiogram is a technique in which an iodine solution is injected into the blood vessels so they can be clearly observed by X ray. "If this is just hemiplegic migraine"—constricting blood vessels in his head that could be causing both the weakness and the asphasia—"the dye could make the spasm in the vessels worse and possibly cause a stroke. But if we *are* dealing with a clot, then I sure as hell want to know about it and begin anticoagulants. But . . . he's already improved a little since he arrived, so maybe he'll get lucky."

"You can't usually see much on a CAT scan at this stage, can you?"

"Not unless he's bleeding. But if he is, we've got to know because then we obviously wouldn't anticoagulate him, and we might be able to drain it. He better hope like hell he's not hemorrhaging. *I* better hope. . . ."

"So how do you know if it's migraine?"

"If he gets better—quickly. If he isn't a lot better in the morning we'll have to do an angiogram. If he's got an artery that's only partly occluded, we can get him on an anticoagulant and keep things from getting worse."

"But not better?"

"It just depends. Whenever you clot off an artery for long enough, you're going to end up with an infarct beyond that spot, meaning dead tissue because of oxygen deprivation. In the brain it just takes a few minutes. But then there's always a period of time before you can tell what was actually infarcted or how much function he'll get back. Jesus, you'd think they'd be done with that scan." He stood up and strode down the hall, then through the doors of the radiology department, past the dark windows beyond which Yoshi lay on a narrow, padded table, his head inside the cylindrical scanner.

"Haven't you got him yet?" Ferrier asked the technician who was seated at a computer console.

"Won't have film for a few minutes, but you can look at the monitor. I don't think there's much for you to see. Hit this key here when you're ready for the next cut."

Ferrier sat in front of the big black-and-white screen and studied the series of cross-sectional pictures of Yoshi's brain, beginning with a small round slice of the top of his cerebrum and ending with a section at the base of his brain that included his optic nerves and eye sockets. He was soon finished looking, and he sighed as he stood.

"Well?" I asked.

"Well, not much. His left hemisphere looks a bit larger, but he's right-handed and I don't think it's edema—swelling—yet. Looks normal for now."

The technician walked up to the console. "We still need to have a radiologist read this, don't we?" he asked.

"Yeah," said Ferrier. "I doubt we're missing anything but we can use all the help we can get with this one. Have whoever is on call come see me in the ICU after he's seen it."

"Will do."

"Thanks. Come on," he said to me as I stared at the screen, the dim oval shape somehow very different from the sections of brain I had seen the pathologist slice.

Yoshi was lying in a bed in the intensive care unit when we saw him again. Dr. Fukuda, wearing black-framed glasses and a sport coat, his knit shirt buttoned at the collar, stood at Yoshi's side, his small hand on Yoshi's forearm. "Very pleased to meet you, Doctor," he said. "How is my young friend?"

"He's been better. I guess you've heard about how he was found at the pool. As far as we know, he didn't hit his head diving or anything. He is weak on the right side, but getting better, and he seems to be asphasic, mute, right now. But we need your help to find out."

"I know a tiny bit about asphasia," Dr. Fukuda said. "I teach linguistics; also Japanese. Yoshi is one of a large group we have here in International Studies who are attempting to learn English."

"How good was his English?"

"Not very impressive yet," Dr. Fukuda said, smiling.

"Would you try to have a conversation with him in Japanese?" Ferrier asked. "Just ask him how he is, how he feels, and let's see how he responds."

The professor nudged Yoshi's arm and called his name. Yoshi opened his eyes and Dr. Fukuda started to speak. Yoshi nodded his head repeatedly, appearing to understand; once he opened his mouth as if to speak, but made no sound.

"Ask him to lift his right arm," Ferrier said, but when the professor did so, Yoshi's right arm did not move. "Now ask him to lift his left arm." Dr. Fukuda translated the request, but Yoshi's left arm remained motionless on the bed. Then Ferrier took Yoshi's forearm in his hands and raised it once. He laid it on the bed again and motioned upward with his thumb. Yoshi promptly lifted his left arm high into the air and held it there. "Ask him to touch his left hand to his nose," Ferrier said, but again Yoshi did not respond. When Ferrier showed him what he wanted him to do, however, Yoshi successfully reached for his nose.

"Well, that's pretty explicit, isn't it," Ferrier said. "He's clearly got a receptive problem right now. He certainly should have been able to understand you normally, shouldn't he?"

Dr. Fukuda was pale. "Yes. I'm sure he should have."

"His chart says he's right-handed. Do you know for sure that he is?"

"No, I'm not sure. But let me think . . . I believe I've seen him sit at one of those writing chairs with no problem—the ones with the arm on only the right side. If one of his friends gave you the information that he is right-handed, he very probably is. Can I place a call to his parents? I think they should know this has happened."

"That would be very kind of you. But if you don't mind, maybe you should wait until morning. He could improve a lot by morning."

"I was under the impression that recovery from stroke was a long process."

100

"It usually is, but I'm not sure yet that Yoshi's had a stroke. You see similar symptoms sometimes with an unusual kind of migraine; instead of an excruciating headache, you get these sorts of symptoms because blood vessels to the head are severely constricted and the brain isn't getting enough blood. I have to tell you, though, that my hunch right now is that this is a stroke. With migraine you normally see a change faster than we're seeing here. But since this happened in a swimming pool, we have to assume that there's a real possibility that he suffered some sort of trauma, even a fairly subtle blow that could have caused him to clot off an artery."

"If it is a stroke, will he be able to talk again?"

"He probably . . . well, it's hard to say until we know what the problem is. But he's young and that's still very much in his favor. The younger you are, the better you tend to recover. Young brains are remarkably good at relearning things."

Dr. Fukuda stayed by Yoshi's bed while Ferrier called the radiologist from a telephone in the nurses' station. I heard him say he was afraid to do an angiogram, heard him say his best guess at the moment was a pale infarct, heard him agree that they would wait until morning to scan him again and to decide about an angiogram. "Thanks, Don," he said before he hung up, "this really does worry me. Poor kid came over here to learn English. Now he may go home not being able to speak Japanese."

Then Ferrier dictated an admission note, outlining what little was known about what had happened at the pool, Yoshi's condition on examination, the argument against an immediate angiogram, and the plan to do no more than monitor him until morning. The same information had to be scribbled into Yoshi's chart before he was finished, and Ferrier added an order to check his vital signs every hour. "Linda, page me with any change, okay?" he said as he handed a nurse the chart. "Improvement or worsening, whatever. And I'll be back in an hour or two."

Dr. Fukuda was standing in the hallway as we left the ICU. "Thank you for coming down," Ferrier said. "Maybe we'll have some good news in the morning."

"Let's hope so. You know, I know his parents. They are old friends of mine. They hope Yoshi will become a politician. Local politics. I'll see you in the morning then."

We walked down the corridor, back toward the emergency

101

room. "I'm not sure the odds are great right now that he'll ever give a campaign speech," Ferrier said, his hands in his pockets, his pace slow enough that I could keep up with him.

"What's a pale infarct?"

"It's the dead tissue in the area beyond a blocked artery. I'm always hesitant to start anticoagulants because you can sometimes bleed into a pale infarct and make matters even worse—causing a hemorrhagic or 'red' infarct. The last thing his left hemisphere needs right now is a big bleed."

Sunday morning was clear and warm, winter at last was waning. Yoshi remained unchanged. His right side was weak, he still could not speak, and his comprehension had not improved. Ferrier had to presume that hemiplegic migraine was not the culprit, and if a thrombosis was, it would be safe enough now to permit an angiogram. Ferrier finished his rounds, seeing both his and Putnam's patients, while the radiologist performed the angiogram.

Two hours later, the evidence on the X-ray film was distressingly precise. Injected with dye, his left internal carotid artery appeared dark and thick to the point beyond the branching of the posterior communicating artery at the back of his brain, where it suddenly stopped: a thrombus. Beyond the thrombus, the unstained artery could not be seen. Because of the interconnections of arteries in the brain, some occlusions pose little problem; the arterial network allows blood to bypass blocked vessels and successfully supply areas that would otherwise become "ischemic"—blood deprived. But in Yoshi's case, the occlusion of the artery appeared to be complete, and somehow the "circle of Willis"—which connects the carotid arterial system of one hemisphere with that of the other—was unable to supply a blood-starved area in his left temporal and parietal lobes—an area that subsequently infarcted, died. A second CAT scan, performed immediately after the angiogram, dimly revealed an area of swelling in his left hemisphere surrounding the infarcted tissue.

Yoshi remained in the intensive care unit and Ferrier checked on him four more times during the day. The strength and coordination in his right leg showed slight improvement. He still could not comprehend Japanese and still could not utter a sound. Ferrier had ordered intravenous heparin, an anticoagulant, which would be introduced to prevent the extension of the clot into adjacent arteries; evidence from the angiogram had shown that the heparin was now indicated.

Ferrier and I discussed whether to see *Desperately Seeking Susan* again or to welcome spring with a wheezing three-mile run, but he opted instead to go to his office to file articles, to pay bills and clean up his desk, to rearrange his bookshelves, and to otherwise kill the intervals between trips across the street to County to check on Yoshi's condition.

Dr. Fukuda's tweed sport coat with leather elbow patches looked as if it would more readily belong to a professor from Cambridge than one from Kyoto; he wore a tan turtleneck underneath it and he beamed as he saw Ferrier walk through the doors that isolated the intensive care unit. It was Monday morning and we had not yet seen Yoshi. "Oh, please come let me show you something," the professor said as Ferrier set his briefcase on a counter in the nurses' station. We followed him to the bed where Yoshi lay, his eyes open, his expression surprisingly alert. Dr. Fukuda went to the opposite side of the bed from where we stood; he waited for Linda, Yoshi's nurse, to join us. "Yoshi," he called after he had waited a few more seconds, his stage finally set. "*Ohiyo.*" *Good morning.*

Yoshi pursed his lips into an oval shape, then held them there for a moment. "Oh . . . ohiyo," he said in a soft and fragile voice.

Ferrier's delight with Yoshi's one-word greeting almost matched Dr. Fukuda's. "*Ohiyo?*" he asked. "Ohiyo, Yoshi, ohiyo. Wonderful. Very good." Linda reached for Yoshi's exposed toes and shook them encouragingly. "Way to go," she said. "We knew we could do it, didn't we?" Yoshi's nod seemed to say "yes, by God, we did," but he did not really understand her; the nod was still simply his ubiquitous way of reaching out. He could say good morning, but nothing more, and when Ferrier asked Dr. Fukuda to help him test Yoshi's comprehension, the professor's visage betrayed his disappointment.

"Really. It's a terrific sign," Ferrier said to Dr. Fukuda as we stood in a short queue in the hospital's cafeteria. "The fact that he can say *anything* is just great. And he says 'ohiyo' on cue. He's obviously receiving the word when you say it. It's not much, I agree, but it's a start—a start I wasn't sure we would have for a while."

"Is there any way he can be tested to find out how much language he'll eventually get back?" the professor wanted to know.

"No. It's strictly the sort of thing that's wait and watch. My hunch right now is that he'll make some real progress. It could easily be a year or more—two, three—before he stops showing progress; or that could happen in a couple of months. Part of the difficulty is knowing how much of his weakness and speech deficit is caused by the infarction, the brain tissue that has died and can't be regenerated, and how much is caused by the swelling around the more severe damage and the associated trauma, which he will get over."

Dr. Fukuda insisted on buying our breakfasts; then Ferrier took his scrambled eggs and grapefruit juice and led the way to a long, empty table.

"Do you think Yoshi is fully aware of his situation?" Dr. Fukuda asked as he sat down. "Does he know what he's lacking?"

"When asphasics have deficits that primarily affect the motor production of speech—Broca's area damage, in other words—they tend to get very frustrated; they often understand everything and know what they want to say, but they just can't *say* it. But people with receptive problems don't usually show similar frustrations. It seems to be different from being deaf or hard of hearing and groping for what's being said. With lots of receptive aphasics, you get the impression that they're not concerned about what they're missing—as if the whole concept of spoken and heard language just vanishes. Yoshi's aphasia is mixed right now; he has receptive and expressive problems. I don't get the impression that he's very frustrated at the moment, but he will be once he's to the point where he's trying to say the word for 'milk shake' and it just isn't there."

"So does his problem comprehending mean that the stroke damaged Wernicke's area?" I asked.

"Well, yeah, certainly his receptive capability is impaired, at least for now. But I can't claim to know precisely what areas of

104

his cortex he infarcted, nor, for that matter, could I tell you where Yoshi's own language centers were, are. They are located in several areas of the dominant hemisphere. That's why it's so common to encounter language problems when the dominant hemisphere suffers a sizable stroke. You expect to see one-sided deficits, like we did with Yoshi, and you expect to have some sort of aphasia, at least temporarily."

"But you cannot be sure about the type of aphasia, is that correct?" Dr. Fukuda asked. He had not started to eat.

"The varieties are amazing. Some people with receptive problems can follow written commands but not verbal commands; some people can write but not read. You can ask them to write a sentence: 'John brought the dog home,' then say 'Gee, it's a pretty day, isn't it? By the way, could you read this for me?' You give them back what they wrote and they have *no idea* what it says. That's called dyslexia without dysgraphia.

"Some people can get information from their sensory centers when they can't get it from their visual centers. If you show them a key and ask them to name it, they'll say, 'Oh, you know, it's a . . . well, for the . . . you know, with a door, you. . . .' But then you put it in their hand and ask them to name it and they say, 'It's a key.' Occasionally the deficit is so subtle that the patient's language function is perfectly normal except that he can't identify colors. Not a vision problem; he's not color blind, he just can't tell you the name of the color of a banana. It just isn't there. In Yoshi's case, it's a shame he wasn't closer to being bilingual. It would have been very interesting to see what he had lost of both languages, and whether he recovered one more quickly than the other. The mother tongue usually tends to come back faster, but sometimes just the opposite is the case. And it would be very possible, for instance, for Yoshi to be able to read the pictographic Japanese alphabet, but not the phonetic one of English, depending upon where his lesions were."

"Yoshi's parents were very appreciative of our call yesterday, by the way. I have a telegram for him from them this morning," Dr. Fukuda said. "It arrived in English, of course. When I go back upstairs I'll translate it back for him. He might understand more of it than we realize, you know."

"He might," Ferrier said.

"And his mother arrives on Thursday. Perhaps he'll have much more to say for her than just 'good morning.' "

At the office, after rounds, Ferrier saw a new headache patient, a new seizure patient, then Wendy Stetham, the young pregnant woman whose seizures had been uncontrolled. But Wendy was no longer pregnant; her six-week-old son Timothy was healthy and very lively and was living with a foster family until his mother's seizures could somehow be contained. During the four-month course of his care, Ferrier had tried to manage Wendy's seizures with a number of anticonvulsants: first Dilantin, then Tegretol, Depakote, Mesantoin, and Mysoline; side effects had limited the use of some, others were simply not effective. She was presently on a daily regimen that included the latter two, plus Tegretol, and although her seizures had become less frequent, they were still too constant to allow her to care for her child. Wendy had recently broken her wrist during the wild, manic, flailing minutes of a seizure.

In hopes of finally stopping Wendy's seizures, Ferrier had admitted her to the university hospital in the city where he was currently "attending"—teaching residents. There she had undergone a neurological and psychiatric diagnostic workup, and the findings were intriguing. In one procedure, with EEG electrodes taped to Wendy's head, she had been injected with a small amount of placebo saline solution, which she was told would induce a seizure. The physician administering the test also told her that a second solution would neutralize the effect of the first drug and would stop the seizure in progress. Following the first injection, Wendy went into a seizure, but the EEG showed only normal brain-wave activity. When she was injected a second time—again with saline solution—her seizure promptly stopped.

During the course of her psychiatric workup, it was discovered that Wendy had given the hospital four different birth dates; she had given conflicting information about her past seizure history, about the universities she had attended, about her relationships with her parents, and about the nature of Timothy's conception: She had been raped, she had repeatedly told Ferrier and her psychiatric social worker, but she told the physicians at the university hospital that her boyfriend was Timothy's father, and that he had gone away to Germany.

Ferrier had long suspected that many of Wendy's seizures were, in fact, "pseudoseizures"—unconsciously provoked by a complicated personality disorder. Yet several EEGs performed over the past months had been positive—they had indeed shown epileptiform activity—and it would have been extremely unusual for Wendy to have broken her wrist in the midst of a pseudoseizure. Wendy's social worker, Katherine Braverman, was now convinced that the pseudoseizures were a means of rejecting Timothy; yet conflictingly, Wendy also very much wanted to keep him to make a point to her parents, whom she felt had rejected her. Katherine had also cautioned Ferrier that she felt Wendy was becoming inappropriately attached to him, hoping he could fill her father's void, or her lover's. "Maybe Timothy and I could live with Dr. Ferrier," Wendy had once suggested as a solution to her problems.

Ferrier had confronted Wendy before with the issue of whether many of her seizures were psychological in origin, and he did so again today. He assured her that he felt it was important to stay on anticonvulsants, but that he believed her epilepsy was actually well controlled. "I agree with you that your goal should be to get Timothy back," he told her, "but reaching that goal is going to involve working hard, on your own and with Katherine's help, to understand yourself better and to be honest with yourself and to prove that you can be responsible for him."

Wendy sobbed, holding her face in her hands. "You just think I'm being too much trouble. You're mad because you think I'm faking my seizures, so now you want to keep Timothy away from me to get back at me."

"Wendy, I have absolutely no reason to punish you. I want to see you happy and healthy and, if it's what you want, with your child. But if that's going to be—"

"You just want to get rid of me," she cried. "Katherine wants to be rid of me . . . and you won't let me have my baby." Wendy's shoulders heaved with each sob; she curled herself forward and buried her face in her lap.

Ferrier said nothing for a moment, then spoke in a quiet voice. "That's not true, Wendy. Katherine and I are committed to seeing you through these things; we're not leaving." He had not said anything more when Bonnie knocked on the door and opened it. "I—I'm sorry to bother you, Doctor," she said, embarrassed by

107

what she assumed she had interrupted. "You have a call from Dr. Whittengen at the university health center. He's got some sort of emergency and needs to talk to you just as soon as possible. I told him I'd—"

"I'll speak with him. Thanks," he said, picking up his phone. "I'm sorry, Wendy. I guess I'd better see what this is." Ferrier's conversation was short. Dr. Whittengen had a patient, a nineteen-year-old student, who had been brought in incoherent. The young man had a high temperature; his eyes were hypersensitive to light, and his neck was suspiciously stiff. Dr. Whittengen had already done a spinal tap; the lymphocytes, infection-fighting white cells, in his cerebrospinal fluid were at alarmingly elevated levels. "I'll be there as quickly as I can," Ferrier said, and he hung up the phone. "Wendy. It's awful to leave you like this. I apologize. But this is something that has to be taken care of immediately. You're going to see Katherine this afternoon, aren't you?"

She looked up; her whole face was wet. "I don't know. I don't care. Just go. Go, will you?"

"Wendy, I. . . . See Katherine this afternoon. Okay?" He did not say anything more before we left.

Dr. Whittengen's worries were well-founded. His patient's symptoms left little doubt that he faced something serious. James Ames, a freshman, had complained to his roommates the day before of a severe headache; he vomited throughout the day and early evening, then slept through the night. He woke not being able to identify where he was or who his roommates were. He mumbled unintelligibly, sometimes shouted, and he had broken out in a steady sweat.

The doctor handed Ferrier the lab report on James's cerebrospinal fluid after Ferrier had hung his jacket on a chair. "What does this look like to you?" he asked.

"Looks to me like you had reason to be concerned." Ferrier scanned the several findings: elevated lymphocytes, raised protein, low sugar, no bacteria, but the pressure of the fluid was almost double its normal level. "Where is he? Let's see how he's doing."

James's mother, who lived only forty minutes away, sat in a chair beside his bed; she held his hand and softly, steadily stroked his forearm, but she could not keep him still. He twisted from side to side, writhing, tossing his head, flailing his left arm. When Ferrier examined his eyes, particularly his left eye, James recoiled as if in pain from the bright beam of the flashlight. Ferrier held James's head and manipulated his neck; it was indeed stiff, and James tried to pull away from Ferrier's hold as though his neck were also tender.

Ferrier conducted his exam quickly, determinedly, without distraction, and I could tell that he was worried by the condition of James's neck; he was worried about his painful response to the light and by his 103-degree fever, but he was most plainly worried when he found that James's left-hand grip was strong, yet his right hand simply refused to close. "Is he right-handed?" Ferrier asked.

"Yes," his mother said.

"Did you check him for herpetic lesions?"

"No sign of anything," said Dr. Whittengen.

Ferrier turned to Mrs. Ames. "Has he ever had cold sores, or do you . . . do you happen to know if he has genital herpes?"

She looked perplexed—what could herpes have to do with his incoherence? "No. Not that I know of. What do you think this is?"

"I'm not sure what Dr. Whittengen has already told you, but the reason he asked me to see James is that he's concerned about an infection in his brain, or possibly in the meninges, the protective membranes between the brain and the skull. We know from looking at his spinal fluid that there's no bacteria that we can detect, so if it is an infection it is probably a viral one, probably in the brain also, which is called encephalitis. If we have an encephalitis that is caused by most viruses, there isn't much we can or need to do to treat it; the body itself can usually knock it out fairly quickly, without too much complication. If it's a herpes virus, however, it's extremely important to treat it just as soon as possible to avoid some serious residual problems. But at least we *can* treat it."

"What kind of problems?"

"Let's go ahead and order an ambulance, and at County we're going to need a head scan and an EEG," Ferrier said to Dr. Whittengen, then turned back to James's mother. "Well . . . potentially like loss of speech. The herpes virus tends to choose the frontal and temporal lobes, parts of the brain where speech is located. Once we get him to the hospital we'll determine as quickly as we can if herpes is our problem, and if it is, well, then we'll get him medicated immediately."

Mrs. Ames, thin and dark complected, seemed suddenly startled, as if assaulted by what Ferrier had said. "I . . . I thought this was just like a high fever or something. You make it sound like it's . . . like it's really serious. Can he . . . make it?"

"I think he can; I think he *will*, I really do, but yes, that's how serious it is."

Fifty minutes later, Ferrier yanked the CAT scan from the light board where it was held. "This is worthless," he yelled. "What the hell am I supposed to make of this? There's nothing here but movement artifact."

"The orders said no sedation," said the technician, seemingly unperturbed by Ferrier's burst of emotion. "We just couldn't hold him still. Sorry. Say the word and we'll try again."

"Why don't I just wait till he's a vegetable to bring him back down? You could probably handle him then."

"Hey, Doctor," the technician said, "we did the best we could." Her voice was cool, controlled; she pushed her hands into the pockets of her lab coat and started to leave the room.

"Where is he now?" Ferrier asked, trying to make his question sound apologetic.

"Intensive care. I think they're doing the EEG," she said without turning around.

During the many months that I had watched Ferrier work, I had never seen him appear so openly scared about a patient's prospects for recovery, so nervous about the quality of his own efforts to ensure that those prospects were good. Ferrier was not yet frantic, but he was anxious and extremely concerned. He moved even more quickly than usual; his voice was tense, his words clipped and terse, his preoccupation nearly total.

If James were suffering herpes simplex encephalitis, treatment had to begin within the next few hours to give him a chance of avoiding permanent brain injury, at best. Without medication, he would probably die. Just a year or two before, 70 percent of the

110

patients whose brains were infected by herpes did die, most of them very suddenly. Now a drug called acyclovir, which interferes with the replication of viral nucleic acids, had become available. Acyclovir could kill the herpes virus and leave the patient with little or no brain damage if it was administered soon enough. But the problem, the nerve-racking predicament, was to recognize how herpes encephalitis differed symptomatologically from other encephalitides and from the various forms of meningitis. In terms of fever, neck stiffness, semiconsciousness, and changes in the cerebrospinal fluid, the several diseases tended to show very similar symptoms. But the herpes virus was unique in its predilection for the cerebrum's frontal and temporal lobes, and in this case, Ferrier was worried by James's asymmetrical symptoms.

James's right-sided weakness and his incomprehensible babbling, together with the other findings, strongly suggested that his left cerebral hemisphere was being invaded by herpes simplex. And the probability that he had not had oral or genital herpes lesions did not alter the likelihood that his encephalitis was herpes-caused: More people who *do not* have histories of other herpes infections contract herpes encephalitis than do those who do. Yet before Ferrier began the intensive, ten-day intravenous course of acyclovir, he wanted to be convinced that herpes was the root of James's illness. Acyclovir, like most drugs, posed manageable yet significant side effects, and it could not be administered simply on the chance that it might be effective. Even more important, until Ferrier knew that James was suffering from the herpes virus, he could not be certain that he wasn't overlooking another cause.

A clear CAT scan would likely have shown swelling in James's left frontal and temporal lobes if it were herpes encephalitis, but a clear scan had been unobtainable. A brain biopsy would have probably been conclusive—a microscopic examination of a bit of brain tissue would have shown the presence of typical herpes virions—but a brain biopsy was dangerous. It meant the possible—and not insignificant—risks inherent in brain surgery, risks that included postsurgical seizures, the possibility of the surgery doing direct damage to the brain, and the remote possibility of anesthetic death. Ferrier's best hope of a solid diagnosis now lay with a simple electroencephalogram.

"We're having quite a rodeo," said Dwayne Steidel, the big, burly EEG technician, an Army veteran who always signed his memos to Ferrier with a smile face. Dwayne stood beside James's bed in intensive care, trying to hold his head still while a nurse pinned his left arm to the sheet, his mother clinging to the other.

"Honey, honey, easy. Honey, be still . . . just a little bit," whispered Mrs. Ames.

"Shit," Dwayne murmured when his wedding ring tore loose an electrode as James suddenly spun his head. "I don't know if we're going to be able to get anything for you to look at." Dwayne struggled to replace the electrode while Ferrier stared at the tracings—looking like little seismographic squiggles—that rolled steadily out of the machine.

"No, no, he's still enough intermittently. Jesus, look at this! Good, all right, yes, this is what we need." Ferrier pointed toward the slow, smoothly undulating waves generated by four electrodes attached to the left side of James's head. In contrast to them, the electrodes attached to the right etched a rapid-fire series of waves, their peaks and troughs spaced only millimeters apart. "Look at the difference between the two hemispheres; the left is dramatically slow." He was suddenly enthusiastic. "Okay. Well . . . we'll get started."

Ferrier told Dwayne that he could stop his struggle with James, and he asked James's mother if he could speak with her in the hallway. He told her he was satisfied that the culprit was likely the herpes virus—the diminished electrical activity in James's left hemisphere had convinced him—and he said he would begin the acyclovir immediately. Mrs. Ames asked if this meant his chances were better; her voice cracked and faltered as she spoke. She bit her upper lip and held it before she finished her sentence. Ferrier told her that James could start to show some improvement a few hours or days after the medication entered his bloodstream, and that his chances of surviving were good. He added that it was much too early to know whether his brain would be permanently damaged, and he put his hand on her shoulder for a second before he rushed away.

Ferrier ordered the acyclovir from the hospital pharmacy and told the nurse who was standing by to prepare the IV drip for it, but not to start it until he returned—he was not sure how much of the drug to administer each hour—it had been a while since he had had to prescribe it. He told the nurse he would be back in five minutes, then he tore through the swinging doors, down the corridor to a service entrance and across the street to his office.

He was frantic now as he rummaged through a long drawer of manila folders, searching for an article he had saved from the British medical journal *The Lancet*, checking the file marked HERPES, the file marked ENCEPH, the one labeled VIRAL INFECTIONS, but not finding what he needed. The drug was too new to be listed in the *Physicians' Desk Reference*; the person he spoke with in the hospital pharmacy could not help; Putnam was out of town. Cursing himself for having misplaced it, shouting to vent his frustration, he ran back to the hospital, his tie flying behind him like an aviator's scarf.

Inside the small hospital library, Ferrier madly flipped through bound issues of *The Lancet*, his finger streaming down their tables of contents, while the librarian did a quick computer search for recent articles on herpes encephalitis. She handed Ferrier a printout listing four articles, one of them from *The Lancet*, just as he found the article he had remembered and thought he had saved. The dosage was easy to find—10 cc's per hour—and Ferrier was buoyant now, calling thanks to the librarian who had seemed to enjoy the brief drama and who smiled warmly at his relief. Ferrier walked quickly past people in the corridors who stepped out of his path in the same way that cars pull over for an ambulance, his shoes slapping the polished floors. He finally slowed as he went through the doors of the ICU, then sat on the edge of James's bed, puffing, sucking in air as he watched the nurse start the drip, the clear liquid acyclovir sliding in drops through the tube that emptied into the saline solution, the race over at last. It was three P.M.—a little more than three hours since Ferrier's first tentative diagnosis.

Bonnie had cancelled the afternoon patients, and we now sat in an orange booth at the Dairy Queen across from the hospital. We had not eaten since Dr. Fukuda had treated us to breakfast at seven that morning, and I was starving, but Ferrier was not hungry and he only drank a Coke. He sat slumped on the opposite side of the table, running the fingers of both hands through his hair, pulling it, staring at the yellow paper cup in front of him.

"So. What now? What are his chances?"

"Of what?" He looked at me without lifting his head.

"Living."

"Well . . . I guess I'm not really worried about that anymore. I've done what there was to do. But he could real easily have some permanent right-sided deficits. And, I mean, the kid might not be able to talk. If he's aphasic a week from now, I'm going to feel pretty shitty."

"Did you screw something up?"

"No, no I don't think I did anything wrong, but it doesn't really matter how confident you are that you're doing the right thing—even an egotist like me—you can't help but be a little terrified that you're the only thing between him and a horrible outcome. I might have missed that diagnosis. Who knows? Maybe I did. What if it's not herpes? What if he doesn't get better? I mean everything points to that diagnosis, but I'm not absolutely sure, and I'm a little scared. In just this setting, people report missing everything from tumors to TB of the brain. I'm going to be scared till he starts to talk to me."

No one knows precisely how the brain reacquires its language functions after they have been impaired. Stroke, trauma, tumor, and invasion by infection can cripple speech, leaving patients unable to make themselves understood or unable to understand, blocked by their brains' dysfunctions from the essential business of communication. Yet brains can and regularly do rekindle language that has been lost. The networks of neurons that once allowed someone to recite "The Cremation of Sam McGee" do not rebuild themselves once they are dead; but somehow new circuits are made—adjacent to damaged speech areas or in entirely new locations—circuits that reshape the expressive network and connect it with the memory in much the same way that the old one was connected, allowing the remembered poem once again to be transformed into spoken speech. The process of relearning language is as fundamentally full of wonder as is its initial acquisition, yet the mystery is that specialized "language neurons" do not grow out of damaged tissue like shoots from a fresh tree stump. Instead, unprogrammed neurons that could potentially be available for a multitude of functions are enlisted into the encoding and decoding of speech. Old brains, very simply, learn new tricks of language.

When children suffer damage to their language centers, they exhibit remarkable facility in reacquiring language, a facility that adult brains cannot match. A right handed five year old who becomes aphasic because of permanent damage to critical areas of his dominant—left—hemisphere often transfers speech functions to his right hemisphere and it henceforward becomes dominant for all aspects of language. But by age fifteen, the mirrored transference of language from one hemisphere to the other is much less likely to occur, perhaps because as the brain matures it loses a special language "plasticity." When language functions are destroyed at age fifteen, they tend to be reacquired in an unpredictable variety of areas—areas elsewhere in the dominant hemisphere, occasionally in both—and the reacquisition is less likely to be complete. By age fifty-five, the prospects for completely reprogramming lost language functions have greatly diminished. In most cases, mature adults recover some of what they have lost, but the recovery is often capricious.

It seems fair to ask why, if the neurons possessed by a five-year-old are intact five decades later, they somehow lose their ability to form new synapses, to build the intricate interconnections that make language—new language—possible. It is a fair question to ask, but the answer is unobtainable. Perhaps it has something to do with the brain growing sedentary, its synaptic processes becoming sluggish; more likely, it is a matter of trade-offs. As the brain matures, it grows ever more skilled and specialized. It becomes expert not just at speaking, but at playing softball and singing camp songs as well, at driving an automobile and fixing faucets and selling convertible bonds, at maintaining friendships and falling in love. In exchange for its remarkably diverse abilities, the specialties we call everyday life, the brain necessarily forfeits some of the flexibility, the malleability, that it had when its cortex was smooth, its fissures still shallow and undefined.

As language becomes entrenched in one hemisphere, brain functions that are related to language tend to lateralize to that hemisphere as well. Logical and analytical thought processes, writing, calculating, and the memories of names and concepts are

115

almost always lateralized to the dominant hemisphere—the left, of course, in about 90 percent of us. What then is the "minor" hemisphere's role? Is it merely a backup, a kind of cerebral spare part?

At the turn of the twentieth century, British neurologist John Hughlings Jackson speculated that it was precisely that. He observed that people with extensive right hemispheric damage tended to be able to function much more closely to normal than did people whose left hemispheres were destroyed. The left hemisphere, he surmised, was probably dominant for *everything*. It remained difficult to deduce what, in fact, was the right hemisphere's role until the 1950s, when neurosurgeons experimentally began to sever the corpus callosum—which connects the two, otherwise separate, hemispheres—in a few patients with severe, uncontrollable seizures, a procedure that proved effective in halting the spread of seizures and one that is still sometimes performed.

The people who had undergone the surgery—so-called split-brain patients—did not seem to suffer gross deficits of any kind, yet tests revealed some subtle abnormalities. In one test, the patients momentarily were shown a photograph split vertically down the middle; the left half was a man's face, the right a woman's face. The patients observed the split photograph with both visual fields, transmitting information about each half of it to the opposite hemisphere. When asked to describe what they had seen, the patients *said* they had seen a woman, but when they were asked to point out who they had seen from a set of photographs, they invariably selected the man. When they were asked to draw pictures of the person they had seen, they drew the face of a man.

These tests, and hundreds more performed subsequently, seemed to demonstrate that although the dominant hemisphere controls language, the nondominant hemisphere has special spatial and visual abilities. In almost all of us, it is the right hemisphere that recognizes faces, shapes, and familiar surroundings; it is far better at perceiving through touch than is the dominant left. Unlike the generally analytical left, the right hemisphere seems to deal with artistic, musical, and emotional concepts. If the left hemisphere is, in general, capable of separating a thing or an idea

116

into its component parts, the right appears capable of recognizing relatedness, of grasping whole situations.

Without the right hemisphere, it also would be difficult, often impossible, to decode the meanings of subtle voice inflections or to comprehend the emotive quality of a statement. "You're going to town?" might be interpreted as a command. On hearing, "Oh, they're coming back," a person with substantial right-hemispheric damage would not know whether the statement implied fear, happiness, or indifference. It is the "prosody" of speech, its emotionality, its conveying and interpreting of meaning through intonation, that is the purview of the right hemisphere—the hemisphere which intuits but cannot decipher, which "feels" but cannot describe, which "sees" but cannot speak.

I had watched Ferrier wait nervously for the outcomes of surgeries on patients with malignant tumors; several times I had seen him endure the apprehensive minutes during patients' grand mal seizures; I had been with him when he performed test after test, each one exhaustive, before at last he was willing to declare a child brain dead. But I had never seen the anxiety in Ferrier, the fear that he might be as helpless as his patient was, as I saw on the day that James's brain became infected, his right side and his speech slipping away from him in the midst of his fevered struggle. Some of Ferrier's anguish certainly had to do with the ominous possibility that James's virus would quickly kill him, but the death of a patient was not new, and Ferrier had even remarked during a black moment in the middle of that long afternoon that a sudden death from encephalitis would not be such a bad way to go. Instead, I am sure that it was the possibility that James would recover from his virus with only part of a brain, a part that could not speak, that so vividly frightened Ferrier.

In many ways, it is speaking and being spoken to that most directly define who we are and how we relate to others around us. The Latin root of the verb "to converse"—*conversari*—means to live with, to keep company with; we converse in order to live with those we encounter. Without speech, each of us would be isolated, terribly alone—and we are not an animal who chooses to live in isolation.

117

At eight o'clock on Monday evening, James's temperature had dropped to ninety-nine; he was still and silent; his mother and father waited in the lounge beyond the swinging doors and were allowed to stand beside him for five minutes every hour. Yoshi's bed was nine feet away from James's; Yoshi was awake, doing little besides watching the nurses who periodically walked past his bed, nodding when they spoke to him; Dr. Fukuda had come and gone before dinnertime.

At seven o'clock on Tuesday morning, James's temperature was normal; he was groggy and did not want to open his eyes; his right side was stronger. When Ferrier asked him if he knew where he was, James mumbled an answer. Where? "Hospital," he said. Ferrier asked him his name. "James," he plainly said. Beside him, Yoshi was eating breakfast, his fork in his left hand. He said "ohiyo" in response to Ferrier, and he tried to say "good morning," but the words would not form in his mouth; he tried again, then gave up, slamming his left fist against the mattress.

At nine, Wednesday morning, James's eyes were open and although he was weak, the strength in his arms was nearly symmetric. "What on earth hit me?" he asked Ferrier. Yoshi was unchanged.

James's parents were standing by his bed when Ferrier arrived at eight o'clock Thursday morning. His father reached to turn off the television; his mother raked James's hair across his forehead. "Are you sure I've got to stay hooked up to this thing for ten whole days?" James asked the doctor. "I've got better things to do, for sure."

"He is missing quite a bit of school," said Mr. Ames as the three of them stepped away from James's bed, but Ferrier said there was no choice but to continue the medication.

"You know, ten days isn't really too big a price to pay when you consider what the outcome could have been."

"We know," Mrs. Ames said, "it's just that he's a theater major, and he's really doing well. He's quite talented."

"I'm sure he is," said Ferrier.

Yoshi's mother bowed when Dr. Fukuda introduced her. She

asked the professor to tell Ferrier that Yoshi's family was grateful for his care, and she offered him a small box wrapped in rice paper. "Just a token, a tie tack, I think," Dr. Fukuda said, and Ferrier bowed a little at the waist as he thanked her for it.

Yoshi held his mother's hand as he tried to repeat the words Dr. Fukuda asked him to attempt. He shook his head with each failure. Mrs. Kurumata bent to her son's ear, saying something, and Ferrier looked at Dr. Fukuda as if to ask what she had said. Dr. Fukuda smiled. "She told him that children are always impatient."

Ferrier nodded; he reached out and shook Yoshi's toes encouragingly. Yoshi sighed, exhaling his frustration. His mother bowed again in Ferrier's direction; Dr. Fukuda still wore a slight smile, and the three of them were silent when we walked away.

5 Houses of Pain

One afternoon each week, Ferrier drives across town to an outpatient clinic called a pain-control center, a facility housed in a flat-roofed office complex within a new industrial park, a place that seemed more likely to be the home of a trucking line or cardboard-box manufacturer than of the practitioners of this peripheral branch of medicine. The center, one of the first of its kind in the country when it was established in 1978, is directed by Bill Steele, a neurologist and one of a burgeoning breed of medical entrepreneurs, a doctor who gave up his own private practice to head a group of physiatrists (physicians who specialize in rehabilitation), physical and occupational therapists, psychologists, social workers, biofeedback technicians, and clerical staff that treats chronic-pain patients from throughout the Rocky Mountains. Their patients are people for whom conventional medical therapies have failed to provide relief and who come to the center as a refuge of last resort. They are referred by many sources—family physicians and insurance companies, chiropractors and Workers' Compensation representatives, by lawyers active in personal injury actions. The patients are people who have been unable to work for months or for years, who report that leisure time is vacant time and that recreation is out of the question, who say that marriages and sex lives suffer, whose days are ruled by pain.

At the growing number of multidisciplinary pain centers around the country today, teams of physicians and therapists work in concert, sharing their views on the best potential treatments for each pain patient—and many centers are showing encouraging results. Yet whether it is treated by one physician or by a team, the cycle of long-term pain that leads to anxiety, depression, fatigue, and low self-esteem remains a difficult one to break.

120

Pain, like memory, is not quick to be erased. With their doctors' help, some patients are eventually able to escape pain's persistent clutch, but many others are not.

Ferrier's job at the pain-control center—one for which he is paid a flat consulting fee—is to examine three patient candidates during each weekly afternoon visit and to help the staff evaluate whether any of the three is likely to benefit from the center's programs, which focus treatment on physical and occupational therapy, individual counseling and group interaction, and treatment of drug dependency. Each prospective patient is examined by a neurologist (Steele or Ferrier or Putnam, depending on the day), a physiatrist or physical therapist, and a psychologist. At an evaluation conference at the end of the afternoon, the staff meet to share findings and impressions, to diagnose collectively the cause of the chronic pain, and to decide whether the patient should be admitted for treatment. There is an obvious impetus for the staff to conclude that their prospective patients should be treated—if they were to turn away too many, the center would find itself without paying customers. Yet in order to attract patient referrals, the center's success ratio has to be high—it has to be able to offer proof that it gets results—so blatantly poor prospects are simply told that the center cannot be of help to them.

On the day I first went to the center with Ferrier, snow still draped the distant peaks but an early summer seemed at hand in town; in front of the building, four patients sat on the thick green grass with soft drinks cradled in their laps, the middle-aged men and one woman looking a bit like students on a break between classes. Inside, seven more patients who were waiting for their afternoon sessions sat on couches in a room filled with vending machines and lunch tables, the walls lined with a series of vapid motivational posters—photographs of couples walking through fields of flowers, others standing pensively at the shores of still lakes, with slogans like Dreams Can Be Captured or Today Is the First Day of the Rest of Your Life. Hung in a small black frame near the reception desk where Ferrier picked up the first candidate's chart and where he asked what office he should use, was a typed quotation from Emerson: "He has seen but half the universe who has never been shown the house of pain."

121

Throughout human history, the alleviation of pain has been one of our species' central concerns. It seems probable that instead of fundamentally pursuing happiness or comfort or some measure of pleasure, we actually dedicate ourselves, as best we can, to the surcease of pain. Perhaps even more than the whispered dirge of death, pain seems to those who suffer it to be the antithesis of life. Pain is greedy, boorish, meanly debilitating; it is cruel and calamitous and often constant, and, as its Latin root *poena* implies, it is the corporeal *punishment* each of us ultimately suffers for being alive.

It was presumably easy for people in primitive societies to reckon with the acute pain that was caused by injuries; lacerations and contusions and the fractures of fragile bones provided obvious sources of pain. But the pain caused by disease—chronic pain that would often endure for years—was mysterious, the sly work of spirits or gods, a disharmony between the sufferer and his or her surroundings. The emergence of shamans and healers in most societies was no doubt directly related to the need for special, pure or insightful people who had the power to deal with pain, who could exorcise it, destroy it, or keep it at bay. Today, throughout the world, attempts to alleviate pain are more often part of the realm of science than of spirituality, yet pain remains mysterious in many ways, and the physicians who treat it often do so with successes that are merely comparable to those of their predecessors who rubbed ashes on their patients' foreheads and touched corn pollen to their fingers and toes.

In the world of contemporary medicine, the very nature of pain is still being debated. Are there special receptors in the nervous system whose sole function is to detect pain? Do discrete pathways relay pain messages to the brain? Or is pain simply the presence of overloaded sensory stimulation—too much heat, too much noise, too much pressure? Virtually everyone who studies pain does now agree that previous distinctions between "physical" and "psychological" pain—or pain that is "real" or "unreal"—are incorrect and have become counterproductive. Except for unusual cases in which a patient, for whatever reason, malingers, claiming to feel pain when he or she honestly feels nothing, the myriad types of pain that patients report cannot be considered imaginary. Regardless of whether pain has its genesis in a shallow

122

wound or a deep depression, it involves neurophysiologic activity in the brain and is therefore a biological reality.

Yet the understanding that pain is shaped by, and persists because of, a complicated mixture of physical, psychological, and environmental factors does little to help define its proper method of treatment. In many instances, the treatment a patient receives for chronic pain depends first of all on the specialty of the treating physician—on the insights and prejudices that his or her particular specialty brings to bear. Surgeons tend to treat pain with invasive procedures, cutting nerve pathways or removing herniated discs. Anesthesiologists inject nerve blocks; psychiatrists probe troubled psyches, and neurologists and internists often prescribe drugs and physical therapy. Unlike the relatively new and booming subspecialty called oncology, which is devoted to the treatment of the many cancers, the field of *angology*, the study of pain, has few full-time participants.

We met the first prospective patient in Bill Steele's office—Steele had gone to Tucson to speak to a convention of health-insurance executives. The patient, a forty-two-year-old black woman named Velma Simms, a divorcée with four grown children, sat in a caned chair, her print dress pulled over her knees. She was cooperative but quiet as she matter-of-factly told Ferrier about the car accident two years before that had left her with a whiplash injury and, later, with steady, aching pain that radiated down her right arm. She had been laid off from her job at an assembly plant following the accident, then fired four months later when she was unable to do the light-duty work to which the company had transferred her. She told Ferrier that she had begun to use her left arm to accomplish simple tasks because her right arm was so painful, that she seldom left her house, and that she had once made plans to commit suicide but had become too frightened to do so. "I doubt I'll try it again," she said. "I don't guess I have the energy." On examination, Ferrier found significant weakness in her right arm and was able to isolate an injured cervical nerve root. "This is a C5 injury," Ferrier said, directing his words to me. "Notice how weak the deltoid and biceps are, how this reflex is virtually gone, and she's lost sensation here."

"There. Oh, gosh, yes, that's the trouble," she said when Ferrier raised her arm above her shoulder, his fingers probing the back of her neck.

At the evaluation conference two hours later, the decision was easy to make. Ferrier outlined the woman's history and his findings and said he felt that she had damaged the fifth cervical root. Her myelogram had not shown a slipped disc, however, and Ferrier called it a "superimposed thoracic outlet syndrome" with muscle overcontraction—meaning a bony irritation of the long thoracic nerve as it exits from the spinal cord at the fifth cervical vertebra. She would likely respond to aggressive physical therapy. Jenny, the jolly, matronly physical therapist, said the woman's slumped shoulders and poor head carriage contributed to her pain. David, the thin, soft-spoken psychologist, said the woman suffered from a posttraumatic depression with suicidal features. The three agreed that she was an excellent candidate for treatment, recommending that she be admitted for a full four-week therapy program. Louise, the stern administrative assistant, made note of their quick decision.

Joe Grabowski, the second candidate, had been referred by the woman at Workers' Compensation who managed his case. He had been injured at a construction site several years before, when a forty-five-pound box culvert landed on the large toe of his left foot. A year and a half later, surgery was performed to fuse a joint in the toe that had been destroyed by the blow. Joe's severe pain decreased following the surgery, but did not disappear; it remained dull and constant. He had worked intermittently in the intervening time, but the pain and lack of mobility made manual labor difficult. Now thirty-seven years old, he was currently suing the construction company and collecting $980 a month in compensation benefits—as much money as he had been making before the accident.

Joe had just spent an hour with the psychologist, and he refused Ferrier's handshake when he walked into the office. He wore a denim jacket and steel-toed boots, and he turned his chair so he could direct his gaze away from the doctor.

"I'm Doctor Ferrier and I'm a neurologist. I haven't been able to read your records yet, so why don't you begin by telling me why you're here."

"You tell me," Joe snapped back, "you're the fucking expert, aren't you? I don't know why I'm here. I sure as shit don't want to be, playing your fucking games."

"Well, then why are you here?" Ferrier asked, his voice rising in response to Joe's shouts. "Who sent you?"

"The jerks at Workers' Comp, I guess. They jack me around about every way they can think of. So they make me waste a whole day with this Mickey Mouse bullshit. Hey, is that all you need to know? Are we through? Can I get the fuck out of here?"

Ferrier paused before he spoke. "You can leave any time you want to as far as I'm concerned. But let me spell this out. I'm a doctor. My job here is to talk to you and to examine you and to see if I can figure out what's causing your continued pain. That's it."

"Well, I fucking know what's causing it," Joe shouted. "My toe is smashed to shit! You don't have to be no fucking genius to figure that out."

"Listen, mister!" Ferrier seemed to rise in his chair; his voice was loud and challenging. "You're going to go too far in a minute. Lots of people smash the shit out of their toe and two years later don't even remember it. I don't know what's bothering you, but I'm going to tell you just one more time that I'm not your goddamn enemy. You can walk out of here right now, or you can cooperate for about fifteen minutes. What's it going to be?"

"Okay, okay," Joe said, suddenly backing down. "Ask your questions, okay?" He sat slumped in his chair and spoke into his lap. "This whole thing has just been such a fucking drag."

Ferrier was able to find out that Joe was suing the company that had employed him for fifty thousand dollars, that he had no other medical complaints, and that he would refuse any new job that would not enable him to work outdoors. He claimed that his injury had not affected his relationship with his wife or daughter, but it did keep him from playing softball. By the time they moved to the examining room, Joe had calmed considerably and Ferrier performed a complete exam, finding the diminished movement in Joe's toe. Coordination, strength, and sensation were normal in both feet.

"Prince of a guy," Ferrier said when it was time to consider Joe's case at the conference an hour later. The others laughed. His diagnosis: chronic pain syndrome related to a fibrous union of the distal interphalangeal joint of the left hallux secondary to the [1980] injury. Jenny's impression: unstable pelvis with feet externally rotated, but probably unrelated to the toe pain. David's "call": adjustment disorder with mixed emotional features. The three agreed that Joe had absolutely no interest in coming to the center for therapy, and on that basis alone, he should not be admitted. Louise noted their recommendations that Joe be reexamined by the orthopedic surgeon who performed the surgery, and that he conclude his lawsuit as soon as possible. Chronic pain has an intriguing tendency to subside when litigation is settled— even when the settlement is not in favor of the person in pain.

"Your last one's a doozy," said the secretary when she handed Marilyn Roybal's chart to Ferrier. "I guess they just wanted to get rid of her down at St. Joe's. I know Dr. Steele was skeptical about doing an eval on her since she's an inpatient, but . . ."

We found Marilyn in a wheelchair at the end of an isolated hall. She wore a hospital gown and a furry green robe; her feet were tucked into furry blue slippers. Her head was slumped so far forward that her face was invisible; her hair was dark and matted. "How are you?" Ferrier asked, stooping to say hello, his words loud and slow.

"I'm about to die," Marilyn mumbled.

"Can you lift your head up?"

"Of course not."

"Why not?"

"Because of the pain. Because it kills me, that's why." Her words were slurred and she spoke them in a sort of moan. "Do you think I like it like this or something?"

"Come on," he said. "Let's roll you into the office so we can try to find out what the problem is."

But the problem was not easy to ascertain; Marilyn could not keep track of the conversation. She told us her friend was waiting for her in the lobby, but in fact, she had been brought up from the city in an ambulance. The pain was in the back of her head, she said, then changed her mind; it was definitely in her neck. She could not be sure when her problems began; it might have been last week, or maybe a month ago, but it could have been last year. When Ferrier pressed her for details, she groaned and shook her head. "Doctor, how the hell am I supposed to know? I'm sick, aren't I?"

"Marilyn, it looks to me like you've been getting a lot of medication at the hospital. Do you know what they've been giving you?" She shook her head. While Ferrier leafed through her chart, she sat motionless, her head still bent, her hands gripping her bare knees. I could see that her hands had recently been manicured, her long nails painted purple; one nail had a thin, diagonal silver stripe.

Ferrier turned in his chair. "Listen to this. She was admitted seven days ago, I think, and since that time this guy Baxter has given her Dalmane, Valium, Tylox, phenobarb, Meclomen, Thorazine, Demerol, Vistaril, Elavil, and Xanax. She's a walking pharmacy. Barbiturates, opiates, heavy tranquilizers. What the hell was he doing?"

"Baxter is a hatchet man," Marilyn said, her words surprisingly intelligible. "Percy, the guy I had before him, was even worse. He's the one that did this to me. He's the one that operated."

In the examining room, Ferrier and I lifted Marilyn onto the table. Despite her inability to raise her head while she sat in the chair, she was able to lie on her back without discomfort, her head flat against the table. But Ferrier quickly gave up his attempts to examine her after he studied her eyes and probed the back of her skull with his hands. She could not attend to the strength and sensation tests he tried to perform, and he clearly did not trust her answers to his questions.

"Do you know where you are, Marilyn? What is this place?"

"It's a hospital, stupid."

"Who is the president?"

"Richard M. Nixon," she pronounced, as though it were a silly question.

"Are you sure? Who is Ronald Reagan?"

"He's the president."

"Then is the president Nixon or Reagan?"

"It depends," she said.

"Okay, good. Marilyn, someone is going to come in and stay with you for a while so we can have a meeting about what we should do to help you. Okay? I need to go try to find out some more about what's been happening with you."

127

"Why don't you ask the hatchet man?" she mumbled.

Jenny, Louise, and David were already in Bill steele's office when we walked in, and they offered us nods of commiseration. "This was the last goddamn thing I needed today," said Ferrier. "That bastard knows this is an outpatient clinic; he's sent people here before. And he had to know she's toxic. Did you see the list of meds he's had her on? I'm surprised she knows her name."

"I couldn't be at all sure about what I was getting from her," David said, "what was behavioral and what was due to the medications. About the only thing I got was that she's thirty-six and that she admits to an abusive childhood and an abusive marriage; this one's her third. She says she has four children; the husband has six, but I couldn't find out if all of them live at home. I didn't get anything about the injury or whatever."

"Neither did I," said Jenny. "I couldn't do a thing with her. Just took her to the toilet and struggled through that with her. Poor thing doesn't know whether she's coming or going. I did notice a surprisingly large occipital skull defect."

"Me too, which I guess relates to a craniotomy done in 1977 that I'm reading about here." Ferrier flipped through the pages of her chart. "Let's see if this explains anything." He silently scanned two pages before he spoke again, his finger tracing the words he read. "Okay, well, from what I can make of this, she was pushed down some stairs at a bar in 1977, hitting her head on a concrete floor. Subsequent to that injury, a CAT showed what they thought was a tumor, so they did the craniotomy. All they found, according to Baxter's note—he didn't do the surgery—were adhesions related to the trauma. Three years later, Marilyn began to have severe headaches, and another scan showed hydrocephalus, so they implanted a shunt to drain the fluid. She got a second shunt a year later, in '82. And these notes don't say anything about seizures, but for whatever reason, she was put on phenobarb and Dilantin at the time of the second shunt.

"Now—" he took a deep breath, "Baxter is totally vague about this recent hospital admission. There's something about a fall at home, but I can't tell if she hit her head, or if the fall was because of a seizure, or what. And depending on how you read this thing, Jesus, she was either admitted to St. Joe's on April 29, May 3, or May 7—take your pick."

"Baxter's a general surgeon, isn't he?" David asked. "Have we had his referrals before?"

"Many," Louise said. "But he's never done this to us before."

"God, this pisses me off," said Ferrier. "Bill should never had agreed to this."

"Dr. Steele talked to him from Tucson. I guess Baxter agreed to take her back if we didn't admit her to the program, but he told Bill he thought she was a very suitable candidate."

"And he thought she could just sleep on a sofa in the lobby, I suppose. We don't know how to get hold of her family. We don't have a decent history. The woman is dangerously overdosed, and this guy thinks he can just ship her up here for a little physical therapy and a day or two of counseling and she'll be fixed right up."

"I could try to get him on the phone," Louise said.

"I think I'll just go ahead and admit her to County," Ferrier said. "The most immediate thing is to get her detoxed. If we detox her over the weekend, maybe by Tuesday she'll be in good enough shape to come back for evaluation. I don't know. How can we get her to the hospital?"

"I guess I can take her in the van," Jenny said. "I'll get some of the guys to help me get her in."

"I'll try to locate the family," Louise said. "Surely St. Joe's has something on them."

"And I'll go up and profusely apologize to the nurses at County," Ferrier said. "When she starts to come off all those meds, she's going to be climbing the goddamn walls."

Ferrier was still fuming as we drove across town to the hospital, blasting the Saab's horn at the slower drivers who moved into his lane. "This is what you call a dump," he said. "This, in fact, is a textbook dump. Baxter doesn't know what's wrong with her; he doesn't want to know. He gets tired of her whining about being in so much pain, so he drugs her out of her head and puts her in an ambulance and points her up here. She can't bother him if she's thirty miles away. I'm supposed to be giving a minor opinion about whether she can be helped by a pain-control program, and I end up admitting her for detox. Now she's my problem, and he's probably playing golf. Very interesting, huh?"

"Is there some way you can report this guy? I mean, this is pretty outrageous, isn't it?"

"You can make sure you don't refer any business to him if you can help it."

"But doesn't the state or the AMA have ethics committees or something?"

"Yes, but I'm not going to call them up about Baxter."

"Why not? It sounds like he's a quack."

"Because I'm just not going to do it, all right?"

"Because the unwritten law is that you have to cover each other's ass. I can't believe you don't want to see him get burned."

"Listen, you don't know shit about this sort of thing. People make mistakes—I mean, the guy's just a surgeon. And it's none of your goddamn business."

"Okay, okay. Excuse me, asshole," I said, then we sat in silence.

Ferrier was seldom reticent to comment privately when he felt one of his colleagues had made a poor decision or was generally incompetent. And in conversations between him and other physicians I would sometimes hear some subtle disparagement of a fellow physician or observe an irritated shake of the head. Yet collectively they were always allies—belonging to the "medical community" seemed to mean something important to them—and Ferrier was no more likely to confront a member of that community through the "proper channels" than he was to slash the fellow's tires. Slow waitresses, confused sales clerks, churlish mechanics, and arrogant attorneys could quickly drive him crazy, but Ferrier was quite understanding of the frailties of the world's physicians. He spoke highly of the quality of medicine that was practiced in his city; he often praised individual internists, ophthalmologists, surgeons with whom he was in steady contact; and his response was verbose and ready whenever someone implied in his presence that physicians were shoddy, unconcerned, or disproportionately paid for their services. He would agree that it was easy to encounter substandard physicians, but he recoiled against the notion that they were proof the profession was flawed.

Ferrier's opinions are not surprising, of course. It would be startling, to the contrary, to find a physician who would claim that all doctors are quacks. Yet doctors probably are more collectively defensive than are artists or stevedores or securities analysts, perhaps simply because they are such easy and ubiquitous targets. And it may be that Ferrier and the thousands of physicians like him are unwilling to call attention to a colleague's rushed judgment or quick and shoddy practice because they viscerally know how seductive that cursory kind of work can sometimes be.

In contrast to the mean and lingering pain suffered by Marilyn, Velma, and Joe—pain seemingly without purpose—the purpose of acute pain is to act as a physiologic alarm system, alerting us to the fact that we are somehow near harm, reminding us to be protective, immobilizing a finger or a foot or a whole body long enough to allow it to heal. Acute pain, the short-term pain that accompanies injury or illness, can be brutal, but it is mitigated by its brevity. Chronic pain, on the other hand, seems very different. It can be transferred to areas of the body that have had no injury; it can last long after nerves or bones or skin have healed and its function, if indeed it has one, only becomes destructive. Although neuroscientists admit that there is much to be learned about the physiology of acute pain, its basic processes are understood. The persistence of chronic pain is another matter, its pathology often mysterious.

When a finger is cut or a toe is stubbed, a number of chemical substances such as prostaglandins, histamine, bradykinin, and others stored in or near the nerve endings at the site of the injury are suddenly released. Prostaglandins quickly increase blood circulation to the damaged area, facilitating the infection-fighting and healing functions of the blood's white cells, antibodies, and oxygen. Together with bradykinin and other substances, present in only minute quantities, prostaglandins also stimulate the nerve endings, causing them to transmit electrical impulses along the length of the affected sensory nerve to its junction with the "dorsal horn" of the spinal cord, a strip of gray-matter tissue running the length of the spinal cord, which collects sensory signals from all parts of the body and relays them to the brain—first to the thalamus, where pain is first "felt," then on to the "sensory strip" of the cerebral cortex, where the pain becomes conscious, its location and intensity perceived.

The "experience" of pain can be lessened or blocked in a variety of ways. As healing occurs, prostaglandin and bradykinin production slackens, inflammation decreases, and fewer pain impulses are sent to the spinal cord. Analgesics like aspirin and Tylenol are effective because they inhibit the production of these same chemicals—thereby similarly limiting pain impulses. Nerve blocks—local anesthesias—performed surgically or with injections of drugs, simply prohibit the transmission of pain or any sensory stimuli along affected nerves. Antidepressants, developed for other purposes, nonetheless sometimes exhibit pain-relieving properties, possibly by altering the transmission of pain information between the thalamus and cortex, somehow affecting the appreciation of pain. Narcotics, acclaimed for their pain-killing properties and cursed because they are often addictive, appear to exert their effects by binding onto the synaptic receptors of neurons in both the brain and the spinal cord that are involved with pain transmissions, inhibiting the impulses or altering them as they travel. In recent years, neuroscientists have discovered a whole class of neurotransmitters produced in the pituitary and elsewhere in the brain that, intriguingly, act similarly to narcotics—dulling pain, limiting the perception of it before it actually vanishes.

The particular problem with chronic pain is that in many instances there is no observable reason for it to exist. Long after healing should have been complete, the thalamus still recognizes pain and the cortex still localizes it to an arm or a shoulder or a lower back, interpreting it as a steady ache or a maddening, burning throb. Sometimes careful examination of a chronic-pain patient will reveal a latent disorder—a slipped disc, a bone spur, a pinched nerve—one that can be treated and the pain relieved. But too often, no latent complications are evident to account for the pain. Analgesics, opiates, sometimes even anesthetics, are unable to limit the painful perception that something is wrong.

Chronic-pain researchers are confronted with a number of perplexing questions and possibilities. Can pain, experienced for long enough, become *learned* in a manner similar to the way in which we learn how to balance ourselves or how to distinguish objects with touch? Is chronic pain somehow entwined with memory, enduring in some sort of remembered state—a reverberating cross talk between overcontracted muscles, their nerves, and the brain? Do some long-term pains become a kind of "sink" for any number of psychological stresses and sublimations that would otherwise be evidenced in other ways? Do back pains and migraines—the two most common chronic-pain complaints, both of them very "real" and often debilitatingly painful—sometimes plague their sufferers because of underlying, unconscious problems?

It is hard to pay attention to someone else's pain. Chronic pain, in particular, is personal; it matters immensely to the one who suffers it, but notwithstanding the most profound compassion or empathy, it is something that cannot be shared or understood. It is perhaps the most subjective of all diseases—and it truly is a disease in the sense that it represents an unacceptable, and sometimes radical, departure from health. Pain cannot be measured; it cannot be discovered with diagnostic tests. Except for the statements of those in pain, there would never be any evidence that it exists at all.

Pain thresholds tend to vary among individuals—women in general seem to have higher thresholds than men—and the types of pain that people find noxious vary as well. Some individuals only marginally affected by the deep, aching pain of broken bones find the sharp, stabbing pain of lacerated skin almost unbearable; some types of pain, particularly those that accompany muscle massage or sexual activity, are actually perceived as pleasurable. In attempting to understand the nature of the noxious pain their patients suffer, doctors are limited to the use of inadequate adjectives: Is the pain throbbing or steady? Is it a burning kind of pain? Dull or sharp? Is it widespread or is it limited to one spot? It is even harder to try to quantify the level of pain. Is this the most intense pain you have ever had? Is it worse than a splitting headache? Is it as bad as having a baby?

Regardless of its intensity or its many manifestations, pain is pervasive; it is the single most common reason people seek medical attention. Seventy million Americans suffer chronic back pain; more than 30 million are arthritics; 20 million suffer from migraine. At any given time, about a million people battle the long-term pain that comes with cancer. Chronic pain in all its guises probably disables as many people as cancer and heart

133

disease combined, and some estimates place its annual cost in medical care, insurance benefits, and lost income at $70 *billion*. Bill Steele's study of the patients at his pain-control clinic claims that those who are successfully treated save themselves and their insurers, over the course of their lifetimes, a quarter of a million dollars each.

But if pain is such a basic problem, and if medicine's mission is to comfort as much as it is to cure, why is pain still so marginally understood? Why are our age-old aches still with us?

"Well, that's like asking why we can't cure colds," Ferrier said as we drove to the hospital Friday morning, en route to check on Marilyn, who lay strapped to a bed in the intensive care unit. "Colds are tough because the whole arena of virology is so complex. It's similar with pain because of what we know about the brain itself, which in fifty or sixty years will look like very little.

"It wasn't that long ago—in fact, when I was in medical school in Edinburgh—that two pharmacologists at Aberdeen isolated peptides in the brain, now called endorphins, which are inhibitory neurotransmitters that latch on to the same receptor sites that the opiate drugs do. As medical discoveries go, this was very exciting. We had known for a long time that the opiates act centrally, on the central nervous system, that they somehow latch onto receptors on the surface of neurons and prevent the transmission of pain information. But the evidence that, in effect, the brain produces its own opiates was startling. For a long time, people had conjectured that the brain had a means of limiting pain transmissions, but I'm not sure many assumed that it did so in much the same way the opiates do.

"That's one of the reasons why long-term use of opiates is such a vicious circle. When you have morphine or heroin or whatever on board over a period of time, your own endorphin activity can drop drastically. You need more and more of the opiates over time to get relief, partly because the endorphins are no longer doing their share. Whether I'm treating patients with peripheral pain or migraine or what have you, the first order of business is to get them off narcotics immediately, and to get them on a daily aerobic exercise program. Twenty minutes a day of any kind of aerobic exercise increases the brain's endorphins. It's not at all clear why, but it seems to be true. It's probably the best single reason, in fact, for people in pain to get regular exercise."

134

"You're going to ruin your reputation if you start bad-mouthing drugs," I said.

"Oh, no, don't get the wrong impression. The opiates can be extremely valuable for certain things. They are great with cardiac patients. They are tremendous anxiety reducers as well as painkillers, and that's exactly what you need for somebody who's having a heart attack. And I think it's weird that heroin isn't legal for use with terminal patients in this country the way it is in Britain. In late-stage cases of cancer where you don't care about addiction, heroin can be a wonderful drug. Opiates can provide real relief for someone's last days when nothing else can, and cancer patients deserve to have it."

At the hospital, Ferrier leaned over Marilyn's bed and asked her if she knew who he was. "You look sort of familiar," she said.

"I saw you at a pain clinic yesterday. Do you remember being at the pain clinic?"

"No."

"I'm Dr. Ferrier. I'm going to look after you for a few days. The nurses tell me that you were able to sleep last night, which is great. You're welcome to sleep as much as you want to. We'll try not to bother you too much. How is your pain this morning?"

"It hurts."

"Is it as bad as yesterday?"

"Are you trying to see how tough I am?"

Ferrier smiled. "No, but we've taken you off your medications, which you're probably going to think was a pretty rotten thing to do, and the pain's not going to be easy for a couple of days. But it's very important that you get through it, just on your own. And I think that before long we can get it to go away. We're going to try anyway."

Marilyn nodded and I followed Ferrier into the nurses' station, a narrow, glass-enclosed room in the center of the ring of beds, one wall lined with a bank of video monitors, their cameras trained on the beds. Three sleepy-eyed nurses in lavender pants and smocks leaned on the low shelf on the opposite wall, their all-night shift over in half an hour. "Yeah, I think she's doing pretty well," Ferrier said to the young, freckle-faced woman who sat between the other two. "Have you had a call from a husband or anyone?"

"Nobody as far as I know," she said. She glanced at the others and they shook their heads. "Any objection if I pull her catheter before I leave? I think she'll be able to use a bedpan today."

"Sure, why don't you. But let's leave her strapped until I come back this evening. I'm not sure she's out of the woods yet, but she does seem to be doing well. Maybe we're going to get lucky."

"Don't think she's been too lucky lately," said the nurse.

Yoshi Kurumata sat on the edge of his bed, separated by a long corridor and two flights of stairs from the bed where Marilyn lay. He wore shorts and a striped T-shirt, and he was attempting to tie the laces of his sneakers when Ferrier and I said hello. Ferrier said "ohiyo" actually—it had become his ritual morning greeting to Yoshi. But three weeks after his accident, three weeks after his speech disappeared, Yoshi could now do much more than speak that single word. He could express himself in simple sentences in Japanese, and he seemed, according to Dr. Fukuda, to understand almost everything that was said to him. His spoken English remained nearly nonexistent, but he did say "how are you" and "I feel fine" each time Ferrier saw him.

Yoshi had been moved from intensive care to a room on a medical ward a week after the accident, two days after his mother arrived. His right side had remained weak, but he was beginning to be able to use a fork in his right hand and he could walk in a kind of clumsy shuffle. Today he was changing hospitals; he was being transferred to the rehabilitation department at St. Luke's Hospital, where he would begin twice-daily sessions of speech and physical therapy. Yoshi's hope was to improve enough that his doctors and parents would allow him to stay in the United States to continue his English studies, but Ferrier and his mother felt, at least for the time being, that Japan would be the best place for him to complete his convalescence.

"Am I . . . stay here . . . now?" Yoshi asked Ferrier as the doctor checked and compared the strength in his limbs.

"No. You're going to go to a new hospital today. Don't you remember us talking about that with Dr. Fukuda?"

Yoshi shook his head, then struggled to find the words he wanted. His face grew flushed as his frustration mounted. "No . . . stay . . . stay . . . America?"

"Oh. Are you going to stay here in America?" Ferrier asked and

Yoshi nodded intently, obviously pleased at having made himself understood. "Well, you're definitely going to stay for a while, while you're in rehab at St. Luke's." Ferrier spoke slowly, his voice soft. "After that, you and I and your mother, also Dr. Fukuda, will have to talk and decide what would be best. But we won't decide until we see how much you're improving. Do you understand what I'm saying?"

Yoshi looked puzzled, but then he grinned and tried to talk again. "Yes . . . speak English." His smile spread across his smooth round face, the right corner of his mouth drooping only slightly.

Lisa Benedict came into the office in the middle of the morning. She wore jeans and a plaid flannel shirt, its collar turned up; her red hair was combed forward as if to hide her delicate face. I had met her before; by coincidence, her two previous appointments had fallen during weeks I was in town. "Gosh, are you always here?" she asked with a slight smile, her voice thin, almost fragile, but sweetened by an Arkansas accent.

"Sorry," I said. "I'm really not here all the time. I guess your timing's just bad."

"No," she blushed, "no, I didn't mean it that way. I'm just surprised you can sit here all day listening to everybody's problems. Doesn't it get you down after a while?"

"It . . . makes me feel pretty fortunate."

"Yeah, I bet it—"

"Listen, I'm sure I can find some work to do in the other room if you two just want to sit and chat," Ferrier said, enjoying his facetiousness.

Lisa blushed again. "Sorry. Didn't mean to ignore you."

Ferrier leaned back in his tall swivel chair. "How are things in the mountains?" he asked, smiling. "You look good."

"They're pretty good. Almost looks like summer."

"Your kids?"

"Fine."

"Your husband?"

"He's . . . fine."

"That was a harder question, wasn't it? Things with him haven't improved much, I take it."

"I don't think it's going anywhere, Dr. Ferrier. About the only

137

time we even talk is when he gives me trouble for coming down to see you. He thinks the headaches are all in my head, I mean, well you know, that I'm crazy."

"Does he know you came today?"

"He drove me down. But then he stormed off when he dropped me off. Who knows if he'll show up to pick me up."

"How are your headaches?"

"Better. Fewer anyway. When I get one, maybe about once a month or so now, it still wipes out about three days if I don't catch it in time. But I can usually catch it."

When Lisa first saw Ferrier four months before, she had been referred by a family practitioner who told her that the "sick headaches" she had always suffered could be treated. Even though she averaged a three-day headache once a week, Lisa was reluctant to see a neurologist, whose consultation would no doubt be expensive, who might prescribe expensive drugs, and who would not understand how much her husband hated the idea of her seeing a doctor. But when one headache was finally so severe that it sent her to the emergency room at the small hospital in the mountain town where she lived—the right side of her head feeling as if it were being torn away—she decided she had had enough.

The headaches she described to Ferrier were almost always right-sided, and they were occasionally preceded by a "funny feeling." As the pain crescendoed, she would invariably become nauseous. Her right eye would grow red and tearful, and she would see bright lights arranged in strange zigzagging lines. She found it almost impossible to sleep during the course of a head-ache. Her children were small and she had to attend to them in the midst of the pain, but when her husband came home from work, she said, she would sometimes lie on a bed in a dark room to get a bit of relief.

Ferrier found nothing abnormal in his examination of Lisa on her first visit and he ultimately diagnosed her complaint as "clas-sic migraine," a variant of the several types of chronic headaches that are caused by the abnormal constriction—and subsequent dilation—of blood vessels that supply the brain and scalp. The actual cause of the acute pain is invariably the throbbing, dilated blood vessels, but apparently in most cases, the dilation is preceded by a vascular constriction whose cause remains unknown. In his letter to Lisa's family physician, Ferrier noted that the strange lights she sometimes noticed as her "classic" headaches began were what distinguished them from those known as "common migraine." The redness and teariness in her right eye were related to elements of a distinct headache called cluster. Yet the diagnosing categories were not absolute, and it was common for a patient's headache symptoms to include elements of several headache types. Many migraine patients were also unfortunate enough to suffer muscle contraction headaches as well—the so-called tension headaches that most people have from time to time, headaches characterized by bilateral bandlike pain, and head and neck tenderness, sometimes including sleep disturbances, depression, and fatigue—headaches capable of causing excruciating pain in their own right. But although Ferrier felt it was probable that Lisa suffered a psychological depression, he believed her headaches were true migraines. "Her relationship with her husband seems to be a source of significant stress in her life," he wrote, "and although she is in a mildly depressive state today, it is my impression that Lisa would still be a migraineur even if her home situation were entirely happy."

Before Lisa left following her first appointment, she and Ferrier agreed that they would try an "abortive" therapy—treating each headache at its first signs of onset. If that method proved unsuccessful, they would then try "prophylactic," or preventive, medications. He prescribed Midrin, a nonnarcotic analgesic containing acetaminophen (the drug in Tylenol), Vistaril, to reduce nausea, and a mist inhaler of ergotamine tartrate that often effectively constricts blood vessels. He stressed that all three medications needed to be taken at the first signs of a headache, and lastly, he wrote a prescription for chloral hydrate, a mild sedative that she should use to help her sleep when a headache became severe. Many patients, he told her, found that if they could get a good night's sleep, despite the pain, they would wake up to find the pain had vanished.

Lisa was pale and tearful when she returned six weeks later; she looked tired and troubled, but she said everything was fine. When Ferrier pressed her, Lisa admitted that her domestic situation was bleak. "If I had any way to provide for the kids, I'd leave," she said, "but I just don't know how I'd take care of them." When he asked if her husband had ever been violent with her or the two children, she said no. "It's just his voice, his shouting. Seems like he's always mad and screaming at one of us about something."

Lisa's headaches were better, however. She said that the ergotamine inhaler had aborted several headaches, but she was not sure that the Midrin had been of much help. With Lisa's concurrence, Ferrier decided to begin her on a course of amitriptyline, an antidepressant that, somehow serendipitously, is often effective for both migraine and muscle contraction headaches. Because of her depression—whether it was related to her home strife or endogenous neurological factors—Ferrier felt that the use of amitriptyline might be particularly appropriate. He also urged Lisa to contact the counselor in her hometown whom he recommended; she was reluctant—her husband would go crazy if he thought she was seeing a shrink. "So don't tell him," Ferrier said. "He doesn't have to know."

"But I don't think I can pay for it."

"We're just charging you what the insurance company pays us. I'll see if Virginia, the counselor, can do the same. Being able to talk things out with her could be every bit as important as the amitriptyline and the inhaler, probably more. These headaches are real. You're not dreaming them up, regardless of what your husband may think. But family situations and depressions can make them much more frequent and more severe. So, as your doctor," he said, smiling, "I order you to go see Virginia."

"You can't order me," Lisa said, wiping her cheeks and returning a bit of a smile. "Taking orders and backing down have got to stop, too, don't they?"

Ferrier nodded. "I think so," he said.

Today's visit followed Lisa's second appointment by six more weeks, and it came a month after Lisa had begun weekly counseling sessions with Virginia. "She's real good to talk to, she really is," Lisa told Ferrier. "I just wish Robert could talk to her, too."

"You don't think he'd agree to it?"

"Oh, God, he'd hit the ceiling." Lisa reported that her headaches came on much less frequently now, and that the ergotamine inhaler could reliably abort every headache she did have, as long as she used it just as soon as she noticed the pain. "I don't know about the amitriptyline," she said. "Maybe it's helping, too."

"I'd like you to stay on it for a while longer. It may actually be reducing the headache frequency, but even if it's not, we're probably getting some depression relief from it." He paused, then picked up a pencil and turned it in his hands. "Lisa, if after a couple more months, if you still don't think you and your husband have made any progress, I would hate to think that you would just put up with a rotten situation forever."

"So would I," she said.

"So you would leave if it came to that?"

"Doctor, like Virginia says, nobody's going to do the leaving for me, are they?"

Putnam was on call on the weekend, and Ferrier and I had hoped to canoe a stretch of a small, runoff-swollen river two hours' drive away. But now he was reluctant to leave town. Before we left the office on Friday evening, Ferrier had briefed Putnam on his current inpatients, among them, Marilyn. He spared Putnam the details of Marilyn's whole saga, but told him that she seemed to be detoxifying without many complications, and he promised Putnam that he had an interesting story about Marilyn's doctor to tell him one of these days. By Saturday morning, my arguments that the clouds that had covered the sky in the night would not ultimately result in rain, and that Marilyn would surely continue to improve were unpersuasive. Ferrier was plainly concerned about her, so we stayed in town, and he checked on Marilyn twice that day and once on Sunday. She berated him for his sadism each time she saw him, telling him she could not figure out why doctors like to hurt people, but her feistiness was a good sign and Ferrier remained amazed at how smoothly her detoxification seemed to be going.

On Sunday evening, we sat on Ferrier's deck with his girlfriend, Jenny Stern, an ICU nurse. The three of us watched the sky turn from blue to a nearly neon red before it turned black behind the mountains, and I told them how it had begun to seem to me that many of Ferrier's patients were the kinds of people that the world simply seemed to pile up on, whose illnesses seemed to be just one element in lives of sad misfortune.

"You mean Marilyn?" Ferrier asked.

"Marilyn, Lisa, lots of them."

"Well, I suppose there really isn't any question that people who lack self-esteem, who don't take active responsibility for their lives, their situations, probably get sick more often than other people, at least with minor viruses, colds, flu, and it's certainly the case with chronic pain, too. You seldom see people who are positive, energetic, motivated, who are riddled with constant pain, whatever the source. You shouldn't overgeneralize, but it seems to be true, maybe because they're simply too busy to be in pain. There have been lots of studies done on the personality traits of migraineurs. Lots of them, a surprising percentage, are people who don't adapt to environmental stress very well; you see lots of people who are rigid, uptight, unable to express emotion, especially anger; lots of compulsives. And you can see why you might expect those kinds of people to get headaches—the tension headaches caused by muscle contraction, anyway. Why uptight people would have blood vessels in their heads that tend to go into spasm is a lot less clear. And why do you suppose that so many more women—three-to-one—get migraines than do men? I have a hunch that it has something to do with the fact that estrogens markedly influence vascular tone—the contractability of the blood vessels. That may be why when women withdraw from estrogens, as they do during menopause, they get hot flashes. But even when estrogens are at steady, low levels after menopause, many women still have frequent migraines, so that may not be the answer."

"Men get cluster headaches more often than women, don't they?" Jenny asked him.

"Something like ten-to-one male. I very seldom see a female with true cluster headaches."

Cluster headaches, sometimes labeled a migraine variant but often considered a distinct disorder, are presumed to be caused by a dilation and constriction of blood vessels that is similar to the cause of migraine. Yet clusters have markedly different features. In addition to affecting men almost exclusively, they tend to occur in "clusters" lasting a few weeks to a few months, most commonly beginning in the spring or fall. In the midst of a cluster, most patients suffer one or more headaches daily, usually at night, usually at the same time every night. The pain, which comes on suddenly and invariably wakes the patient, is reported to be among the most excruciating of all types of pain, rising behind or around one eye, sometimes spreading to the whole side of the head, causing redness or tearing of that eye, nasal congestion, flushing, sweating. The pain is usually described as steady and can be so severe that it seems unsurvivable. The duration of each headache is relatively short, however, very few of them lasting more than two hours.

There is no increased familial incidence of cluster headache, as there is with migraine, and there is as yet no explanation of why attacks begin at a certain point during the year or of why they suddenly end. Consumption of alcohol can trigger a single headache during a cluster series, but it seems to have no bearing on when the series starts. Studies have shown no common personality traits among cluster sufferers.

I remembered one of Ferrier's cluster patients whom I had met during the winter, a twenty-three-year-old Mercedes mechanic who was otherwise very healthy. At the time I met him, he was in the midst of a cluster, experiencing one headache each day lasting thirty to forty-five minutes. Each headache reliably woke him at one-thirty in the morning, *always* one-thirty. The pain, he said, was like being stabbed in his eye, the blade of the knife reaching deep inside his head. He said he could not be sure how long each cluster lasted, a month or six weeks perhaps, and he guessed he had about three clusters a year. He had seen a variety of physicians during the two years since his clusters began and he had tried a number of medications. Nothing seemed to work to prevent the headaches and nothing but the inhalation of oxygen stopped one in progress. Except for the oxygen, which was stored in a tall green tank beside his bed, his only alternative was to wait, to endure the agonizing minutes. He wanted Ferrier to write a prescription for him for a new tank of oxygen; his insurance company would pay for it only if it were prescribed by a physician. Ferrier took his history, examined his eyes and the blood vessels beneath his scalp, discussed the issue of alcohol, then gladly wrote the prescription.

"What in the world causes the cycles? Why the same time every day?" I asked as the sky darkened at dusk.

"Nobody knows. There may be some metabolic factor that initiates the vasoconstriction phase cyclically, but I don't know."

"What medicines do you usually start people on?"

"Sometimes ergotamine, which is a drug derived from a mold that grows on rye, works with cluster, as it does with migraine. And short courses of steroids, normally prednisone, can be very effective at breaking a cluster cycle. Drugs like lithium, indomethacin, Sansert, and cyproheptadine can sometimes prevent subsequent clusters from starting. The problem with cluster is that many medications work well when you begin them, then for some reason lose their effectiveness. A few patients have to resort to the oxygen."

"How does oxygen help?" asked Jenny.

"Well, the arteries that supply the head and brain dilate or constrict to regulate the amount of blood, and therefore oxygen, the brain gets. Presumably, what happens is that when you start breathing pure oxygen, your blood oxygen shoots up and the arteries constrict in response. Once the throbbing, dilated vessels have shrunk, the source of the pain is gone."

We sat outside long after dark; the air was warm and fragrant; locusts called from the high grass in the alley. "We should have gone canoeing," Ferrier said.

"You're about thirty hours too late to realize that," Jenny admonished him.

"Yeah . . . I just . . . I don't know. I end up thinking I just ought to be around. Not that I can ever do too much, but whenever I've got a patient in the ICU I hate to think that if something happens they'll end up saying, 'Well, we tried to get hold of Ferrier, but of course he was out screwing around.' "

"But you're not on call. Who the hell would expect you to be around?" she asked. It was obvious that this was not the first time that Ferrier's work habits had been at issue between them.

"But there's always something I ought to be doing. That's the trouble with this profession. You never get things over with. Nothing is ever finished."

"That's ridiculous," I said. "I've been around a lot when you've told patients you don't need to see them anymore. You finish with them."

144

"Yeah, I know, but . . . there's always somebody with the same carpal tunnel syndrome or the same cluster headache out in the waiting room. I mean, it's all laid out for me. I'm always going to be adjusting Mrs. Pembroke's medications, or trying to manage Lisa's headaches in the midst of a shitty marriage, or confirming MS for the millionth time. All of it endless."

The straps had been removed from Marilyn's arms by the time we saw her on Monday morning. Her short hair was combed; she looked pale and tired, but her bright green eyes were wide open. She curled her purple-nailed fingers around the telephone receiver she held to her ear. "Just a minute," she said into the mouthpiece when Ferrier walked up to her bed.

"Who is it?" he asked.

"My husband."

"Tell him I'd like to talk to him when you're finished."

Marilyn nodded and said just a few more words before she handed him the receiver. Ferrier took the phone and stepped as far from the bed as the cord would let him.

"You look like you're feeling better," I said.

"I don't know what's worse—to be all doped up and in awful pain or to have the pain straight. Are you a doctor, too?"

"Yes," I said. It wasn't the first time it had seemed easier to lie than to give a more involved answer. I saw Marilyn wince and shut her eyes. "Are you okay?"

"Had a flash of something for a second," she said when she opened her eyes again. "When do I get out of here?"

"Are you sure you feel good enough to go anywhere?"

"Doctor, I haven't felt good for about five years, frankly."

"Maybe they'll be able to be of some help. I know they are going to do whatever they can."

"I won't hold my breath," she said. "What about you? You're not involved, I take it."

"I'm just watching him work."

"Watching me lie here is more like it. Do me a favor, will you? Tell him this isn't a joke. Tell him I hurt like hell and I need to take something for it."

"I'll tell him," I said as Ferrier brought the phone back to its cradle.

145

"Tell me what?" he asked.

"That I need to take something for this pain."

"I know you do," Ferrier said. "We're going to start you on a new regimen this morning. It's a powerful drug, and it's very safe, and I think it may help you a lot. It's quite strong, but you'll still have to put up with some pain while you're withdrawing from your other medications. Then, assuming you're doing even better tomorrow, we're going to take you back to the pain-control center where they'll decide whether they think their program can help you."

"What if they don't? Are you going to send me home? Don't send me home yet. Jesus, he hates it when I'm sick."

"We won't send you home till we get you well. Okay?"

"Good luck," Marilyn said.

Ferrier was writing in Marilyn's chart when her nurse stopped to look over his shoulder. "Let's put her on an aspirin and Tylenol schedule, 2QH," he said, turning to speak to her, "and don't tell her exactly what it is she's getting. I've just told her she's going to be getting some strong medicine. How's she eating?"

"Well, she's starting. She's better with fluids, but I think she's starting to get an appetite."

"Let's see how she is this afternoon. I'm pretty impressed with how she's getting through this."

"What's the etiology of the pain?" the nurse asked.

"We haven't tackled that one yet," he said as he closed the chart.

"That's kind of cruel to give her aspirin and Tylenol and to tell her they're going to help, isn't it?" I asked as we walked through the swinging doors that isolated the ICU, then down a quiet corridor.

"They make us take oaths saying we won't be cruel. They just don't trust us."

"But they won't do her any good."

"I hope they will. You don't give placebos to psychosomatics only. It's pretty well understood now that placebos can actually stimulate endorphins, and when they do, the placebo response actually blocks pain. They don't necessarily work by psychologically tricking you; they can also help your brain battle its own pain."

146

"How was the husband?" I asked, remembering the phone call.

"Seemed like a jerk to me. Didn't ask me a single question; just heard me out. I asked him if he'd been able to come up to see her yet and he said no, he's been working overtime. God, sometimes I wonder if there are any good relationships in this world."

Was it true? Did pain tend to plague the very people who already had to bear too many problems? Did poor relationships and an inferior sense of self tend to breed nagging pain and other elusive kinds of illness? There is no question that mental and physical health are intimately related, and "stress" is popularly made the culprit of everything from hypertension to headache, from irritable bowel syndrome to sinusitis. Yet stress, the great scourge of the late twentieth century, could surely be defined as nothing more than the evidence of being alive. It seemed to me that for every one of us, facing stress and reacting to it was as inevitable as sucking in air. And if we now knew that many chronic pains bore a relation to stress and a variety of psychological issues, would we decide years hence, armed with a better understanding of the brain and the body, that cardiac disease, diabetes, and cerebral stroke were also the products only of stressful lives? Surely we would not blame multiple sclerosis on a poor self-image, would we?

They were questions I could not answer. But I nonetheless had a vague and rather shallow hunch that there was, or ought to be, a middle ground in the debate about whether disease, by its very nature, was "psychosomatic"—the physiological expression of psychological concerns. Yes, many cases of labile hypertension, duodenal ulcer, allergy—and much of chronic pain—were certainly psychogenic. But on the other hand, if the psyche was capable of becoming disordered, if it could periodically get out of whack, surely we could expect the same of the complex *corpus* itself.

Perhaps the debate between what is physiological and what is psychological will one day be entirely moot. Perhaps then we will know enough about the brain to explain the thing—the web of neuronal processes—we now call the psyche. Perhaps one day we will explain our responses to bad marriages and bleak predicaments solely in terms of the physical—the physical brain, conscious and unconscious, and the physical body, both of them adapting, changing, decaying, struggling to stay alive.

When we got to Ferrier's office, the first patient was Richard Randolph, the man whose wife had insisted he switch to another neurologist. But the new neurologist was even more un-cooperative than his wife, Julie, felt Ferrier had been, and his office was an hour away from home.

Julie rolled Richard into Ferrier's office, then sat in a chair beside him. "Yes, we're back," she said. "Thought you were rid of us, didn't you?"

"I'm glad you're back," Ferrier said, "always glad to see you. Where's the fellow—I can't remember his name—who was look-ing after Richard?"

"Bill," Richard said with a broad smile.

"I fired him," Julie said. Her words were abrupt. "He turned out to be a lazy leech. And Richard wouldn't try to do the things he ought to do for himself when Bill was around. He'd just let Bill do them. It didn't work out."

"Oh . . . well," said Ferrier.

The reason for their visit today, Julie said, was that Richard was smoking entirely too much pot. He smoked six or seven joints a day, starting right after breakfast. Julie had a suspicion that it was the marijuana consumption that had made the tremors in Richard's arms much worse in recent months, making it even harder for him to feed himself or to brush his teeth. "Don't you think seven joints is a little carried away?"

Before Ferrier responded, Richard spoke up, still smiling. His words were slow and slurred and hard to understand. "My wife . . . Doctor . . . doesn't realize that I need to . . . smoke some pot to put . . . up with this life." Then his smile disappeared. "It's the only way I can stand it."

Each of us, I think even Julie, was stunned by what he said, and no one spoke for a time. When Ferrier finally said something he addressed himself to Richard. "I certainly won't pretend to tell you how to cope. It would be arrogant of me to act as if I know what's best as far as this sort of thing goes. You're the one who has to live in the chair, and I don't think you have to be some sort of Spartan about how you deal with things." He turned to Julie.

148

"I wonder if you and I wouldn't be doing exactly the same thing if it were us."

"I don't mind a little marijuana," she said, "but it's getting to the point that it keeps him from trying—at all." Her voice broke as she spoke.

"Is that true, Richard?"

He looked down at his lap, his wrists curled and lying on his thighs. "I . . . I do what needs to be done."

Ferrier asked Richard to hold out his arms. An erratic tremor was visible when he did so, and the tremor was much worse when he tried to touch his fingers to his nose. Richard chuckled as his fingers flailed about in front of his face.

Ferrier closed Richard's chart, then stared at its manila cover. "I don't know what to say. I think it's possible that the pot is having a worsening effect on the tremor. I'm not sure of it, but it's possible. I wonder what you would think, Richard, of trying a test—not smoking anything at all for a week to see if it changes anything." Richard did not respond. Julie nodded her head. "If you notice a real difference you might be glad to know it, to know what effect the marijuana has. Something else we could try would be for you to agree not to smoke before five in the afternoon, something like that. What do you think?"

Richard was not smiling. He turned his head to look at Julie. She returned an inquiring stare before he turned away.

"Richard?" she asked.

"It's really not the . . . business of either of you, is it?" he said. "But I will agree to . . . wait till the afternoon just to . . . make peace."

Ferrier said he could agree to the deal, but Julie only reluctantly accepted it. She had been convinced several months before that Ferrier was too easy on Richard, and today's consultation did not change her opinion. She and Richard agreed to return in a month and the three of them would then assess whether the reduced smoking had had a beneficial effect. For the first time since I had met them, I was able to empathize with Julie's anger. This Richard was not the man she had fallen in love with long ago. He was no longer her friend and husband; he was her ward. Of course she still cared for him, but it was *his* damn disease that had shattered their dreams. Richard's MS had plainly claimed two victims.

"Why do I feel like I'm the big bad guy every time I come in here?" Julie asked over her shoulder as she maneuvered Richard's chair through the open door.

There was a message on top of the next patient's chart—a message, marked urgent, to call Virginia, the counselor who was seeing Lisa Benedict. Ferrier set the chart and a heavy stack of EEGs on his desk, then dialed the number and turned on the phone's speaker so I could hear the conversation.

Virginia said Lisa and her two children had been waiting in a car outside her office when she arrived for work that morning. Last night, Lisa explained, her husband hit her—once in the face and a second time in the stomach, then he left the house. Lisa collected clothes for the kids and for herself and drove away; the three of them spent the rest of the night in a truck-stop cafe in a nearby town.

"She says she's determined not to go back," Virginia told Ferrier, "but she's scared. I put her in touch with a shelter down your way; she should be there by now. The husband doesn't know about me, but he does know you. Lisa asked me to call you and tell you. She thinks he might try to find her through you."

"Well, good. I appreciate the call, and maybe this will finally get this resolved. When you talk to Lisa again, tell her not to worry about her husband getting in touch with me. Tell her you know for a fact that I'm a mean son of a bitch. And ask her to call me, if you would. Did she mention what precipitated the fight?"

"She said she got a headache, a bad headache, and I guess he just blew up."

6 Impeded Pathways

It is a debate that will not become a *Newsweek* cover story, and the evening news will never address it, but there is an ongoing argument in the medical community these days about whether there are too many practicing neurologists, about whether too many more are now being trained, and about what kinds of diseases and disorders they should properly treat. It is a debate spawned by the recent explosion of research in the neurosciences—research that the clinicians take part in only peripherally but that has direct bearing on the types of treatment they can administer—and by the emergence of neurology as a small but visible, and increasingly attractive, medical specialty.

Until recently, neurology was strictly considered a *subspecialty* of internal medicine. Following medical school and a general internship, physicians entered a three-year neurology residency only after completing a residency of at least two years in internal medicine. Before they focused their training on the diseases of the nervous system, they had to become versed in the treatment of the circulatory, respiratory, digestive, and endocrine systems as well; they had to *specialize* in the function of all the body's internal organs, in other words, before they could *subspecialize* in the physiology of the brain. Throughout Britain and in much of the United States, prerequisite training in internal medicine is still the rule. But at many medical schools, independent departments of neurology have been created, and residents can now enter those departments with as little as a single year of internship in internal medicine. Proponents of the former curriculum believe that a firm grounding in general medicine is essential if future clinicians are to appreciate the interrelatedness of body function and to be adept at treating the common and important problems they will encounter. Advocates of the latter argue that there is so much to learn about brain anatomy and physiology, about the rare and difficult diseases of the nervous system, and about the revolution in diagnostic tests and procedures, that neurology must be studied as a specialty in its own right—parallel with surgery or pediatrics—and that the sooner its study begins, the better. For now, partisans of this view remain somewhat in the minority, but there is no question that as understanding of the brain and its dysfunctions burgeons, there will be increasing pressure for the discipline of neurology to assert its independence.

At present, there are about five thousand neurologists in practice in the United States, roughly eleven hundred of whom hold faculty positions at teaching hospitals. Those numbers, surprisingly, rank their discipline as a very small one, equivalent in size to nephrology, the study of the function and treatment of the kidneys. Yet several studies now claim that because of neurology's increasing appeal to medical students and because of the creation of a number of new neurology departments at medical schools around the country, there will be seventy-five hundred neurologists or more in practice by 1990, an increase of 150 percent since 1985. Will the number of new neurologists meet or exceed patient demands? Should their expertise be focused on rare disorders or on common neurological complaints? Again, there is argument.

The Office of Graduate Medical Education of the federal Department of Health and Human Services estimates that neurologists currently see far more patients who complain of chronic debilitating headache than any other disorder, followed in terms of incidence by cervical and lumbar back pain, herpes zoster (shingles), brain injury, and the effects of long-term alcoholism. Stroke, epilepsy, parkinsonism, dementia, multiple sclerosis, and nerve and muscle diseases are seen far less frequently—their *combined* incidence little more than one tenth the per capita incidence of serious headache. Could internists and general practitioners just as successfully treat neck and back pain, shingles, and many types of headache as do neurologists, freeing the latter to treat less frequent but potentially more serious conditions? Is long-term treatment by a neurologist necessary in the management of multiple sclerosis, Alzheimer's disease, paralysis following spinal cord injury, and other disorders that are now only marginally treatable? Most neurologists would agree that patients with both major and minor neurological disorders *could* be treated by physicians outside their specialty, but they would certainly argue that the quality of care the patients received would inevitably be reduced. And, of course, this question also concerns them: Could seventy-five hundred neurologists survive economically if they saw only patients with uncontrolled seizures, unusual types of strokes, subdural hematomas, tumors, and rare disorders like Tourette's syndrome?

In an era in which health-care costs consume 11 percent of the gross national product, the shape and substance of clinical medical practice surely bears scrutiny, both from within and from without. "Cost-effectiveness" is the catchphrase of the day, and the medical community struggles to find an acceptable balance between competent and complete treatment on the one hand and reasonable cost on the other. As the issue pertains to neurology, the cost-benefit balance is a precarious one. Is it cost-effective for a neurologist with a minimum of five years of resident training following medical school to devote one third of his or her practice to the management of migraine headache? The question is not a rhetorical one—migraine can be a catastrophic disorder and it plagues millions of people, but migraine is not life-threatening and its therapies are reasonably straightforward. Perhaps migraine and other common complaints should be treated principally—and more cost-effectively—by medical generalists instead of specialists and subspecialists. If so, then surely there should be fewer neurologists—who treat only major neurological illnesses. But on the other hand, perhaps a relatively large number of practicing neurologists should treat virtually all nervous-system complaints, including the basically benign pain syndromes, their numbers thereby resulting in constrained, competitive costs. This is the fundamental issue: Should neurologists serve solely as consultants to general physicians or should they also be the providers of "primary" care?

During my months with Ferrier I was surprised to discover that the disorders that paid his mortgage and kept his neckties current were not the mysterious and dramatic maladies, not the notorious

153

diseases of his discipline, but rather the kinds of disorders that virtually every one of us suffers at one time or another—pain and numbness caused by pinched or irritated nerves, the long and agonizing legacies of whiplash injuries, headache, of course, and sometimes simply fear—fear borne by a variety of strange and unaccounted sensations.

Propped on Ferrier's desk each morning was a schedule typed by one of the secretaries, listing the time of each of the day's appointments, the name of each patient, and, for every new patient, the name of the referring physician and some clue as to the problem. "HAs" meant headache; "SZs?" meant the question of epilepsy; an "MVA" was a motor vehicle accident; "numbness" and "neck pain" went unabbreviated. If Ferrier were to see ten patients on a hypothetical day, three of the ten would have chronic headache. At least two more would suffer "mononeuropathies"—damage to individual nerves such as the median nerve at the wrist or the ulnar nerve at the elbow, often the result of an injury; two would likely be seizure patients. Of the remaining three, one might be parkinsonian; the second might complain of unexplained numbness; the third would be recovering from stroke. During the course of a given week, Ferrier might see three patients with multiple sclerosis, four who had suffered traumatic injuries to their brains or spinal cords, one who was losing her memory.

Beginning in early summer of the year I was on hand, Ferrier and Putnam agreed to take part in a long-term study conducted by the university medical school of the kinds and percentages of cases that were treated by neurologists in their region. Ferrier guessed that when the data was finally compiled, his own mix of patients would closely resemble those of his regional colleagues, and that the regional norms would parallel the national statistics with one important exception: Ferrier and other Rocky Mountain neurologists unquestionably see far more multiple sclerosis than the national average because of their location in the disease's high-incidence zone. In contrast, Ferrier sees few cases of amyotrophic lateral sclerosis, ALS, sometimes referred to as Lou Gehrig's disease, a disease that exhibits no regional bias in the United States, and whose national rate of incidence of new cases per year is approximately the same as the national incidence of

MS. Ferrier treats so many multiple sclerosis patients that it was surprising for me to discover that it occurs nationally only as often as ALS. Stated another way, it was shocking to learn that ALS is so common.

Each of us harbors his own nightmares—secret, never-spoken fears of being disabled, of surrendering health and its fundamental freedom to the cruel snare of disease. The word *cancer* makes most breaths quicken; the sight of someone else in a wheelchair makes many of us anxious and strangely uncomfortable; sometimes the barest news of another person's illness can spawn our own sudden and similar symptoms. When I had begun to watch Ferrier work months before, as winter crawled into the piedmont and people prepared for its frigid stay, I had wondered how I would respond to a regular exposure to illness. I had heard stories that some medical students spend their first years convinced that they have every disease in the textbooks. It was certainly possible that I would suffer similar hypochondrias, but luckily, I did not. At first, to be sure, I was absolutely arrested by every patient and every sinister disease I observed. I paid rapt attention to each person's history, and I remembered each one vividly weeks later. I was fascinated by the microcosmic worlds of the hospitals—the people who suffered and the people who were paid to work, day in and day out, to try to relieve their suffering. It seemed to me that one could encounter the very essence of living and dying inside an intensive care unit.

Yet over the months, my attitudes and attentions changed, perhaps inevitably. As I met more and more patients, each one seemed less unique; the hundreds of patients' predicaments seemed less poignant, and, like Ferrier, I began to forget their names. By spring, the hospitals seemed only a little different from schools or even from supermarkets—all three of them simply places that were full of a broad and bustling mix of people, some administering services, others receiving them. There came a point during the long, languid days of summer when I could watch Ferrier examine the victim of an automobile accident to determine whether he was brain dead, then a few minutes later listen to him discuss with the family of a thirty-year-old victim of a brain-stem stroke whether she should be taken off her respirator, and I would no longer be stunned by those experiences for the rest of the day. Both tasks were common and required aspects of his job—they were literally all in a day's work—and once they were completed, there were always CAT scans to read, new patients to examine, and new diagnoses to deliver before the day was done. The drama, the frightening importance that I initially perceived in so much of Ferrier's work was somehow tempered by its familiarity.

At the end of June, however, eight months after I had become a medical spectator, I spent time talking with two of Ferrier's patients whose ordeals with disease captured my sympathy as completely as the illnesses of those earlier patients had done. Twenty-three-year-old Alan Dunn was a finance student who had undergone an eighteen-month battle with acute idiopathic polyneuritis—usually called Guillain-Barré syndrome—a disease that, when it was at its worst, had left him unable to move except to speak and to lift his head a few inches off his pillow. But by now, Alan was almost completely recovered, having gone from health to total paralysis to health again in a tumultuous year and a half. Peter Koppel was a seventy-two-year-old widower, the retired regional head of a federal housing program, who had been diagnosed with ALS more than a year before. He could no longer walk or feed himself, he had recently moved into a nursing home, and he would not recover. He would be dead in another year, perhaps in two.

In the cases of both men, I was impressed by their brave and buoyant responses to adversity, to having been done in bodily by their diseases but not in spirit. And the two diseases themselves were fascinating, disturbing, one of them truly demonic. Both men had countered their conditions with generous spirits, with humor, and with hope. It was Alan Dunn's hope, he said, his belief that he could indeed recover from Guillain-Barré, that kept him going during the months that he simply stared at the ceiling of his hospital room. Peter Koppel, a warm, dynamic man with many friends, simply hoped his ALS would kill him quickly.

In the weeks before Christmas in the year that his problems began, Alan Dunn noticed the muscles in his arms and shoulders seemed to be strangely weak. But he was in the midst of final exams and was consequently getting little sleep, and he wondered if the pressure and lack of sleep were the culprits. Influenza might be to blame—several friends had recently had bouts with it—but except for the weakness, Alan felt normal. Then, following a workout with weights at the university sports center a day or two after Christmas, his weak arms grew sore for the first time, the muscles tight and painful and lethargic. The next day, the soreness had spread to the muscles in his legs, and by New Year's day, he was having trouble walking. "I knew something serious was probably happening, but I just kind of blew it off at first," Alan told me, thinking back on his initial reaction to his disease. "I had a pretty good denial mechanism, I suppose. But then I was having a hard time climbing stairs, and I remember that I fell down the steps to my apartment on my way to see Dr. Ferrier for the first time. By then I knew I finally had to do something."

When Ferrier examined Alan on January 5, he found tremendous weakness in all the muscle groups of his upper and lower extremities. Alan's arm and leg reflexes were diminished—evidence that his disorder was focused in his peripheral nervous system; the reflexes would have been increased had the problem been in his brain or spinal cord. His sensory exam showed a slight loss of temperature sensation in both legs. It had been more than two weeks since Alan first noticed the weakness, and Ferrier was curious whether he believed the weakness had stabilized or if it was getting progressively worse. Alan was sure that he was noticeably weaker today than he had been before, and with that information, Ferrier phoned the admissions department at St. Luke's Hospital.

There were several conceivable causes of Alan's sudden and dramatic loss of strength, all but one of them unlikely. Diphtheria damages the peripheral nerves that stimulate muscles in the arms and legs, but its first victims are almost invariably the cranial nerves that supply the muscles of the head and face. Blurring of vision and difficulty with chewing and speaking are often its first neurological symptoms, and Alan had no such complaints; his cranial nerves were normal. And in recent weeks he had not suffered a sore throat or respiratory infection that might make diphtheria a suspect. Lead poisoning can produce a similar "polyneuritis"—damage to multiple peripheral nerves—but it rarely affects nerves that supply muscles in the legs, and Alan could not think of any instance in which he might have been exposed to lead. Polio was a remote possibility, but polio paralyzes muscles asymmetrically, and at onset, the polio virus produces fevers, headache, and irritability. In the case of acute porphyria, an inherited disease and an even more unlikely culprit, muscle weakness is usually accompanied by severe abdominal pains, hallucinations and psychosis, and the excretion of dark red urine. Alan, almost certainly, did not have porphyria.

What he did have, Ferrier presumed, was Guillain-Barré syndrome, a polyneuritis characterized by its sudden and sometimes dramatic onset and by a rapidly progressive weakness of the limbs that can result in total paralysis. In the most serious cases, nerves that supply the muscles in the head and trunk are also affected and death from respiratory failure can occur unless the patient is artificially ventilated. Ferrier explained to Alan that since it was probable his weakness had not yet stabilized, it would be safest if he were hospitalized, where he quickly could be placed on a respirator if one were required. It probably wouldn't come to that, Ferrier assured him, but it could be suicidal to ignore that possibility.

"A rush really went through my head when he told me that," Alan recalled. His voice was soft; he spoke slowly and without emotion, as though Ferrier's frightening words had been spoken to someone else. "I was worried when I went in that it was muscular dystrophy or one of those diseases I'd vaguely heard of—and it wasn't that—but then here he was saying that there was a remote chance that I'd be dead in a few days. It was really a shock, but at least he wasn't saying I'd never walk again. Right from the start I knew there was a chance that I could recover completely, so at least I had something to keep me going. I called my parents from his office and tried to explain things to them as calmly as I could—they were pretty freaked out, of course. Then a friend drove me up to St. Luke's. I didn't leave for four months."

Guillain-Barré syndrome, first described by a team of French physicians in 1916, is an autoimmune disease of the peripheral nervous system, which comprises the forty-three pairs of nerves projecting from the brain and the spinal cord that "innervate" the body's muscles. Similar to multiple sclerosis, a disease that affects only the central nervous system—the brain and spinal cord— Guillain-Barré destroys the myelin sheath that surrounds and protects the axons of nerves in the peripheral system, ultimately interrupting and blocking the transmission of impulses to distant parts of the body. MS and Guillain-Barré are alike in that in both diseases, some strange immunological malfunction causes myelin to be attacked as though it were a foreign antigen. Yet the two diseases are very different. MS affects only the myelin that is produced and contained in cells called oligodendrocytes, which are present solely in the *central* nervous system. The myelin in the *peripheral* nervous system is made by Schwann cells, and it is only this peripheral myelin that is vulnerable to attacks by Guillain-Barré. Unlike the common relapsing-remitting course of multiple sclerosis—the disease progressing over the course of many years—Guillain-Barré normally reaches its peak of severity in just two or three weeks—some cases resulting in no more than mildly weak hands or feet before improvement begins, others, like Alan's, resulting in a period of total paralysis. Unlike MS, Guillain-Barré shows no geographic or ethnic predilections, and it affects men and women in equal numbers. Unlike those who suffer MS, most Guillain-Barré patients return to normal or near-normal health.

The two diseases do share this in common: The cause of neither is known, but viruses may trigger the autoimmune processes of both. Neuroscientists have as yet been unable to isolate a specific Guillain-Barré virus or bacterial agent, and it is unlikely that they will ever be able to do so. Yet about half of all Guillain-Barré patients report that they did suffer mild, flulike respiratory or gastrointestinal infections in the weeks before their neurological symptoms appeared. And intriguingly, in an outbreak of Guillain-Barré syndrome in 1976, many of the cases reported were people who had recently been vaccinated against the swine influenza virus. But although the disease may, in fact, be triggered by an infectious agent, there is no evidence that it is contagious. No one "catches" this sudden syndrome of peripheral nerve demyelination, but it does seem likely that a virus or viruses that do no more to most of us than to keep us away from work for a day or two, do, in a few cases, spawn this dangerous, and potentially grave, immunological derangement.

On Alan's admission to St. Luke's Hospital, Ferrier ordered pulmonary function tests to determine whether the nerves supplying his respiratory musculature had already been compromised, but Alan's respiration was normal. Ferrier ordered blood screens for hepatitis and mononucleosis to see if either of those diseases was responsible for triggering Alan's weakness, and a urine test to check for the presence of lead, porphyrins, or other toxins. All were normal. Nerve conduction velocity tests, however, were markedly abnormal. The transmission of impulses in the major nerves of Alan's arms and legs was very slow, indicating that he indeed was suffering a neuropathy—a disorder affecting the nerves—rather than a myopathy—a malfunction of the muscles themselves. Further, protein levels in his cerebrospinal fluid, drawn by a spinal tap, were elevated, providing additional evidence that the demyelinating process of Guillain-Barré was underway.

By the end of his first week in isolation in a private room on a busy medical ward, Alan could no longer walk and could barely raise his arms against gravity. At the end of two weeks, he could not sit upright, and even though he would try valiantly to do so each time Ferrier made his rounds, he could not wiggle his toes. After a month in the hospital, eight weeks after he had first felt weak, Alan's legs were motionless, and his arms and trunk were motionless as well. His facial muscles remained virtually intact; he could open and close his eyes, chew, and speak; with effort, he could lift his head off his pillow.

"Most people with Guillain-Barré get to their worst point about three weeks after it starts," Alan told me, "but I was unusual. I never did need a ventilator, but I just kept getting worse and worse to the point where I couldn't move. I remember that at the worst point I couldn't figure out any way to get to the knob for the television, and it was just a few inches away. You feel pretty helpless when you have to ask someone to turn on the TV for you. You can't do anything—except watch yourself waste away."

When I asked Alan if there was ever a point when he felt like giving up, as though the possibility of recovery was just too remote, he hesitated. "I always tried to think positively," he said. "That was the one thing I had some control over. But there was one Saturday during the time when I couldn't move when Dr.

Ferrier was off and Dr. Putnam was on call. I asked Dr. Putnam what he felt about everything and he was real open and told me that I was a bit of a mystery. He said I definitely wasn't a typical Guillain-Barré patient and that there was a chance that I had a type of the disease—it's called chronic relapsing polyneuropathy—where you don't recover. They didn't really think that was it, but I just didn't perfectly fit either pattern. Well, I had all weekend to think that over and to be terrified that maybe I wouldn't get better. And I was really pretty mad at Dr. Ferrier; I thought he had been keeping this from me. When he came in on Monday morning, he could tell I was really bothered about something, and I told him I wanted to know exactly what was going on. He sat on the edge of the bed and said that there was a possibility that it was the chronic relapsing type, but that there was no way to know, at least for now. Somehow, he made me feel that he actually did expect me to recover. I calmed down, but I still remember that as being the worst time. I mean, I was physically handicapped, but mentally and emotionally I was fine, and I didn't want to be protected or to have decisions made for me. That would have made things even worse. It was always important for me to be able to do whatever I could. I learned how to use my neck to reach for food instead of having to be fed. My occupational therapist rigged up this thing for me so I could turn the pages of a book with my teeth, but I could never make it work very well, so for a month or so I just quit reading and listened to language tapes. I thought it would be a good time to learn Spanish."

Early in Alan's hospitalization, Ferrier had begun him on a trial of prednisone, an immunosuppressant steroid often prescribed for autoimmune disorders, one that has shown limited success in halting the progression of Guillain-Barré. At first, it was difficult to determine whether Alan successfully responded to the drug; it may have prevented the demyelination of the autonomic nerves supplying his heart, but perhaps those nerves would have been spared in any case. However, when Ferrier tried to decrease the steroids on two occasions, Alan's condition worsened and both he and Ferrier became convinced that the steroids were helping. With or without prednisone's help, Alan did improve. During the long months of his advancing paralysis, physical therapists had regularly exercised Alan's arms and legs to try to avoid atrophy of his muscles and contracture of his joints and tendons. Early in his hospitalization, Alan still had enough muscle control that he could assist them with the passive movement of his limbs; then, for a long and frustrating stretch of time, he could only watch while his therapists performed his daily calisthenics for him.

But one morning at the end of March, Alan's immobile hands seemed to come very tentatively to life. If he concentrated, he could almost make a fist. With Ferrier and his therapists cheering him on from his bedside, Alan at last could wiggle his toes again. The gains were subtle; they were as slow as his slide into paralysis had been, but they were verifiable victories—proof, to Alan at least, that he would be animate again. "A couple of weeks after the first wiggles, I could move my arms a little, and my legs a little, and I got to start doing extensive PT. After so long when time just hardly seemed to pass at all, I finally had things to do, to fill up the day, and I actually remember it as an exciting time. It was almost like I was a professional athlete. I had PT twice a day, OT twice a day; they would lower me into the pool late in the morning and I'd do pool work with a therapist, then after lunch I could go back to the pool if I wanted to. Sometime in April, I got to where I could roll myself in a wheelchair and I would cruise all over the hospital in the evenings—I got to know every nook and cranny of that place. Everything was a discovery, a challenge. When I got enough movement back in my arms that I could reach out and press an elevator button, it was such a triumph."

Using crutches to support himself, Alan walked out of St. Luke's Hospital at the end of the second week in May and moved to his parents' home in the city. He had difficulty negotiating stairs, his muscles remained rather weak, and he continued to receive intensive physical therapy. A month after he was discharged from the hospital, he suffered a relapse, severe enough that he could no longer walk with the assistance of crutches. Ferrier again tried a high dosage of prednisone, but its effects seemed to be minimal; Alan did not bounce back, and his fears that the disease was taking a chronic relapsing-remitting course returned.

Discouraged by his setback, but by no means ready to resign himself to it, Alan decided to try to assert some personal control over his recovery. During his long months of inactivity, he had read much about Guillain-Barré and related disorders and about how patients with a variety of autoimmune diseases had shown dramatic improvement with biofeedback, meditation, and similar relaxation therapies. In July, Alan began a daily relaxation program, doing a series of anxiety relieving exercises after each meal and before he went to bed. "I didn't have a miraculous cure or anything, but right away I felt there was definite improvement. A month or two later, my parents and Dr. Ferrier and everyone else agreed that I was making real progress again."

On November 6, Alan was able to walk the few blocks from his parents' house to a neighborhood school to vote—the first time in eleven months that he had walked without assistance. In January, a year after Guillain-Barré had begun to affect the pathways of his peripheral nerves, Alan returned to the university to finish school. After graduation in June, he hoped his finance degree would help him find a job in the health-economics field. He had not been particularly interested in medicine or health-care issues a year before, but his illness had altered both his perspectives and his plans. "I'll see how things go," he told me when we talked a week after he had walked with ease up the steps of a stage to receive his diploma. "I would just need about another semester to meet the premed requirements. If I don't find something I really like, maybe I'll end up going to medical school."

By June, Ferrier had begun to see Alan only every three months. The two occasionally spoke on the phone to discuss adjustments in his medication, and at the June checkup, which I observed, they agreed that he would continue a very low dosage of prednisone, taken every other day, for about a year. When there was nothing more for Alan and Ferrier to discuss that day, Alan and I moved to the conference room to talk. He spoke about how lucky he had been—lucky that it had not been a fatal disease, lucky that his peripheral nerves at last did regenerate, lucky that the disease struck him when it did. "I was covered by my parents' medical policy. But if the Guillain-Barré had begun six or seven months later, when I had graduated, I would have been excluded from their policy and, you know, there would have been a real good chance that I wouldn't have had one of my own." I asked if he knew what his illness had cost.

"I think it's around three hundred thousand dollars. I'm probably a good case to use in this whole health-care cost debate. Maybe if they had just closed me up in my parents' basement for a year I would have had exactly the same recovery. But then, maybe it was the monitoring and the treatment and the therapy that got me through it. Maybe otherwise I would have been one of the Guillain-Barré patients whose lungs stop. From my perspective, it was worth what it cost."

At the end of our conversation I tried to get Alan to confess that his illness had been a nightmare, a horror, a mean and capricious kind of calamity. He crossed his long legs, sat back and listened to my coaxing, brushing back the blond hair that fell about his thin and ruddy face. I couldn't imagine, I said, watching my body break down piece by piece. Then later, lying motionless, just a warm and speaking corpse, I told him, I could not imagine enduring the glacially slow passage of time, the clock on the wall a mocking reminder of my predicament. But Alan wanted nothing to do with my melodrama, and he brushed my suggestions aside.

"It changed me; there's no question about that," he said, countering with the same quiet control that had long been his best ally. "I learned a lot about myself in the process—and I'll never take my health for granted again, that's for sure. But it wasn't the worst thing that could have happened. Everyone has things they have to deal with."

At the end of the afternoon, Ferrier and I drove to the nursing home where Peter Koppel lived. Dark thunderheads, so big they seemed to diminish the mountains, rumbled and groaned in advance of their rain. The air below them was hot and moist, and we drove with the Saab's windows open, the wind whipping Ferrier's hair into his eyes. "Alan's an interesting guy," he said. "When we talked about the possibility of Guillain-Barré when I first saw him, he seemed to take it all in stride. I wanted to repeat myself; I wasn't sure that he'd understood what I'd said. And during the months in the hospital, he really hung in there, always optimistic, learning quite a lot about Guillain-Barré, about the peripheral nerves and the basic musculature. His patience and his conviction were probably what turned the corner for him."

"He said there is still some question about whether his case was straightforward Guillain-Barré or the relapsing-remitting type."

"That was an unknown for quite a long time, and I'm sure he told you that we were all scared there for a while. But I'm pretty convinced now that his was an unusual Guillain-Barré, one that had a strange, slow course—more than a year instead of six weeks or so. He hasn't had any sort of relapse in almost a year, which makes me more comfortable, but the reason he's going to stay on the low dose of prednisone for another year is basically for safety's sake."

"When you first see someone like Alan, how do you distinguish between whether the problem is actually in the nerves or the muscles?"

"There's a nerve-muscle system that is referred to as the motor unit, comprised of one neuron, which is the nerve cell that lives in the spinal cord, its axon, or peripheral nerve fiber, that delivers the nerve cell's impulse, and the muscle fibers that contract when they are stimulated by that impulse. It's a pretty simple system, really. Every muscle fiber in the body is innervated by only one neuron, but each motor neuron normally supplies numerous muscle fibers. With motor units that control fine movements—the extraocular muscles of the eye, for instance—the neuron innervates only something like three or five muscle fibers. But with gross movements—say, a motor unit of a large leg muscle—one neuron may control two thousand muscle fibers. And in healthy people, it's incredibly reliable. Virtually every large discharge, or so-called action potential in a given motor neuron, leads to the contraction of *every* muscle fiber it supplies—whether three or three thousand.

"With sick people, people who have some sort of motor unit disorder, you get two basic symptoms—weakness and wasting of muscles—because muscle action and muscle bulk are the tangible results of the functions of the motor unit. But the problem can lie with the motor neuron itself, as it does with ALS, with the peripheral nerve fibers, as in Guillain-Barré and all the other peripheral neuropathies, or in the muscles themselves—disorders called myopathies, including the various muscular dystrophies, which are inherited muscle diseases. And there is also a fourth category—the disorders like myasthenia gravis that affect the neuromuscular junction, which is the synaptic cleft between nerve

165

endings and muscle, where a neurotransmitter is discharged by a nerve impulse so it can bind on receptors on the muscle, causing the muscle to contract. With myasthenia gravis, the receptors on the muscle are destroyed by an autoimmune process. Both the nerve and the muscle itself are unaffected, but since the neurotransmitter can't bind successfully, the transmission is blocked and the muscle isn't stimulated."

"So how do you narrow it down?"

"In the clinical exam, one of the first things you look for is distal versus proximal weakness. For reasons that no one knows yet, the neurogenic disorders—problems with the nerve cells and nerve fibers—tend to cause distal weakness, meaning weakness at the ends of the limbs. The muscle disorders tend to cause proximal weakness—weakness of the limbs near the trunk. But there are plenty of exceptions and you certainly can't depend on those distinctions. One thing that is very helpful is that you sometimes see what are called fasciculations—spontaneous twitches of muscles at rest. Muscles that are actually diseased don't tend to fasciculate; muscles that are normal but that are denervated because of a nerve disorder, do. And again, nobody knows why, but fasciculations are far more common with nerve cell diseases like ALS than with diseases of the nerve fibers. We look for loss of reflexes, which are common with nerve diseases, and for sensory loss—and in most cases, electrical studies really complete the picture. Are the nerve conduction velocities slowed, as they are with Guillain-Barré and the peripheral neuropathies? Are the durations of each muscle potential increased, as they are with chronic nerve disorders, or decreased, as happens with muscle diseases?"

In the months that I had sat in the black chair at the flank of Ferrier's desk, I had never met a patient with muscular dystrophy—or any muscle disease that I could remember—and I had never seen him examine a patient for whom muscle disease was the principle suspect. Was that just a coincidence, or were muscle diseases even within a neurologist's purview? I asked him if muscular dystrophies were rare.

"I read one estimate of about ten thousand current cases in the United States, which, if correct, certainly wouldn't make them the most common disease around. Neurologists do treat muscle diseases, but the reason I don't see many cases is that one of the major Jerry Lewis dystrophy centers is down in the city. When a GP or a pediatrician here in town sees a boy with weak and wasted muscles, especially in the shoulder and pelvic areas, a characteristic waddling kind of gait, and, of course, a family history, there is usually no need to send the boy to me or Putnam. The possibility of Duchenne dystrophy is so strong that the patients go directly to the Jerry Lewis center, where the muscle specialists are, and where what they can offer is really tremendous. I mean, whatever else you can say about Jerry Lewis, he has supplied that particular group of disease specialists with a tremendous amount of money, so much that, in some cases, they're willing to help people who don't have strictly defined dystrophies. They often offer a lot of assistance to ALS patients."

Big raindrops began to splatter the windshield; lightning cracked, and the interior of the black cloud above us glowed like a light bulb for an instant. I pushed the console button that closed the sunroof.

"I'm not sure why the telethon approach leaves me with such a bad taste in my mouth," I said. "Maybe it's just the notion of cheerleading for little kids with tragic diseases—getting at the purse strings by tugging at the heart strings. I don't know."

"It raises money. And that's the bottom line with the health industry—both basic care and research. They take enormous amounts of money. You can tax everyone to come up with the money or you can try to get it through charitable donations. There aren't many other options."

"You can let the insurance companies collect it via outrageous premiums. I suppose it's pretty stupid not to carry some decent health insurance, but if you do stay healthy, you end up making a mighty substantial donation to somebody else's health care."

"That's why some sort of basic national health insurance would make so much sense. If everybody was insured—by a giant consortium of the existing insurance companies or whoever—the costs to each of us would have to be reduced. One of the reasons medical care is so expensive now is that we claim to be capitalistic about it all—you get just the medical care you pay for. But we're really too compassionate for that. Nobody is simply turned away because he doesn't have the cash. The hospitals, doctors, everyone ends up getting back the money they spend on indigent care or uncollectible accounts from the people who do pay. A national health plan would simply make the system a lot more fair because it would involve everyone."

"Don't let the AMA hear you touting socialized medicine."

"Only the insurance. I've worked under three different systems so far—the National Health in Britain, which is far better than it's usually made out to be, by the way, the Canadian system, and here. The one that I think works the best is the Canadian, where the insurance is provided by private companies who are overseen by the government. The government regulates the premiums they can charge and the fees the doctors and hospitals can charge, and the overall costs are kept in check. Doctors don't raise their fees like crazy to pay for millions in malpractice coverage because patients, who get long-term coverage for a very reasonable cost, aren't so likely to sue."

"But in this country, they simply charge the bejesus out of everyone."

"In United States hospitals, standardized payment is actually underway. You've heard of DRGs? Diagnostic Related Groups? Medicare now pays hospitals a fixed rate for a given patient's stay, depending on the diagnosis. Medicare pays so much for a broken hip, X dollars for an appendectomy. If the hospital actually spends more than the given rate, they have to make up the difference; if they spend less, it's profit. DRGs seem to me to be the wrong thing for the right reason. Rather than base the standardization on diagnosis, where there are so many variables, it ought to be based on procedures—so much for an angiogram, et cetera—and on length of stay. From my perspective, I certainly don't think that hospitals and doctors keep people in longer than they need to be just to make more money or, for that matter, kick them out before they're well just because Medicare has cut them off, but that's the accusation, of course. One thing about the current DRG payment system, which Medicare calls 'prospective pricing'—you can bet your ass that the insurance companies are waiting until the right moment to follow suit."

"What are your insurance rates like?"

"I pay a stupid amount, just like everybody else."

"No, I mean malpractice premiums."

"Oh, Jesus, they're something like twenty-five hundred dollars a year. But guys like Holly and Burns and other neurosurgeons probably have to pay four or five times that much, maybe fifteen thousand dollars a year. In some parts of the country, neurosurgeons pay well over fifty thousand dollars, all of it ultimately paid by the patients, or the patients' insurance companies—which means by the rest of us. With clinicians like me, there is the *possibility* of being sued; for surgeons, it's a certainty at some point or other."

"What kinds of things could you get sued for?"

"Anything I do, basically, but I suppose missed diagnoses would be the main things. Like if you ever diagnosed someone with migraine and five weeks later they died of a glioblastoma, some families might get a little upset. Nobody can take a joke anymore."

I laughed.

"Seriously. That's the kind of thing that gives you nightmares. Missing a diagnosis scares me more than making a poor treatment decision or even losing a patient. We're not supposed to be able to fix everybody, but we are supposed to know what's wrong."

Physicians like Ferrier are pulled in two opposing directions, it seemed to me. On the one hand, and for very valid reasons, they are encouraged by both hospitals and patients to limit costs, to forgo elective procedures and unnecessary tests, to shorten inpatient lengths of stay. Yet, on the other hand, to avoid the threat of malpractice suits they are pressured to do everything possible for their patients, to order each expensive diagnostic test, to exhaust every therapeutic possibility, to keep their patients hospitalized until they are entirely well. The companies that insure patients urge adequate care that is as inexpensive as possible. And the companies that insure doctors recommend exhaustive and inevitably expensive treatment. Also caught in this confusing middle ground, hospitals must offer responsible care to avoid litigious entanglements with their patients, but they must attempt to do so at a reasonable cost if they stand a chance of staying in business.

The economic crisis in American health care is one that will not be abated with simple solutions, and its proportions are increasingly alarming. In the early 1970s, premiums paid to private health care insurers in this country totaled about $22 billion annually. Little more than a decade later, yearly health insurance premiums had reached $85 billion and seemed certain to continue to rise. Although fees charged by physicians for clinical care rose substantially during that period, it was the price of hospital care that climbed most dramatically, in part due to inflation, but largely because of the costs of employee wages and benefits and the costs of improved medical technology. In order to provide adequate care at an average hospital, four people must be on duty, round the clock, for each occupied bed. A CAT scanner, now a fundamental diagnostic tool in all but the smallest hospitals, costs about $1 million to purchase and an additional $1.8 million to operate for a period of ten years. Should hospitals try to reduce costs by cutting their staff-patient ratios to three or even two to one? If they did so, wouldn't some patients inevitably have to be neglected, placing their health and even their lives at greater risk? Should hospitals decline to purchase CAT scanners and the new magnetic resonance imagers even though they can often eliminate the need for additional—and costly—diagnostic procedures or exploratory surgery? Should they buy the machines, at whatever price, and simply pass on their costs to patients and their insurers?

Unlike the compromises we make when we buy cars or clothes or tropical cruises, few people are willing to sacrifice quality to save money when it comes to buying health care. When we are well, we grouse, with reason, about the ever-increasing cost of insurance and medical care. When we—or friends or loved ones—are seriously ill, cost becomes no object and everything possible simply must be done. Later, healthy again, we are astonished at what it cost to get there. How should physicians and hospitals properly respond to these dual demands of their patients? As a society, how can we strike a balance between responsible care and restrained cost?

In Dr. Ferrier's case, should he concern himself solely with a patient's condition and with the means at his disposal to treat him, or should he temper the scope of the patient's treatment with coincident efforts to save the patient some money? Ferrier obviously believes that physicians can and should be trusted not to be spendthrifts with patients' and insurance companies' dollars;

he opposes Medicare's prospective pricing because he knows that each patient's illness and progress is individual. Yet surely the lack of economic restraint on physicians and hospitals prior to the era of prospective pricing played a role in the rocketing of health-care costs.

Ferrier and his colleagues are not employees of the two hospitals where they have staff privileges. They bill their patients (or their insurance companies) directly for the services they provide. But the physicians and the hospitals in Ferrier's community, and in cities and towns throughout the country, do offer each other substantial financial support. Without doctors' admissions, the hospitals would have no paying customers. And without the availability of hospital services, the doctors' means of providing service—and being paid for it—would be drastically reduced. The challenge for both individual physicians and large medical institutions, working in concert, is to provide medical care that is cost-contained *and* comprehensive.

It is a challenge that has not been met in recent years and probably will not be fully met in the future, and it is a failure that, ironically, is caused in part by one of medicine's proud successes. The average life expectancy for both men and women has increased by four years over the last decade, the same span of time in which health-care costs have risen so markedly. People over age seventy-five comprise the fastest-growing age group of the population, and they are the segment of our society that requires the largest single share of total health services. The quality of medical care has played a direct role in allowing us to live longer lives. Yet by living longer, we have added significantly to the strain on our collective ability to pay for the services that keep us alive. We have discovered that few things are inexpensive, least of all, perhaps, the purchase of longer and healthier life.

The nursing home, a low, elongated building that looked like it was recently built, was sided with red cedar and surrounded by a sloping green lawn. Pansies grew in the stone planter that encircled a flagpole, and daisies grew in the beds by the main door. Inside, a wide, waxed linoleum corridor reached away toward an administrative area that looked like a cross between a nurses' station and a hotel's registration desk. A carpeted lounge, filled with sofas, overstuffed chairs, card tables, two television sets, and a spinet piano, flanked the corridor on the right. Except for a thin man in a sweater, asleep in a chair with his mouth wide open, the lounge was filled with women, perhaps a dozen of them, two of them watching a game show on television, the rest simply sitting, their hands in their laps, staring, saying nothing. An empty dining room and a series of smaller public rooms, their windowed doors all closed, were on the left. Three women in dresses sat in straight-backed chairs against a wall lined with photographs of mountains, and they watched us walk toward them.

"Didn't you bring Carl?" one of the women asked us as we passed, her voice fading in disappointment.

"No, I'm afraid he didn't come with us," Ferrier said. We stopped. "Are you expecting him?"

"We'll be late," she said. "Bernice will give up on us and cut the cake without us. They've already thrown the rice."

"She thinks she's supposed to go to her daughter's wedding," said the woman who sat beside her. "We'll explain to her. Sorry."

We smiled and walked away. At the desk, Ferrier explained who he was and that we had come to see Mr. Koppel.

"Yes, Doctor. Yes. We're expecting you," said a plump and friendly woman in a sage green uniform, her brown hair wrapped in a bun. "We thought you might like to see him in our little library. We can close it off for you. He said he would rather do that than to have you go to his room."

"Fine," Ferrier said.

The woman handed him Mr. Koppel's chart and showed us the library—one of the small rooms we had passed—and said she would be back in a moment with Mr. Koppel. The bookcases contained only a few hardcover books; two long shelves of paperbacks were neatly stacked, and several shelves were empty. Magazines were laid out for inspection on a mobile cart and the day's papers were spread on a round table. Ferrier sat down, opened Mr. Koppel's chart, then asked me to look at something. I moved behind him and read the first page:

To My Family, My Physician, My Clergyman, My Lawyer:

If the time comes when I can no longer take part in decisions for my own future, let this statement stand as the testament of my wishes. If there is no reasonable expectation of my recovery

172

from physical or mental or spiritual disability, I, Peter Garrison Koppel, request that I be allowed to die and not be kept alive by artificial means or heroic measures. Death is as much a reality as birth, growth, maturity, and old age—it is the one certainty. I do not fear death as much as I fear the indignity of deterioration, dependence, and hopeless pain. I ask that drugs be mercifully administered to me for terminal suffering even if they hasten the moment of death.

This request is made while I am in good health and spirits. Although this document is not legally binding, you who care for me will, I hope, feel morally bound to follow its mandates. I recognize it places a heavy burden of responsibility upon you, and it is with the intention of sharing that responsibility and of mitigating any feelings of guilt that this statement is made.

It was dated and signed by Mr. Koppel and by three friends who had witnessed his signature.

"That's probably a good idea, isn't it?" I asked.

"Yeah. He's right. I don't think it means much legally, but we probably all ought to make a statement like that. You'd be amazed at the family members, the ministers, the doctors even, on occasion, who believe that you've got to keep the patient alive—keep their heart pumping at least—no matter what the cost of the situation. Even if the patient is brain dead, it doesn't matter, because they think there is always the chance for a miracle." He stood up and walked to the window. "I'm not sure I've seen one of those kinds of miracles, but maybe my attitude's bad. I have seen some very moving deaths, good deaths, I mean, that seemed fitting, beautiful." The rain ran in sheets down the window. "In Mr. Koppel's case, well, he's basically ready to go; he wants to go. With ALS, his cognitive processes are in perfect health. He's as sharp and delightful as he ever was; he perceives everything very acutely. And what he has to perceive is that his body—which for seventy-some years was brought to life by the motor unit that we were talking about—now has no life. The integrity of his muscles is fine, but because the motor neurons are destroyed, there aren't any impulses to travel the pathways. Finally, his breathing will fail, and when that happens, he'll be able to die. Part of my job these days is to try to tell him not to be impatient."

The network of neurons that fill up the skull and the thin, vulnerable tube of neural tissue that courses through a series of holes in the spinal vertebrae are the parts of the nervous system that most readily capture our attention. The brain and spinal cord comprise the *central* nervous system, the control center for the rest of the body, one that both voluntarily and automatically monitors the body, maintains it, adjusts it, protects it. The brain and spinal cord play a role in virtually every physiological activity—from swallowing to sweating, from listening to the music of Charles Mingus to making love. Yet without the many millions of minute fibers of the peripheral nervous system, fibers that supply every organ, every muscle, every scaly patch of skin, there could be no communication between brain and body. The brain would languish like an unprogrammed computer, and the body would be functionless—some marvelous machine that could never be powered up.

The spinal cord descends about eighteen inches through the bony vertebral column that surrounds it—from the big hole at the base of the skull, where the cord joins the brain stem, to the first lumbar vertebra in the lower back. In addition to its encasement in bone, the spinal cord is protected by three layers of meninges—similar to the membranes that surround the brain—as well as by cerebrospinal fluid that cushions the cord and protects it from shock. The oval cord, never more than an inch wide, has a white outer layer of myelinated nerve fibers, some of which carry sensory signals up the cord to the brain, others which transmit motor signals from the brain down the cord and out to the body. Within the white matter is a gray column of nerve cells that, in section, resembles a butterfly—the "anterior" (front) portion of its two wings controlling muscle movement, the "posterior" (back) portions receiving peripheral sensory signals.

At intervals along the cord, nerve roots sprout from the four wing tips of the butterfly, the two on each side joining to become part-sensory, part-motor spinal nerves that exit from gaps between each pair of vertebrae. Because the spine grows longer than the spinal cord, some of the thirty-one pairs of spinal nerves sprout out of sync with their exit holes and must grow down from the spinal cord in a fan of roots called the *cauda equina*, the horse's tail, before they can escape.

It is the thirty-one pairs of spinal roots, plus the twelve pairs of cranial nerves that connect directly with the brain, that comprise the peripheral nervous system. Although the optic nerve is technically an extension of the brain itself, it is commonly considered a nerve and it is one of three cranial nerves—together with the olfactory nerve and the acoustic nerve—that have no motor function, the three only receiving information. The accessory nerve and the hypoglossal nerve, which control movement of the neck and the tongue respectively, have no sensory role, solely sending motor impulses to muscles in the neck and tongue. The remaining seven cranial nerves, which control eye movement, chewing, facial skin, and taste sensations, and the automatic regulation of the body's internal organs, have both sensory and motor functions.

There are four main groups of spinal nerves: the eight pairs of cervical nerves that exit from vertebrae in the neck supply the diaphragm, chest, arms, and hands; the twelve pairs of thoracic nerves below them supply the trunk; five pairs of lumbar nerves in the lower spine supply the front of the legs and feet with sensation; and five pairs of sacral nerves supply the soles of the feet and the backs of the legs. The lumbar and sacral nerves also move the legs and feet and control bowel and bladder function. All of the spinal nerves receive information and transmit it as well.

Anatomists group these forty-three peripheral nerves into two groups—the "somatic," voluntarily controlled system, and the "autonomic" system, which cannot be controlled at will. The somatic system is comprised of those motor and sensory nerves that make voluntary movement possible. Sensory nerves bombard the brain with information from skin sensors and from ears, joints, and muscles, outlining their own condition and defining the environment they encounter. In turn, both consciously and subconsciously, the brain acts on the information, controlling balance and initiating gross and subtle movements by transmitting motor impulses.

Under the control of the autonomic system are those processes that do not appear to be under the brain's conscious control—the operation of the internal organs and glands and the function of the body's complex coping mechanisms—processes that are kept in a kind of tenuous balance by two opposing subsystems. The "sympathetic" subsystem speeds up internal activity, increasing heart rate, dilating pupils, stimulating glandular secretions, and transferring blood supply from the intestines to the brain and muscles. The "parasympathetic" subsystem does just the opposite, acting to thwart increased activity, and maintaining steady, clockwork functions. The autonomic system, which is principally controlled by the brain's hypothalamus, alternately speeds us up and slows us down in a constant series of subconscious adjustments, increasing adrenal activity, stimulating us to fight or flee to avoid immediate danger, or calming us, steadying us, quelling anxiety. Even digesting food and emptying the bladder involve a "debate" between the sympathetic and parasympathetic systems.

The successful function of both the somatic and autonomic systems depends on an incredible array of nerve pathways— some, like those that allow the reflexive pulling away of a hand from a hot stove, involve only the sending of a sudden sensory impulse in a small group of fibers from temperature receptors in a finger to the nerve's root in the spinal cord. There, stimulated by the sensory impulse, a motor neuron in the gray-matter interior of the cord transmits a motor impulse that leads to the almost immediate contraction of the muscles that lift the hand away.

But if the object that is touched is a harmless kitten, for instance, the sensory and motor processes are much more complex, the pathways longer. Sensory impulses from touch receptors travel through the spinal cord to the brain stem and cerebellum, where they are decoded and amplified, to the thalamus, where the soft fur is probably first "felt," and on to the cerebral cortex, where it is finally "understood" that the fur is indicative of a cat. If the cortex decides it would be nice to pet the cat, it initiates motor impulses that are modified by the cerebellum and the basal ganglia—fine tuning the requests for muscle movement, insuring that they will be smooth and accurate—before they travel down the spinal cord to the point where, stimulating the motor neuron, the impulses continue on through long nerve fibers to the muscles in the hand. Innervated by a rapid-fire series of such impulses, the muscles relax and contract rhythmically, allowing the hand to stroke the kitten's back or rub it behind the ears.

In disorders of movement like Parkinson's disease, or in people with damage from MS, the peripheral nerve pathways remain clear, but the impulses they carry are faulty; the resulting movement is unrefined, sometimes halting, sometimes wildly inaccurate, because of damage to the brain's basal ganglia or cerebellum. When the pathways themselves are impeded—as they are with Guillain-Barré syndrome, and as they were with Peter Koppel's amyotrophic lateral sclerosis—movements are weak, but they are basically accurate and smooth as long as movement remains possible. Confoundingly, sensory pathways are normally unaffected; sensory axons are usually spared in the demyelinating process of Guillain-Barré, and sensory neurons seldom degenerate in tandem with the motor neurons in the brain and spinal cord that are assaulted by ALS. When his disease had progressed to paralysis, Mr. Koppel could still feel cold air on his arm, and the subtle touch of his trousers against his legs. But he could not move his arm out of the way or shift the position of his motionless legs—nor could he have obliged a patient cat.

"Here we are," said the woman in the uniform as she rolled Peter Koppel through the doorway. He smiled broadly; Ferrier walked toward him, crouched by his chair and took his hand. "Good to see you," he said.

"And you. How have you been?" Mr. Koppel tried to turn in his chair. "Thank you," he said to the woman as she turned to go; she smiled and made a little wave.

"I've missed seeing you at the chamber concerts," Ferrier told him.

"Oh, gosh. Those things don't start until eight-thirty, and I'm usually fast asleep by then. I miss the music, but . . . that's the way the cookie crumbles." Mr. Koppel wore dark trousers and white tennis shoes. His lace shirt was open almost to his waist and he wore a choker of large turquoise stones around his neck. His hair was curly and gray, hiding his ears, and his face was smooth and handsome; I had not expected this retired man with ALS to be a 1980s Bohemian. "No, this is where I'm located pretty much full time these days," he said.

Ferrier introduced me, then asked how he was adjusting to the nursing home.

"This is a pretty good place," he said, "perfect for me, really.

177

But heavens, I'm seventy-two and I feel like a kid. I'm by far the youngest person here. And most of the patients are women, you know. I think these ladies enjoy having a young buck join them at the dinner table. Some of them offer to feed me." He flashed a smile; his words were sightly slurred. "It takes some getting used to; they make you eat at ridiculously early times of the day, but that isn't catastrophic, is it? And the first few times these good-looking twenty-year-old nurses hold your penis for you while you pee, that's an interesting experience, but it doesn't bother me. I'm lucky to be in a place like this."

Ferrier asked him about his movement; he did not examine him, but wanted to know whether Mr. Koppel felt he had deteriorated since their conversation a month before.

"Oh, yes, definitely. Last time we talked I still had a little use of my hands, didn't I? When I was still at home I remember that I could scratch my nose, that sort of thing, which I can't do now. When I come in here to read the paper, the only way I can turn the page is by grabbing it with my mouth."

"What about swallowing?"

"It seems like things get stuck a little more often lately. I haven't choked yet, but I have to be kind of careful. And my tongue feels like its getting kind of thick, but I guess it's really just that I'm losing some of the use of it. I hope I don't get to the point where I can't talk."

Cancer had killed Peter Koppel's wife twelve years before, and it was a year after her death when he wrote the statement asking that no heroic treatment be administered if he, too, should become ill. He remained healthy until 1982, when a malignant mole, a melanoma, and surrounding lymph nodes were removed from his left armpit. Regular checkups since then had revealed no spread of the cancer, and his health seemed good again until his left hand began to grow weak fourteen months ago. Soon he noticed that he had difficulty manipulating objects in his hands; he was unable to extend the fingers of his left hand, and his right hand was also weak. Physical exertion would sometimes produce sudden cramps in muscles throughout his body.

When Mr. Koppel first consulted Ferrier, he told him he had noticed no loss of sensation and that he felt no pain in his hands. When Ferrier asked him if the muscles in his hands ever seemed to twitch for no apparent reason, he said yes, as a matter of fact, they did. On examination, Ferrier found significant distal weakness in Mr. Koppel's left arm, minor proximal weakness in that arm, and slight weakness in his right arm and both his legs. He found no sensory loss in any of the extremities, but he did find elevated reflexes and observed subtle fasciculations in the muscles of both arms, both legs, and the pectoral muscles of his chest. An electromyogram, in which Ferrier inserted a needle electrode into the muscle tissues, confirmed the fasciculations and showed that when each of the muscle groups tested was contracted, motor unit potentials tended to be longer and stronger than normal. Nerve conduction studies in his left arm showed that motor nerve velocity was slowed across his wrist, but sensory velocity was normal.

Ferrier's findings were troubling. The fasciculations meant that a muscle disease was an unlikely cause of the weakness and the accompanying muscle atrophy, as did the slowed nerve velocities. The asymmetry of the weakness, the generalized cramping, and the absence of sensory abnormalities made motor neuron disease the likely root of the problem. In order to rule out the unlikely possibility that Mr. Koppel's symptoms were caused by a slipped disc or an arthritic vertebra pressing on his spinal cord, or by a tumor of the cord itself, Ferrier scheduled a myelogram—a procedure in which an opaque dye is injected into the cerebrospinal fluid surrounding the spinal cord in order to delineate it clearly on an X ray. A week later, a myelogram performed at St. Luke's Hospital demonstrated that the discs separating his fourth, fifth, sixth, and seventh vertebrae showed minor encroachment into the space occupied by the cord, but both Ferrier and the radiologist who performed the procedure agreed that the minimal nature of their displacement—especially in the absence of pain—could not explain the diffuse nature of the weakness, now involving all four extremities. Mr. Koppel had had a week to consider that ALS was a strong possibility, and before he left the hospital, Ferrier told him the diagnosis now had to be considered firm.

In France, it is called Charcot's disease because it was Jean Martin Charcot who, in a series of lectures delivered between 1872 and

1874, first delineated the symptomatology and pathology of this mean and insidious motor disease. Charcot, widely considered to be the founder of the discipline of neurology, recommended that the disease be referred to as "amyotrophic lateral sclerosis"— *amyotrophic* a reference to the neurogenic atrophy of muscles, *lateral sclerosis* an appellation for the scarring in the lateral columns of the spinal cord. Unless it is abbreviated, as it most often is, the name is an awkward one, however, and many neuroscientists now refer to ALS solely as "motor neuron disease." In the United States, it is also popularly known as "Lou Gehrig's disease," named after the "Iron Horse" of the New York Yankees, the team's first baseman and cleanup batter from 1925 until 1939, when ALS forced him to retire from baseball. Gehrig was an enormously popular figure—before his illness and after—popularity that is reflected in this singular case in which a disease is known by the name of one of its sufferers instead of one of its discoverers.

Although it is an uncommon disease—occurring in between one and two people per hundred thousand—ALS has afflicted a number of well-known figures in addition to Lou Gehrig: actor David Niven, jazz musician Charlie Mingus, composer Dmitri Shostakovich, astrophysicist Steven Hawking, and former U.S. Senator Jacob Javits among them. ALS strikes men almost twice as often as women, but it shows no racial or regional biases except among the native Chamorro people on the island of Guam, who, inexplicably, suffer as many as one hundred times the cases of ALS as the worldwide average. Epidemiologists obviously suspect that some sort of genetic factor plays a role in the incidence of the disease on Guam; worldwide, however, only about 10 percent of the reported cases show a familial pattern that suggests inheritance.

In its most typical form, ALS strikes people in their fifties and sixties, first manifesting itself as a weakness and seeming lack of coordination in a hand, suspiciously involving the whole hand instead of the portion of the hand governed by a specific peripheral nerve. The muscles in the hand begin to waste, subtle fasciculations appear, the weakness progresses and slowly spreads to the arm itself, to the opposite hand and arm, and to the legs. In some patients, weakness begins in the shoulder muscles, and in others, it first affects the muscles in the mouth and throat, resulting in mushy and lethargic speech and in difficulty swallowing. As the disease progresses and weakness gives way to paralysis, most of the body's muscle groups are ultimately affected. Eye muscles are usually spared, the sphincter muscles are normally unaffected, but arms and legs are virtually always immobile in the late stages of the disease, and the muscles that maintain the respiratory pump usually become so weak that aeration of the lungs becomes impossible, leading to carbon-dioxide unconsciousness and death. Although ALS patients have been reported to have lived with the disease for as many as twenty years, most succumb to it within three years following diagnosis. No one survives it long enough to die of other causes.

Unlike Guillain-Barré syndrome, ALS is probably not an auto-immune disease; in the absence of inflammation surrounding affected motor neurons, it does not appear to involve an immunological disorder. It is classed as a *degenerative* neurological disease—one in which nerve cells are destroyed without evidence of attack by viruses, bacteria, or the body's own antibodies—and as such it is akin to Parkinson's disease and Alzheimer's disease, both of which affect different and distinct nerve cells, all three of which sometimes occur in combination, the triad representing, by far, the most common degenerative assaults on the aging nervous system.

Although neuroscientists know that the disease affects only motor neurons in the brain and spinal cord, its cause remains a mystery. In the early years of the twentieth century, syphilis was believed to be the cause of ALS; later reports blamed the disease on an epidemic of encephalitis that occurred at the end of World War I; in more recent years, researchers have speculated that toxins such as lead, mercury, manganese, and a variety of petroleum by-products are its cause, yet no strong evidence has ever emerged to implicate any of these as etiological sources. As they do with so many neurological disorders, scientists now suspect that a viral agent may play some role in the disease's genesis, although attempts to isolate an ALS-related virus at autopsy so far have failed. And the possibility remains that ALS, as well as Parkinson's and Alzheimer's diseases, are the geriatric outcomes of genetic defects in three discrete types of cerebral tissue—defects present since birth that result in nerve cell destruction only in the later decades of life.

181

Peter Koppel was on no medication—none has ever reliably been demonstrated to slow the disease's progress—and Ferrier continued to see him on a regular basis solely to monitor his decline, to ensure that he was as comfortable as possible, to answer his questions, and to assure him that he was an ally in his commitment to die with dignity.

"One of these days I'm going to catch pneumonia or something," Mr. Koppel said, his wheelchair facing the rain-splattered window, his neck turned slightly so he could look directly at Ferrier while he made his point. "You remember our deal. When it happens, you're not going to admit me to the hospital, and you're not going to pump me full of antibiotics. No respirator. I don't want to be double-crossed, now." His words were spoken softly, and they were shaped more by conviction than emotion; he watched Ferrier for a reaction.

"Listen. I promise you I am not going to double-cross you." Ferrier twisted himself in his chair. "I'm with you on this. But you're getting way ahead of yourself. You've been here for less than a month; you're still getting used to this place. What if it happened tomorrow? Is everything taken care of, everything settled?"

"Well, no, not entirely, but there aren't a great number of things that I have to deal with yet."

"So relax. Take your time. Take care of them when you can, but there's no rush. Mr. Koppel, you could live for another year; you could live for two or three years. There's no way we can predict it. You'll probably be good and sick of me before we part company."

Mr. Koppel smiled. Then his smile faded and he spoke. "I guess my experience with my wife kind of terrifies me. It's selfish, I suppose, but I don't want to suffer the degradation she did."

"If I'm around, if I don't go before you do, I'll do everything I can to ensure that that doesn't happen. But in the meantime, and there may be a long meantime, things can be okay. You can read all the books you've never had a chance to read, listen to all the Beethoven and Mahler symphonies you can stand. You can have some wonderful conversations with your friends."

"My friends have been marvelous. I guess I suspected that when I moved here many of them would find this place too depressing and would visit a lot less. But I've got constant company. And if I didn't tire out so quickly, I could have a dinner invitation every night of the week."

"Well, accept as many as you're up to. You know, in a funny way, you can be a great help to them now. What is happening to you will happen to some of them some day. Hearing something of what you've experienced, what you've learned, will be very valuable, very comforting down the line."

"An old friend of mine, a widow, asked me the other day if I expected to see my wife again when I died. I had thought about that some, sure, even before the ALS, but I guess I'd never formed an opinion. Are you a religious person, Doctor?"

"No, but I—"

"Well, I have been, never the most devout person in the world, but I have always believed in God. Yet I never gave much thought to the issue of an afterlife, heaven, hell, or just *finis*. Now that I know I won't live too much longer, you would think that it would be a big issue for me. But what's interesting is that it really isn't. It may be a silly analogy, but I just feel like I'm very tired and I'm looking forward to a good long sleep. It's not a suicidal feeling; it's not that I can't stand living anymore. It's just that I'm tired. It's been a long day."

Ferrier pushed Mr. Koppel's chair out of the library a few minutes later and rolled him into the main lounge where he would wait for dinner. "I agree," Ferrier told him. "I think you did find a good place to hang your hat."

Before we left, Mr. Koppel asked me how often I came to town to tag along with the brain doctor. I told him I was in town for a week at least every month. "I'm sure I'll see you again," I told him.

"I hope so," he warmly replied, as if, on my next visit, he expected to be alive.

Outside, the rain had ended. There was no sun, and clouds still seemed to seal off the hills that surrounded the city, but the air was cool and sweet with moisture. Rainwater ran in the gutters and steam rose from the asphalt.

As we drove toward St. Luke's Hospital, where Ferrier had to read three EEGs and to see Yoshi and a Down's syndrome patient who had suffered a massive stroke, he said, "He's quite a guy, isn't he? Most neurologists would agree that this is the most terrifying disease in the discipline—it's like having a front-row seat at your own dissolution—but his response is so . . . wise, in a way."

"I guess I was expecting him to seem really tragic. The ALS certainly is, but he . . . tragic isn't the right word."

"This is what is hard for people to understand—how I keep from being real depressed in this business. Part of it is that you become callous. I'm sure that's part of it, but there is another aspect. Some of the most profound things, and some of the dying, are not depressing. You end up feeling good in a way that has to do with having learned something from someone else."

I could not be sure exactly how I felt after having met Peter Koppel and Alan Dunn, but I knew that I would remember them, and, for a change, I would remember them more as people than as patients. Neither man's saga of disease frightened me, and my reactions had little to do with a sense of good fortune at having escaped their fates. Unlike the ubiquitousness in this college town in the Rocky Mountains of a disease like multiple sclerosis, and unlike the tumors that had grown, uninvited, in the innards of so many friends and acquaintances, these two diseases that affected the ability to command muscles to move seemed remote, exotic, impossible. Statistically, at least, I would probably be immune.

Yet what they had both experienced was compelling, I suppose, because I could not imagine it. What would it be like to have the meat on my bones betray me, simply cease to flex and relax because it was no longer connected to my brain? If I could recover, would I fight for recovery with Alan's optimism, his will? If recovery was not an option, would I surrender to death as gracefully as Peter Koppel was doing?

What I ultimately wanted to believe about myself and about these two men was that none of us was unique. I wanted to believe that Alan Dunn and Peter Koppel represented aspects of the human spirit that are shared by all of us. We are all terminal cases, after all, yet we struggle fundamentally to live. I wanted to believe, and perhaps I now had evidence that would allow me to, that as long as there is hope for health, for life, hope itself is a juice that flows in our veins and that sparks the synaptic connections in our brains. I wanted to believe that when hope is extinguished, as it sometimes has to be, its absence induces a splendid kind of fatigue that can only be met with sleep.

7 An Insidious Swelling

Vera Bridgewater had been behaving a bit strangely. She would stand idly in the shower for half an hour or more, neglecting to wash before finally turning off the water. She would puzzle in front of her clothes closet for long periods, unsure of what she had meant to find. Food tasted strange, she said. At age sixty-nine now, she often felt tired and "fuzzy" and she frequently wet her bed because she was "just too comfortable to get up." According to her twin daughters, one of whom she lived with, she did not seem to be depressed. In fact, she found most things rather funny. She would often laugh at sad stories on television, be amused by a cat at the side of the road that had been run over by a car, and she even chuckled one day when she heard that an old friend had died.

Mrs. Bridgewater's husband had been dead for eight years, and she had adjusted well to widowhood, yet Gail Sebring, her family physician, suspected that her lethargy might, nonetheless, be attributable to a subtle depression. Dr. Sebring prescribed amitriptyline, an antidepressant, and after a month, during which time Mrs. Bridgewater seemed unchanged, she increased the dosage. At the end of two months, Mrs. Bridgewater seemed to be worse and Dr. Sebring referred her to Ferrier. Could her symptoms actually signal a toxic response to the amitriptyline? Was this the early onset of Alzheimer's disease? Or did her unusual lethargic and euphoric symptoms represent another, as yet unsuspected, disorder?

When Ferrier first saw Mrs. Bridgewater during the second week of August, he soon decided that a diagnosis of Alzheimer's could safely be rejected. Her short-term memory seemed strong. She knew that an airliner crash was the big story in the news that week, and when asked what medical problems the president had recently suffered, she said he had been operated on for colon cancer. She performed the serial seven test with ease, subtracting seven from a hundred, from ninety-three, from eighty-six, from seventy-nine more rapidly than Ferrier himself could have done. She remembered what she had eaten for dinner the night before, and for breakfast that morning, but when Ferrier asked her to interpret the proverb, "People who live in glass houses shouldn't throw stones," her answer seemed too concrete when she told him she guessed it meant that rocks can easily break glass.

Ferrier felt that the amitriptyline might be the culprit—her symptoms had worsened since she had gone on it—yet her daughters were convinced that they had begun long before she started taking the antidepressant. He suggested that she stop it for the time being, and he scheduled blood tests and a head CAT scan to look for other causes.

A week later, Mrs. Bridgewater and one daughter returned to Ferrier's office, and he gave them a firm diagnosis. The CAT scan had shown the presence of a baseball-sized tumor—an enormous growth that, surprisingly, should have been causing far more severe symptoms—lodged between her skull and the frontal lobes of her cerebral cortex. Ferrier explained that because of the tumor's location, and because it appeared to be surrounded by a clearly delineated capsule, it was very likely benign. But it would have to be removed. Mrs. Bridgewater's daughter looked shocked and relieved in the same instant; yes, Ferrier assured her, the surgery should ease or entirely relieve her mother's lethargy, her confusion, and her strange behavior. Mrs. Bridgewater herself thought the news was amusing. "A tumor?" she asked with light-hearted disbelief, as though the doctor had told her he had found a bunny rabbit inside her brain. She laughed and turned to her daughter to see if she had shared the joke.

Ferrier had told Mrs. Bridgewater about her tumor on a clear and sweltering Tuesday, and before she left his office, he had called Ed Holly, a neurosurgeon whose office was a floor below. "I'd be glad to see her," Ed Holly said. "Have her call my girls. I can probably see her this afternoon."

After he had seen Mrs. Bridgewater in his office, and after he and Ferrier had examined her CAT scan films, as well as the films from an angiogram that further defined the location and nature of her tumor, Ed Holly scheduled the surgery for Friday. When he called Ferrier on Thursday to say that everything was set, Ferrier turned on his phone's speaker so I could hear their conversation. In the background, I could also hear the whine of a motor that sounded as if it belonged to a food blender; it was only a few minutes after eight in the morning, and I assumed Holly was still at home.

"Mrs. Bridgewater's resection is set for seven tomorrow morning," he told Ferrier.

Ferrier turned toward me, his eyes bright, a trace of a smile on his face that seemed to say he had thought of something brilliant. "Ed," he asked, "would you mind some company? I don't think I'm seeing anybody until ten tomorrow." Then he asked if I could join them as well.

"Don't see why not," Ed Holly said. "I think the hospital'll make him sign a form saying he won't try to help or anything, but it shouldn't be a problem. Give me his name and I'll take care of it." The motor in the background seemed to strain, its high whine growing shrill as it labored; perhaps it was his day off and he was at work in his wood shop. "And listen. Roger is going to be late tomorrow. He's got to do a deposition before he comes in. You can assist if you want to."

"I'm sure your regular nurse-tech is a much better assistant than I am," Ferrier said. He turned to me again. This time, his eyes seemed to say, *can you believe what I've gotten you into now?*

"Don't tell me what I already know," Ed Holly said. "I'm sure there's plenty of reasons why you're a sorter and not a surgeon." The motor screamed, then seemed to bind up. It stopped. "Well. Sounds like Roger is about inside. I'd better go to work. See you tomorrow."

At last I realized that Ed Holly had called from an operating room. The motor I had heard, Ferrier said, was a surgical saw, cutting through a patient's cranium. It was arresting enough just to hear it, to suddenly comprehend that before the intricate and delicate work of brain surgery begins, a bit of rough carpentry must be accomplished. What would it be like to *watch* Ed Holly work, to see his scalpel make its smooth incision in Mrs. Bridgewater's scalp? I wasn't sure a single day was enough time to prepare myself to see him lift out a piece of her skull like the lid of a jack-o'-lantern.

"So. Now you'll see what the surgeons do for a living," Ferrier said.

"I thought you didn't like surgery," I said.

"You ought to see what it's like. And it never hurts me to see the inside of somebody's head. It'll be interesting."

"What if I turn green?"

"Another reason for wearing a mask," he said.

Ferrier had confessed long ago that he could never have been a surgeon. "They're technicians. They have to be good at what they do, obviously, but can you imagine years of it? I'd be bored to death." And Ferrier was not alone in this particular prejudice. Clinical specialists of every stripe tend to assume that surgeons comprise the blue-collar branch of their profession. Surgeons are the "saw-bones" who do the dirty work, the craftsmen whose work is sometimes curative, but that seldom requires *thinking*. They have the bedside manners of mafiosi and the bank accounts of computer whizzes. And anesthesiologists, their partners in the invasive procedures of the operating theaters, are even harder to understand. Their incomes are equally impressive, but their discipline is one that is characterized only by hours of gaping boredom and seconds of genuine terror.

If the surgeons and anesthesiologists are aware of these tongue-slightly-in-cheek characterizations, they do not appear to be bothered by them. Self-doubt and hypersensitivity are not their stock in trade. Besides, they know full well that *they* are the true practitioners of the medical art. They do direct battle with diseased bodies, while the clinicians try timidly to *understand* illness, to cooperate with it, to coax bodies back to health. As the surgeons see it, the clinicians are ultimately "sorters"; their job is a clerical one—screening patients to determine who needs to take two aspirins and who must meet the knife.

Yet despite their preconceptions, despite their separate perspectives and the differences in the way they tackle their trade, Ferrier and Putnam work well with Ed Holly and Roger Burns, almost exclusively referring their surgical patients to the two neurosurgeons—unless, as happened occasionally, the patient opted instead to be operated on by someone with a wider reputation in the city, by a friend of a friend in Philadelphia, or by someone on staff at the Mayo Clinic. Both Holly and Burns were well liked and respected by the local medical community; they were technically very competent and, most important in Ferrier's mind, they were medically *conservative*. "The only kind of surgeon you ought to refer your patients to," he told me, "is one who is *less* likely to recommend surgery than you are. If he's too anxious to open everyone up, you'd better shop around. I'm not sure what I would have done if I'd come to practice in a town like this and discovered that its only two neurosurgeons were eager-beaver types—or were incompetent, for that matter. You seldom encounter a really poor surgeon these days, but occasionally you run into one—the kind of guy who always has his scrub nurse close up the patient because he's got a tennis game in twenty minutes."

Throughout the rest of that Thursday, I could think of little else but the prospect of observing Mrs. Bridgewater's surgery. Emergency rooms and intensive care units by now had begun to seem almost commonplace, but an OR was another matter. This would actually be my second trip to an operating room. My first visit had been twenty years before, and my only memory of that experience was of the hazy minute or two before an anesthetist injected sodium pentothal into a vein in my arm. This time I would be wide awake, and regardless of what astonishing things I observed, I would have to portray a kind of veteran calm, a careful nonchalance. Yet if seeing the surgery was anything akin to hearing the straining whine of the saw, nonchalance could be a difficult role to play.

Ferrier, however, had patients to see in the midst of my anxious imaginings, and I tried to put them out of my mind as I listened to the morning's consultations—a retarded four-year-old American Indian girl whose parents were suing the hospital where she fell from her crib as an infant; a forty-four-year-old real estate saleswoman who would progressively lose her vision to the point of blindness during the course of her migraine headaches; and an eighteen-year-old boy who had tried to commit suicide two months before, and whose psychiatrist suspected his periodic aggressive outbursts might, in fact, be temporal lobe seizures. He also saw Lisa Benedict, the migraine patient from the town in the mountains who had left her husband in May.

Lisa and her two children had moved home again in early June, and her husband had found an apartment in the same town. He still would not agree to joint counseling, but he told Lisa he wanted to work things out. He wanted the marriage to survive, he said, and they agreed that perhaps a separation would be beneficial for them both. Lisa's headaches had not worsened during the traumatic three months since she had last seen Ferrier, but neither had they disappeared. She still depended on the ergotamine inhaler to abort the most serious headaches, but she felt it was time to quit taking amitriptyline. Ferrier did not object, but he cautioned her that, without it, her headache frequency might increase again.

"I don't think it will," Lisa said. "I think a lot of the tension that the amitriptyline was helping with is gone now, and the tension was probably the reason why I was having so many headaches. It's just . . . I don't feel like a crazy person, and I'd rather not be taking an antidepressant."

Ferrier smiled. "And I agree with you. Shall I write that on your chart? 'Lisa is not a crazy person.' " He looked up from his pretended scribble. "What's in store for you and your husband?"

"Well. He comes over for dinner sometimes. And you know, he's much sweeter to the kids now that he's not living with us. I guess I know now that I would like to be married to Robert, for whatever reasons, but I don't want it to be at any cost. I feel like I kind of woke up that night he hit me."

"Has he woken up, do you think?"

"He . . . Robert's a very private person. Even back when we were happiest, I didn't ever know much about how he felt about things. Right now . . . I guess he's probably realizing we all mean something to him. I hope so."

"Is he helping you three financially?"

"He is. Virginia, my counselor, asked me about that, too, and I guess maybe that's a good sign. He's been real good about coming over just as soon as he gets his paycheck. I suppose that says something, doesn't it?"

Ferrier put his arm around Lisa when they walked out of his office and down the corridor a few minutes later. They had agreed that she would not return for six months, but he assured her that she should call if her headaches got bad again. I heard him say, "The worst thing about you getting healthy is that I won't see much of you anymore," before their voices grew faint.

By five o'clock, Ferrier had seen his final office patient of the day, and there were only two patients to see on rounds before he was finished—Yoshi, who would leave St. Luke's Hospital to return to Japan in two more days, and Mrs. Bridgewater, who by now had checked into County Hospital for tomorrow morning's procedure.

Yoshi had lost weight since his accident; his once-pudgy face now looked lean and almost adult. His dark eyes seemed to offer assurance that he had been through a bad time. According to Dr. Fukuda, Yoshi's Japanese was steadily improving; he could walk without difficulty, but his right arm remained uncooperative. And he did not want to return to Japan. "In Japan," Dr. Fukuda had told Ferrier when they discussed finding a suitable rehabilitation program for him in his own country, "people with disabilities are often treated unkindly. There is not much understanding. Sometimes you see people laughing and joking about someone on the street in a wheelchair. I know it worries him. Also, I think he does not want to go home looking defeated."

Ferrier's visit with Yoshi that afternoon was short. He compared the strength in Yoshi's arms, watched him walk from his bed to the window and back, then asked him to read the English words on a chart his speech therapist had supplied. Yoshi had no trouble with words like *pen, ball,* and *banana,* but *tomorrow* and *empty* eluded him. He successfully mimicked the movements Ferrier made with his mouth, then lay back on his pillow, assuming the daily routine was done.

"I know you have mixed feelings about going home," Ferrier said, his hands gripping the footboard of the bed. "Dr. Fukuda explained things to me, and I don't blame you for being worried. But it's home, you know. Your parents want you to come home, and from what I've been told, they have found a very good program for you. I would be glad to have you stay, but I do think you need to be in a place where Japanese is the language you're going to be around. Learning English can wait; there will be plenty of time for it. Right now, I think it's important to concentrate on the Japanese. Do you understand what I'm saying?"

Yoshi nodded, his mouth curling into a slight smile. "Yes, yes, thank you," he said, as he did every day.

Down the hill and half a mile away at County Hospital, Vera Bridgewater wore a checked robe and lay in a bed beside a vase of roses. Her twin daughters sat in chairs between the roses and a second, unoccupied bed.

"Well, Mrs. Bridgewater," Ferrier said as we walked into the room, "what brings you here?"

She giggled. "Well, I guess you're going to take out that tumor, aren't you?"

"Dr. Holly is, actually, but I'm going to be there to make sure he does a very good job."

"How long do you think it will be before she's out of the recovery room tomorrow?" asked the daughter who lived out of town.

"Well, it depends on how quickly everything goes, but she should be awake by noon or so. We'll probably keep her in the ICU for a couple of days, just to make sure everything's as it should be, and I'll check on her there late in the afternoon." He turned to his patient. "Mrs. Bridgewater, I want you to remember something for me. I want you to remember these roses. When I come visit you tomorrow, I want you to tell me that it was the roses you were supposed to remember. Okay?"

"Okay, I'll try to," she said, smiling as though this doctor certainly made strange requests.

"It's going to go real well," he said, turning to each of them as he spoke. "We don't expect any complications, and other than having a short haircut for a while, you're going to do splendidly."

The second daughter followed us out to the corridor after Ferrier had said good-bye. She wanted to know if she and her sister could expect their mother to be immediately improved following the surgery. It was hard to say how quickly changes would be evident, he told her. But they ought to come within weeks rather than months. "It's a very large tumor," he said, his voice low as he spoke in the direction of her mother's doorway. "It's putting pressure on a big portion of her cortex, a part that controls thinking and that's involved in a person's emotional responses. With that pressure gone, she certainly could become her old self again."

"Wouldn't that be something," she said.

Ferrier and I ate gyros that night in a restaurant filled with photographs and murals of the Greek village of Santorini. Bouzouki music played from a stereo behind the bar while I interrogated him about what was in store for us in the morning. Would I watch from some sort of observation balcony? No, such facilities only existed at teaching hospitals, he said. Would he actually assist Ed Holly? Not if he could help it. Would Mrs. Bridgewater be under a general anesthetic? Yes, of course. Would Ed Holly mind if I occasionally asked a question? Not if it was a good one.

I was beginning to be genuinely excited—nervous, nonetheless, but intrigued by the brief opportunity to see this ancient and ritualistic art in practice, this medical manual labor that was at once murderous and curative, a healing craft whose principal tool was a sharp and gleaming scalpel. And I would see, I presumed, a bit of a *living brain* through a square window in bone.

Yet I had seen the CAT scan images of Mrs. Bridgewater's tumor—meningeal tissue gone mutant and grown wild, so large that perhaps all there would be to see until it was excised would be the tumor itself. How would Ed Holly know precisely where it would begin and end? Was it difficult, in the wet, red dish in which he would be working, to distinguish the unwelcome tumor from Mrs. Bridgewater's healthy and ever-so-delicate frontal lobes?

"Not with a benign tumor, it isn't," Ferrier said. "Most of them have a capsule, made of a kind of fibrous tissue, that nicely separates them from healthy tissue. That's why we have been willing to tell Mrs. Bridgewater and her daughters that there is such a strong likelihood that it's benign. It's obviously grown out of the meninges, and most meningiomas are benign, for one thing. It's got a very clear demarcation on the CAT scan, for another, and the angiogram shows a typical pattern of blood vessels reaching into the tumor—benign tumors usually have few blood vessels.

"Malignant tumors, on the other hand—and this applies to every organ—are very vascular. On the films, you see hundreds of blood vessels reaching into them, and that's one of the reasons malignant tumors are so debilitating. They grow very quickly and invite in much more blood than an equivalent amount of healthy tissue would, and they succeed in robbing the rest of the body of nutrients. And malignant tumors have no capsule. Instead of seeing a nice sharp edge of the tumor, like with Mrs. Bridgewater's meningioma, you see fingers of tumor reaching, spreading *into* the tissue around it. That's where the term *cancer* comes from, from *crab*, from the reaching out and grabbing motions of a crab.

"Surgery on benign tumors is largely curative; they are relatively easy to resect—you can get the whole thing—and they seldom grow back. But surgery almost never cures cancerous tumors. By its nature, cancer is a disease in which you see the tip of the iceberg. The spread of malignant cells into surrounding tissues and into the rest of the body via the lymphatics, the blood, or cerebrospinal fluid is virtually assured unless they're caught very early. Surgeons do biopsies to determine the type of tumor, and they do what they call debulking procedures with malignant tumors—meaning they take out a chunk of the given tumor—a procedure basically designed to decrease their size for a while so they don't sap the patient so much. But even when they take out every bit of malignant tumor that they can see, the microscopic cells remain behind—and then ultimately grow."

"When you first see a patient," I asked, "are there symptoms that tend to distinguish benign tumors from malignant ones?"

"No, it's more complicated than that. The presentation of a brain or spinal cord tumor totally depends on where it is located, on what neuronal activity it affects. Some patients with tumors—either benign or malignant—first present with seizures; some lose arm function or speech and look like they've had a stroke. In Mrs. Bridgewater's case, she has the symptoms—the inappropriate emotional responses, the unusual behavior—that are common with a variety of frontal-lobe problems, hematomas, cell loss caused by dementias, strokes, and tumors. The symptoms are often the same, but there can be several causes.

"I have another patient—who I'm seeing sometime this week,

by the way—a young guy with melanoma, a horrible kind of cancer that begins in the pigmented cells of the skin. He remembers that he had a funny mole on his chest that he scratched off, but what first took him to see the doctor was severe morning headaches. For a neurologist, that is the one symptom that tips you off very early that tumor is a possibility. With most other headaches—migraines, clusters, muscle contraction—if you wake up with a headache, it will tend to get worse throughout the day. But when a patient tells you that he wakes up with an excruciating headache that gets better as soon as he gets up, you pay attention. When you're lying in bed, fluid may leak out of blood vessels and collect around a tumor—one that may be very vascular, remember—and then swell and cause a lot of pain. But when you get up, gravity causes the excess fluid to leak back into brain blood vessels and to move toward your feet, and the headache improves or disappears. So a symptom of that kind of headache can be very telling, but . . . many malignant brain tumors never involve any pain or headaches at all."

"Do most cancerous tumors in the brain spread there from other parts of the body?"

"Not most, no. In older people, I'd say perhaps 50 percent of the tumors you find are metastatic, meaning they have spread from a primary tumor elsewhere in the body. And for some unknown reason, tumors from some other organs—particularly the lungs, breasts, and large bowel—and from the pigmented skin cells, tend to metastasize to the brain. In younger patients, in the age groups in which cancer isn't so common, probably 80 percent of all brain tumors are primary, meaning they begin as a mutation of brain cells.

"What's interesting about the primary brain tumors—and there are dozens of specific types, distinguished by where they are found, what they look like, and how they tend to grow, both benign and malignant—is that almost all of them are tumors of the brain's glial cells, the supportive cells that insulate and nourish nerve cells. Tumors of the nerve cells themselves are quite rare, and that may be because, unlike all the other cells in your body, they aren't constantly duplicating themselves. You're born with all the nerve cells you're going to get; you don't grow new ones. And since nerve cells don't grow, they aren't prone to mutate and then to begin to grow wildly. Also, who knows why this is the case, but primary brain tumors just don't metastasize to other parts of the body. There are isolated reports of it happening— the kind of thing that, if you see it, you write it up—but it's extremely rare."

"Do benign tumors ever become malignant?"

"Well," he said, his answers to my string of questions keeping him from his gyro, "tumor, which in Latin just means 'swelling,' is also referred to as neoplasm. A neoplasm is any new, abnormal growth. Both benign and malignant tumors are neoplasms, but under that one blanket category there are hundreds of different kinds of tumors with different characteristics, including, yes, benign tumors that become malignant. And while there are logical reasons for a beginning medical textbook to have a major chapter on a disease it calls cancer, an oncologist, a cancer specialist, will tell you that he or she treats dozens of very different diseases— each with its own cell of origin, prognosis, treatment, chances of metastasizing, rate of growth, et cetera, et cetera."

There wasn't even time for coffee on Friday morning. It was six-thirty when Ferrier awoke, and I was still sleeping soundly when he hollered out to the living room. We dressed quickly and drove to County Hospital, walked in a back door, then through swinging doors marked SURGERY, NO UNAUTHORIZED PERSON-NEL, where we encountered a nurse who knew we were coming. I signed the photocopied form she handed me, then we followed her into a small locker room where she took down from a cabinet pale blue surgical shirts and trousers for us both. She took paper caps, masks, and shoe covers from three covered cardboard bins and laid them on a counter. "When you're dressed, put your shoes back on and the booties over your shoes," she said. "Don't go in till your masks are up, don't touch anything in the OR, especially nothing green, and . . . oh, there's a pocket in your pants. Take your wallets with you. It happens."

"I could use a cup of coffee," I said as I sat down on a bench to pull off the pants I had put on fifteen minutes before.

"You'll wake up," Ferrier said.

We soon looked like facsimiles of surgeons—the short-sleeved, V-neck shirts as big as maternity blouses, the balloon pants held

196

up by drawstrings, our booties in place, the caps, like paper soup bowls, pulled snug over our heads, the soft metal arches of the masks bent across our noses.

"No matter how rough it gets in there boys, remember that your country's damn proud of you," Ferrier cracked, trying to sound like a platoon sergeant as we walked through a second door and into the scrub room. I looked at him inquisitively as we walked by the row of sinks. He shook his head. "Not us."

Beyond the windowed doors we walked through next was a surprisingly small operating room. I was expecting an enormous circular arena, I suppose, but instead, the room was square, about a quarter the size of a basketball court, its ceiling ten feet high, its overhead lights very bright. Ed Holly, looking chubby in his surgical scrubs, stood in front of a light board mounted on a wall near the doors, studying Mrs. Bridgewater's X rays and angiogram to determine precisely where he would cut through her cranium. Ferrier introduced me. "Welcome, welcome," Ed Holly said, holding his ungloved hands in front of him. "I take it, John, that you're going to let the rest of us do the work today," he said to Ferrier.

"I'm rusty," Ferrier said.

"Fair enough. But you two can keep us honest. We'll get started here in a minute."

"Where do you want us, Ed?"

"Well, why don't you stand over there to start with. And then once we're in, I'll have you come up to the table."

As we turned in the direction of his gesture, I was startled—as though I had not expected her to be present—to see Mrs. Bridgewater, anesthetized already, her shoulders high on the inclined table, her head shaved except for the gray strands at the nape of her neck, her pale scalp now painted with orange disinfectant—a nurse, standing on a stool above her, scrubbing her scalp with a brush. In the silent fog of anesthesia, stripped of her hair and painted, she had become another person, someone I had never met. If I had been told she were dead, I would have readily believed it.

But she was very much alive. The anesthesiologist, his giant nose distorting his mask, sat crouched on a stool beside the table, monitoring her vital signs, checking the drugs—cyclopropane and other anesthetics—that kept her "asleep" and the oxygen that kept her alive, saying "whenever you're ready" in muffled tones through his mask as he caught Ed Holly's eye.

Ferrier and I stood against a wall near the head of the table, next to an electrocardiograph monitor that was held fast to a cart with white adhesive tape, adjacent to a white plastic board where strategy could be mapped out with marking pens. A few feet away, one nurse counted scalpels, sutures, tongs, tweezers, and absorbent pads that were arranged in rows on a tray that flanked the table. Another nurse covered Mrs. Bridgewater with sterile paper drapes, her body, her face, disappearing beneath the pale green blankets. A third nurse, her gloves already on, helped Ed Holly into his gloves before he stepped to the table, gently rubbing Mrs. Bridgewater's orange scalp with his thumb as if to reassure her. "Shall we, people?" he said as his eyes made a sweep of the assembled parties.

The human brain is housed in a hard bone box and bathed in a crystalline fluid. No organ in the body is more fragile than the brain; none is better protected. On the exterior of the head, even the hair offers a bit of protection from glancing blows and extremes of temperature; the scalp is an amalgam of epidermal and dermal tissue, fat, blood vessels, and tough connective fibers. The cranium beneath the scalp is not one bone, but eight of them, fused together in ragged joints called sutures. The interlocking bones of the cranium form a rigid dome, guarding the brain like a bony vault.

Between bone and brain are the meninges, three distinct layers of protective membrane. Outermost is the dura mater, the "hard mother," a thick, leathery, unstretchable sheath; beneath it is the "spider's web," the arachnoid, an elastic membrane that encloses and confines the cerebrospinal fluid in the so-called subarachnoid space. The pia mater, "soft mother," is the thinnest layer of the meninges. It clings closely to the brain's irregular surface and supplies the surface with blood.

The brain has a ravenous need for blood. It receives about one-fifth of the body's total blood supply—one and a half pints per minute—yet it accounts for only about one-fiftieth of the body's total weight. Unable to store oxygen or glucose—as muscles can, for example—the brain depends on its large and steady blood supply for its constant nourishment, oxidizing about 400 kilocalories of glucose each day, roughly one-sixth of the whole body's glucose consumption.

In addition to delivering an uninterrupted flow of oxygen and glucose, blood is the raw material from which the cerebrospinal fluid is created. Choroid plexuses, tiny swirls of blood vessels that lie in the ventricles—four linked cavities deep within the brain—continually transform components of the blood into a clear fluid that fills the ventricles and flows, via ducts, to the subarachnoid rim of both the brain and the spinal cord. The fluid protects the brain and spinal cord from careening dangerously into the hard cranium and vertebrae that surround them each time the head is turned or the back bent.

Ed Holly began his assault on Mrs. Bridgewater's meningioma by slicing a three-sided flap in her scalp near her hairline, laying the four-inch square of skin back along the hinge of its uncut side, exposing the yellow frontal bone of her skull, quickly stopping the flow of blood from the incision with rows of metal clamps called hemostats. He scraped away the bone's waxy film—the periosteum—before he asked for the drill.

"Test it, sir," said the nurse as she handed him the drill, connected by a hose to its power source in the ceiling. The drill whined and Holly watched its bit spin for a moment before he put it to work. As the drill augered in, moaning as its bit bore down, flecks of bone flew up and away from the deepening hole, littering the drapes that covered Mrs. Bridgewater and splattering Ed Holly's shirt, until a guide on the shaft of the bit stopped it at its proper depth. Three more half-inch diameter holes followed, the four of them marking the corners of a three-inch square. With the protruding blade of a pneumatic band saw, Holly cut four straight lines, connecting each hole to the next, severing the square from the bone to which it belonged, then lifting it out with two pairs of forceps.

Before he made an incision in the dura, the first layer of meninges, Holly's assistant—dressed like the rest of us except that her cap had a festive floral pattern—used a tool that looked like a plastic turkey baster to "irrigate" the opening, squirting it with saline solution to clean away fragments of bone and bits of blood. A second nurse took the piece of Mrs. Bridgewater's skull and placed it in a bath of saline in a stainless-steel dish, where it would remain until the surgery was all but finished.

"How you doing?" Ferrier asked me in a whisper.

"Okay," I said. "With the drapes, it's as though she really isn't a part of this."

"The drapes are important to help keep things aseptic, but it's probably just as well to depersonalize it a bit, too, so the surgeon can focus in on just what's under his hands."

The anesthesiologist, still crouched on his stool, steadily checked his instruments and made notations on a plastic clipboard. One nurse made a steady series of trips between a supply cabinet and the draped tray adjacent to the operating table, where another nurse arranged and counted tools. The assistant in the floral cap, standing on a short footstool that made her as tall as Ed Holly, stayed close to the square cavern now, keeping it clean, the liquid that squirted from her baster dripping into a plastic bag, big as a garbage sack, suspended from the end of the table. After Ed Holly had used a small scalpel to sever a flap of Mrs. Bridgewater's dura, then did the same to the thin arachnoid layer, exposing for the first time the soft white custard that was her tumor, he asked Ferrier and me if we would like to watch its resection from over his shoulder. "Close as you want," he said as we moved behind him, the lights flooding the gaping focus of his endeavors and illuminating the red stubble of a recent haircut visible beneath his cap. "Only one rule," he said without turning to look at us. "If you faint, please fall *away* from the table."

Twenty minutes into the surgery now, its pace slowed markedly. Although the tumor—so big it filled the bone window through which it was visible—was contained by a thin capsule, the delineation between brain and capsule appeared subtle, obscured by the similarities in color and texture of the two tissues, obscured as well by the steady ooze of blood and cerebrospinal fluid. Working in concert with his assistant, Holly began the delicate, deliberate work of finding the frontier of the tumor, cauterizing each minute blood vessel that reached into it with the burning tip of an electrical probe, then, its flow of blood blocked, severing the vessel with a scalpel. Joined in this slow and rhythmic series of procedures was the placement of absorbent gauze squares, called patties, into the opening to blot the seeping fluids, each white patty trailing a long black, X-ray-opaque string to prevent it from becoming lost once it was soaked with blood. As Holly lifted each stained patty out with a pair of forceps and placed it in a tray, a nurse, who seemed to have no other job, counted it to be sure that the number of patties that went into the cranial cut corresponded with the number that came out.

Half an hour after Holly had begun to separate the soft meningioma from the shell of brain and membrane in which it had grown, Roger Burns walked into the operating room, his hands held away from his shirt. "Is that you, John?" he asked Ferrier as he plunged his hands into the translucent gloves a nurse held open for him. "What's the occasion?"

"Protecting my patient," Ferrier said.

"Ed's not as bad as all that," Burns said, the creases at his eyes signaling the smile that was hidden by his mask. "How's it coming?" he asked Holly as the assistant who had been standing on the stool stepped down and moved away.

"No show stoppers. Big tumor though. I'm having trouble getting underneath it. I think I'll need to debulk it a bit so I can fold it in on itself and get some room to work."

"Any evidence of malignancy?"

"Not to look at. Seems to be a straightforward meningioma. But with this size, I'm amazed this lady functioned as well as she did." As he spoke, Ed Holly made a quick, deft cut in the dome of the tumor itself and, with the help of forceps in his left hand, lifted out a pebble-sized piece of tissue. "Let's biopsy this," he said to the assistant in the floral cap as he dropped it into a tray. The anesthesiologist announced that he was going to give Mrs. Bridgewater a pint of blood, and readied the drip line that would deliver the blood into a vein in her arm. Roger Burns pattied the hole Ed Holly had made and used the hollow, stainless-steel tip of an aspirator to suck out still more fluid from the surrounding cavity before the two surgeons began to work in tandem to collapse the tumor into the hole Holly had cut. As they pulled the edges of the tumor toward its center with forceps, a quarter-inch space appeared between its lateral edges and the tissue that was pressed beside it. *There it was. There was Mrs. Bridgewater's brain*. I saw only a glimpse; it looked much like the tumor looked—gelatinous, fragile, more readily red matter than gray, but it was brain nonetheless. I was seeing, as if through a keyhole, a bit of cortex where thousands of neurons were still engaged in their synaptic chatter despite Mrs. Bridgewater's anesthetic sleep, despite this drastic surgical invasion. I was seeing—it struck me as such good fortune—a sliver of living frontal lobe.

The two men worked for half an hour or more, Burns steadily cauterizing vessels, the tool he held in his hands crackling like an insect lamp as it seared, causing a faint odor of burned tissue to drift toward us, the aspirator that he alternately applied sucking loudly, Holly probing with scalpel and forceps, tugging gently at the encapsulated tumor, finally reaching underneath it and lifting it out in a single piece, bigger still than a golf ball, Burns quickly cauterizing the several tiny vessels that had torn as the tumor came away.

Again the turkey baster was employed to irrigate the open cavity, and the aspirator vacuumed away the fluids and the scattered detritus of tissue. All that remained within the bony cavern now were the flaps of meninges and a concave portion of Mrs. Bridgewater's cortex, its surface a pale and rumpled gray sponge riddled with small red blood vessels. The longitudinal fissure, which separated her right and left cerebral hemispheres, was visible as it coursed, top to bottom, across the cut. "Here," said Holly, stepping aside and motioning me forward. "Have a look. Her frontal lobes will reshape somewhat and fill up part of the space the tumor occupied, but I doubt that they will fill it all. As far as function goes, we'll have to see, but it came away pretty cleanly for a tumor its size, so she may see quite a bit of improvement."

"If the lobes don't expand back out completely," I asked, "will the space there just be hollow?"

"Whatever space there is will fill with cerebrospinal fluid, which is dandy. All we do is close her up nice and tight and leave her to her own devices. I'll order Dilantin as soon as we finish to guard against the possibility of surgery-induced seizures, and Dr. Ferrier may want to continue it for quite a while, I don't know, but other than that. . . ."

Finishing the surgery was solely Ed Holly's province. Roger

Burns stepped away from the table, shed his gloves, and said good-bye before he walked out of the operating room, en route to the surgeon's lounge where he could read the morning paper before, an hour from now, he would be back at work at this same table. Holly's assistant in the floral cap repositioned her stool and stepped onto it, the two working quickly to tie tiny sutures into the layers of meninges, sealing the flaps, replacing the piece of frontal bone, which was deemed healthy enough to reknit with the bone around it (a plastic prosthesis would have been used otherwise), stapling the bone securely in place—Mrs. Bridgewater's cranium domed and solid again—suturing her scalp with black thread that gave her bald pate the appearance of having been through a brawl.

The anesthesiologist, silent and secretive throughout the operation, still crouched on his stool, clipboard still in hand, his job still very much in progress. The nurses, their demeanors noticeably cheerier now, completed the counting of tools and patties— nothing had been sewn inside—and Holly's assistant began to bandage Mrs. Bridgewater's head as he thanked them all. Then he sighed as if officially to pronounce the procedure finished.

Ferrier and I walked with Holly through a maze of doors to a waiting room where Mrs. Bridgewater's daughters sat together on a long couch. The appearance of three of us, still dressed in scrubs, seemed to make them anxious for a moment before Holly, his mask around his neck now like a bib, his face round and freckled, smiled and said it had all gone well.

This was the reward of surgery, wasn't it? The enveloping tension, the labored pace, and the very real possibility of failure was mitigated by this ceremonial announcement, this assurance to family members and friends that the invasion was over, the surgeon-soldier's mission accomplished. I had noticed beforehand that when celebrated heart surgeons and the men who had recently removed the president's cancerous colon tumor went before the television cameras they invariably still wore their scrubs, and now I understood why. A stethoscope around one's neck was no kind of uniform at all compared to the baggy blue blouse and trousers, the cap—sweat-stained at the temples and forehead— and the dangling mask. They comprised a uniform that belonged to a small elite, to a secret and proud society, one whose work was seldom watched, whose healing rituals were seldom observed.

The Greek root of the word "surgery" is *cheirourgia*, meaning a skill or handicraft, and what a mysterious craft these surgeons have mastered, most of the rest of us believe. And surely they believe it themselves. They are somehow akin to the magicians who draw rabbits out of hats and saw ladies in boxes in two, bowing for applause, but never betraying their methods, their tricks. "It went very well," Ed Holly said—and that was all he said. He could have explained, "We put your mother into a sleep so deep it was almost death. We sliced her open and drilled into her skull, cut out a ballooning growth beside her brain, and despite it all, we made her better." But there would have been no magic in that kind of statement. It would have said too much.

"We're so appreciative," said one of Mrs. Bridgewater's twins, laying a copy of *Redbook* on the couch.

"Yes," said her sister, tears welling in her eyes, "yes, we really are."

Ed Holly smiled again and nodded; he said he thought their mother would be awake within an hour—two at the most—then excused himself. Ferrier told them he would see them and their mother again at the end of the day, and we walked back into the surgical wing—the secretive, enigmatic place where incisions are made.

I felt strangely euphoric for the next few hours—relieved that I had not embarrassed myself by falling away from the table, lucky to have been a waking visitor to this secluded world of medical handiwork, awestruck, I'm sure, to have seen *inside* another human being, if only briefly—to have visual assurance now that the gray brain that had been my occupation for these months was indeed lodged inside each skull.

But my euphoria vanished by midafternoon. It fell flat and empty as I listened to Ferrier's conversation with Wayne Byers, the melanoma patient he had mentioned to me—a man my age, a newspaper reporter who did the kind of work I did, who, like me, had hoped to encounter old age. But Wayne Byers was host, as he sat in the deep leather chair across from Ferrier's desk, to five malignant tumors—one in his left lung, another in his liver, three in his brain.

Ferrier had first seen Wayne Byers in April, in the emergency room at County Hospital, where he had come in the dark hours of one morning complaining of an unremitting headache. He had had the headaches for several nights, but the one that brought him to the hospital was far worse than the rest. It would subside a bit when he got up and walked, or sat in a chair, but in bed the pain was unbearable. He could not keep fluids or food down, and he would sometimes see strange sparkling lights. He had never had similar headaches, he told Ferrier, but his mother had suffered migraines for as long as he could remember. It was Wayne's girlfriend, pale and frightened, standing beside the table on which he lay, who told Ferrier about the enlarging mole on Wayne's chest when Ferrier asked about his recent medical history. Wayne had scratched the mole in his sleep since winter, she said, and she had noticed not long ago that it was gone.

Concerned that Wayne's sudden onset of headaches might be caused by a hemorrhage or by dangerous intracranial pressure caused by a buildup of cerebrospinal fluid, Ferrier ordered a CAT scan that night and waited at the hospital while it was performed. The films he saw forty-five minutes later bore disturbing news. A large hematoma—a hemorrhagic clot—was visible in Wayne's right frontal lobe, a very likely cause of the headaches. Another mass, poorly defined, was located in his left occipital lobe; a third, very small mass appeared in his right parietal lobe. The frontal hematoma could have had several causes, but the presence of two other brain lesions made it likely that it represented a hemorrhage within a tumor—malignant tumors, in particular, are prone to hemorrhage because they are intricately laced with blood vessels. Ferrier was afraid that the CAT scan offered all too convincing evidence that the multiple sites in Wayne's brain were the metastatic spread of malignancy from elsewhere in his body— tumors originating in the brain are seldom seen in multiples— and the mole, now unavailable for biopsy, was a sadly suspicious source.

Ferrier admitted Wayne to a ward that night, and the following day he ordered an angiogram—to better define the nature of the hematoma—and a series of bone and liver scans, blood tests, and chest and abdominal X rays were performed in search of other potential tumors. The new films revealed what appeared to be a lesion deep in Wayne's liver as well as a lesion lodged in his lung.

Yet before a firm diagnosis of metastatic disease could be made, at least one of the lesions would have to be biopsed.

No malignant cells were found on his skin surrounding the site where the mole had been; repeated efforts to extract a piece of the liver lesion with a so-called "skinny needle" were unsuccessful. Finally, in consultation with Roger Burns and an oncologist named Larry Schorr, Wayne agreed to a craniotomy. Burns would open his cranium, locate the hematoma, remove it and as much of the tumor as possible, and a biopsy of the tumorous tissue would either confirm or dispel the three doctors' presumption that a small malignant tumor of the melanin-producing cells—the pigmented cells that give color to the skin—had spread via the bloodstream to the three other organs.

Wayne was operated on a week after he had first come to the emergency room. The resection of the hematoma and surrounding tumor was successful, but the pathological report confirmed what had seemed almost certain: the tumor contained malignant melanoma cells.

Following the surgery, Wayne was principally in the care of Dr. Schorr, who began twelve days of radiation therapy to the lesions in his brain in early May—as soon as his craniotomy incision had healed. Four weeks later, Schorr began a five-day systemic trial of DTIC, an anticancer drug regimen that, statistically, had a one in five chance of killing some of the several tumors. At the end of June, scans showed that the five tumors were still present in his brain, liver, and lung, but none appeared to have grown, and a new, sixth tumor was not in evidence.

The DTIC had made Wayne bald by the time Ferrier saw him on June 26. He was pale and weak and more than a little blasé about his medical ordeal—"frontal lobish," Ferrier would call it, an unemotional, sometimes slightly euphoric "affect" that was common with a variety of kinds of frontal lobe damage. Wayne was unable to return to the newspaper, his girlfriend was in the process of moving out of his apartment, the periodic sieges of DTIC made him violently ill, minor radiation burns on his scalp were slow to heal, but, sure, he said, everything was fine. Other than this detached affect, Wayne's neurological exam that day was entirely normal. His only complaint was continuing mild headaches, but he had suffered no excruciating headaches since he had gone on a daily dosage of Decadron in the days before his surgery.

Wayne's exam was normal again on the August day that I met him, and he was still soft-spoken and matter-of-fact, his answers to Ferrier's questions never composed more than a few words. He wore a white gauze turban around his head, evidence of a second surgery performed just ten days before, surgery deemed necessary because the tumor in his frontal lobe again had begun to enlarge. He wore a snap-button western shirt, khaki pants, and sneakers; his hands were folded in his lap, and he seemed to scan the bookcase behind Ferrier as he spoke, his words a barely audible mumble. I could not imagine that a reporter could be so shy, so silently reserved—but surely this Wayne was much different from the one who had been a feature writer. This Wayne, his frontal lobe impinged by an insidious swelling, had acquired a pallid personality that was simply one more grim product of his disease.

"Yeah. Yeah, I feel okay," Wayne told Ferrier when he pressed him to be open. "Between the weeks when I'm taking the chemo, I feel pretty normal. Just kind of run down, I guess."

"Headaches?"

"Not really. Oh, occasionally, but none of them are a problem."

"Are you sleeping well?"

"Yeah. Pretty good."

"How have you been spending your time?"

"Oh, at home mostly. Reading. TV. A friend from the paper and I are supposed to go hiking tomorrow."

"Well, you must be feeling pretty good if you feel like getting out into the mountains," Ferrier said encouragingly.

"Yeah. We'll see. Dr. Schorr said I can do pretty much anything."

"How's your girlfriend? I don't remember her name."

"Jean. Fine."

"Are you still seeing her?"

"She comes over sometimes. I think I probably scare her a little. But. . . ."

I am not sure why, but I wanted Wayne to cry, to tell Ferrier that he was frightened, to say he hated to be alone. Or why wasn't he cheerful, offering platitudes about making the most of each day, telling Ferrier he had come to appreciate so much that he used to take for granted? I would have been glad to hear that he had renewed a lapsed religious faith, but he said nothing of the sort. No, everything was fine. No, nothing was worrying him. Yeah, sure, he felt okay.

Ferrier was uncomfortable as well. I could sense that Wayne's detachment frustrated him and left him feeling helpless. He wanted Wayne to be vulnerable, to be anxious, confused, full of questions. But Wayne needed no help, and there was little for Ferrier to say. Somehow, it seemed to me that Wayne's illness was not something he should experience as if he were sleepwalking. Shouldn't illness be, by its nature, emotive, cathartic, even catastrophic? Shouldn't we all *feel* the ugly claws of the crab when it comes to that? Perhaps not. Perhaps Ferrier and I should have considered Wayne fortunate, lucky that the swelling inside his head made him passive, detached, disinterested. Perhaps it was a kind of blessing that Wayne was simply okay.

Ferrier assured Wayne before he left that he was doing very well—at least he could offer him his optimism. The two of them agreed that Wayne would remain on the Decadron, as well as the Dilantin that had been prescribed to prevent surgery- or tumor-caused seizures. Since his ordeal began, he had not suffered a seizure, and Ferrier was hopeful that he could remain free of them. Already assaulted by five tumors, and by the X rays and drugs that were meant to kill them, surely Wayne could be spared the trauma of seizures.

Wayne agreed that he would return in a month. As he stood in the doorway, he seemed surprised that Ferrier would offer to shake his hand, but he acquiesced. "Have a good hike tomorrow," Ferrier told him.

"Yeah," Wayne said. He seemed to have forgotten about the hike.

This is the disease that is synonymous with death, the disease that one in three Americans will encounter during their lifetimes and that nearly half will *survive*, but which, nonetheless, is regarded by most of us as the most terrifying diagnosis imaginable. The cancers—oncologists now identify about 120 different malignant diseases—are the maladies in which the genes that

208

have, for decades, successfully directed the creation of normal cells undergo a mysterious transformation. Permanently altered, these *oncogenes*, no longer bound by their genetic codes, produce—through a process that remains unknown—drastically abnormal cells, ugly, crude, quickly growing cells that eventually invade the healthy tissues that surround them.

It is currently presumed that virtually all of us regularly produce mutant cells that are quickly killed by our bodies' immune systems. But somehow, in some of us, small masses of mutant cells are able to elude otherwise-vigilant white blood cells. These tumorous cells grow unchecked, strangely unrecognized as the rampant, rule-breaking invaders that they are. The tumors, having no purpose but their own chaotic replication, rob nutrients and blood supply from surrounding cells, destroying those cells in the process, eventually interfering with the function of the organs in which the tumors arise, their satellite cells often spreading, still undetected, to distant sites where new tumors begin their grotesque growth.

As recently as the 1930s, virtually all cancers were lethal within five years following diagnosis. Notwithstanding the surgical resection of tumors and their treatment with high-dosage radiation—therapies in practice since early in the century—malignant diseases usually meant death. By the 1950s, surgical and radiation therapies had grown far more sophisticated, and they were joined by "chemotherapies"—potent and often highly toxic drugs designed to kill microscopic cancer cells throughout the body's systems. This triad of therapies made it possible for roughly one in five cancer patients to survive for the five years that are generally considered evidence of a cure. By 1970, one in three cancer victims reached the five-year plateau; today, the survivors' numbers have grown to very nearly one in two. Immunotherapies, like interferon, designed to goad the immune system into joining the cancer-killing effort, are now also a part of the therapeutic arsenal, and geneticists and cellular biologists are gaining ground in their efforts to come to grips with the mutational transformations that begin the cancer process.

The five-year survival rates of some types of primary not-yet metastasizing tumors are now remarkably high—93 percent for thyroid cancer; breast cancer, 74 percent; 85 percent for uterine cancer; and even 80 percent for melanoma that is treated before it spreads. These statistics surely represent, in part, better methods of treatment, but perhaps most important, they reflect successful efforts to convince the public that early detection plays a fundamental role in survival—the survival rates for all types of metastatic cancers are still discouragingly low. And several intractable primary cancers remain very difficult to treat successfully. Only about 15 percent of patients with stomach and lung cancers are ultimately cured; primary brain tumors remain fatal for four patients in five.

"Our ability to pick up tumors in the brain has taken a big leap forward with the CAT scan," Ferrier said, still at his desk at the end of the afternoon, both of us still unsettled, disturbed by Wayne's demeanor and by his dark prognosis. "The MRI could do an even better job." The MRI, or magnetic resonance imager (until recently called an NMR, or nuclear magnetic resonance scanner) is a new diagnostic device just now being installed in hospitals around the country. Unlike the CAT scan, which measures the absorption and displacement of X rays by the body's bones and tissues and, with the aid of a computer, transforms those measurements into a visual image, the MRI measures the displacement of hydrogen atoms within tissues of varying density when bombarded by intense, but harmless, magnetic fields. "A CAT scan can pick up a tumor as small as about one centimeter. The MRI may be twice that good. And finding tumors early is still the name of the game. The earlier you start to treat a malignant tumor, obviously, the less the chance it will have to spread, and the more likely it is that radiation or chemotherapy, or both, can kill it. Or even that some very benign surgical therapy can be curative. The tragedy with Wayne—and you never know about this sort of thing—is that if that mole had been excised right when it started to get weird, there might have been a very different outcome."

"What are his chances now?" I asked.

"Oh, God, they aren't good at all," he said, surprised that I had to ask.

"I don't understand why neither the radiation nor the chemotherapy seem to be making much headway for him."

"Malignant tumors are tenacious. They are good at one thing, and that is growing, despite our crude assaults on them. I suppose you could theoretically give every cancer patient enough radiation to completely zap every tumor, but you'd surely kill the patient in the process. Even at its best, radiation is a very clumsy therapy. It can't distinguish healthy cells from mutant ones. All it can do is destroy tissue. And surgery doesn't ever have much hope of being a curative therapy because so much cancer is microscopic, and it's interlaced with healthy, essential tissue. You can't simply remove an entire liver or a whole brain. That's why chemotherapy is the ultimate magic. It isn't yet, God knows, but that's where the real hope is.

"The reason Wayne lost his hair, and the reason why he and other patients get so horribly ill on DTIC and many of the other current anticancer drugs is because they act on fast-growing cells. Malignant cells grow very rapidly, so these drugs are able to find them and kill them, often very effectively. But they also kill hair cells because hair grows quickly. And the cells in the lining of your gut undergo a complete turnover every eight days or so— very fast—so inevitably, the chemotherapies attack them, too. What has to come, and I'm sure it will at some point, is the magic bullet for malignancies, a drug or drugs that only recognize and act on mutant cells. There is a lot of exciting work going on now to try to find viruses or antibodies that can lock on to only one cell type—the patient's cancer, for instance. If they can be found, it might be relatively easy to chemically attach anticancer drugs or radioactive substances to them. Together, they would be a very precise and sophisticated kind of attack."

"Wouldn't it be preferable to concentrate on finding an effective way to prevent cancers in the first place?"

"Well, my God, you can't imagine the amount of cancer research that is being done—on every conceivable front. But no, I doubt we'll have a cancer vaccine in the next decade, if ever, partly because there seem to be several causes."

"So you don't think viruses will eventually be implicated in cancer the way they seem to be with so many other diseases?"

"There are several animal cancers that are known to be caused by viruses, but there are just one or two human cancers—such as a lymphoma that occurs only in Africa—that are caused by an identifiable virus. Otherwise, the researchers simply haven't

211

found a single or several viruses at the root of cancer—and it isn't for lack of looking. So no, I don't think virology is where the big breakthrough will come. And there may never be a breakthrough that is just overwhelming, say, similar to the polio vaccine or something. We may simply continue to get better and better at treating specific cancers."

"But prevention is out of the question?"

"No, of course not. Prevention is really where we are having success today. Early detection is a kind of prevention—preventing cancer from getting a firm hold, from getting out of hand. And we know unquestionably that some cancers have environmental causes that everyone is aware of—dozens of toxic chemicals, exposure to radiation, tobacco, several dietary triggers, obviously. We know exactly how to prevent lung cancer, for instance. If no one smoked, lung cancer would almost disappear. The picture isn't nearly as straightforward with other cancers. The dietary question is very complicated; we really can't say absolutely what foods *must* be avoided, what foods *must* be eaten. And I don't mean to imply that all types of cancer have an environmental trigger. I don't think that's the case at all. I had a patient in his sixties who died about a month ago. He had a glioblastoma—a very lethal, fast-growing tumor in his left temporal lobe whose first symptoms were some language problems and confusion. Before he died he became completely aphasic. He had worked for something like twenty years at a nuclear weapons processing plant, handling plutonium. It's very hard for me not to presume that his cancer had an environmental cause, especially because the documented cancer incidence among workers at that plant is pretty high. I can't prove medically that the exposure to plutonium gave him his cancer, but I can certainly suspect it. On the other hand, with most of my brain tumor patients—patients with primary tumors—I don't see evidence of any obvious environmental cause. Somehow, in some awful way that I wish I understood, these people just have glial tissue that begins to mutate, and to grow."

Ferrier still had dictation to finish, and he had promised a lawyer that he would finally review the typed deposition she had delivered to him two weeks before, but he wanted to check on Mrs.

212

Bridgewater. Coatless on this rare occasion, he walked across the street to the hospital, and I trailed him in the sweltering heat, the sun roasting the black asphalt, making it spongy beneath our feet.

Mrs. Bridgewater lay in a bed in the intensive care unit, her eyes closed, her head wreathed with gauze. A nurse adjusted the saline drip above her bed. "Has she been awake at all?" Ferrier asked.

"Yes. Off and on. She's said a few words."

"Mrs. Bridgewater," Ferrier called, touching her forearm, then calling her name again. "Can you wake up for a minute?" She opened her eyes and scanned blankly, groggily, before she found his face. "Hello, there. How are you?" he asked.

"Fine," she said, her voice faint.

"Are you in any pain?"

"I don't think so." She was groggy enough that she wasn't sure.

"Do you know who I am?" he asked. She closed her eyes again, too sleepy to respond, but he pressed her. "Mrs. Bridgewater, wake up. Tell me. Do you know who I am?"

She said. "Well, I guess you're Dr. Ferrier, aren't you?"

"Very good. And where are you? What is the place?"

"Hospital." Mrs. Bridgewater was too tired to talk, but Ferrier insisted. He asked her what date it was, and she knew the date. He asked her who had come to the hospital with her, and she knew her daughters' names. She could raise her arms and legs; she could squeeze Ferrier's fingers tightly in her fists. She was *alive* again.

I wanted to whisper to her, "My God, Mrs. Bridgewater, you're some kind of Lazarus. Do you know what has happened? Do you know what I saw them do to you?" For some reason, seeing her now was the most astonishing event surrounding her surgery. Almost a corpse when I first saw her that morning, her head painted orange and so very sound asleep, she had seemed to be someone other than herself. Then, her cranium opened like the top of an egg, she was simply a specimen; the rest of her hidden beneath the sterile drapes at that point, only her tumor bore attention. She seemed to disappear, almost to die. She had no role in the procedure other than to be the sleeping subject who allowed her head to be invaded by saw and scalpel. But now, only hours later, her bald head hidden by white bandages, she was whole again, stapled and stitched and aware of who she was. It remained to be seen whether the surgery would cure her confusion and end the inappropriate emotional responses, but it was immediately clear that the procedure had done her no harm. The tumor was gone and she had safely returned from the table. Ed Holly was right; it had gone very well.

Ferrier sat on the edge of her bed. "Do you remember when I saw you last night, I asked you to remember something for me?"

"You did?"

"Yes. Think real hard. What did I want you to remember?"

Mrs. Bridgewater closed her eyes, and she kept them closed. It was a difficult question. "Oh. Well, I don't know. Did you ask me to remember my flowers?"

Ferrier was scribbling in Mrs. Bridgewater's chart when he was paged over the hospital's intercom. He called the switchboard operator and was transferred to the emergency room. He listened silently to the person on the other end, then said he would be right there.

It was Wayne Byers. His friend from the newspaper had stopped by his apartment after work to make plans for tomorrow's hike and had found Wayne on his kitchen floor, his body convulsing wildly. The seizure subsided during the wait for the ambulance to arrive, but Wayne had a second seizure en route to the emergency room, and a third seizure had begun just before Ferrier was paged.

Lying on an examining table, surrounded by three nurses, an ER physician, and Ferrier, Wayne's arms and legs flailed violently, crashing into the table, into his torso and head, hitting the people who stood beside him. There was no break between each seizure now; one followed another with frightening incessancy.

"The friend who found him said he ran out of Dilantin a week ago, and he's pretty sure he didn't refill it. His level is zippo," said the doctor on duty. "I assumed you'd want to go ahead and load Dilantin now. The drip's all set."

"Damn it! He told me an hour-and-a-half ago that he was taking it twice a day," Ferrier said. "Yeah. Okay, let's get it started."

The five people had to struggle to secure Wayne's limbs with straps, fighting to quiet one arm long enough to insert a needle into his forearm and to secure the needle with tape, but they were successful within a minute or two, and in three minutes, Wayne was still. His eyes were open and glassy, glazed by the storm of seizures; his tongue was swollen and sticking out, his breathing labored. The doctors and nurses stepped away when they were sure the seizures had stopped, their faces flushed, shining with perspiration.

"I guess you'll admit him, won't you?" one of the nurses asked Ferrier.

"I'll call in an admission note in just a minute."

"No rush," she said. She and another nurse walked out of the room and toward the receiving desk. The ER doctor had already gone to attend to another patient, but the third nurse remained, monitoring the drip, straightening Wayne's legs, laying his arms at his sides. Ferrier sat on a supply cabinet, his eyes red, his face damp and weary, staring at his patient.

"Are you okay?" I asked.

"This is exactly what we didn't want to have happen," he said, sounding as if he, too, had been betrayed by the onset of the seizures. "I mean . . . Jesus, the poor guy." He dropped his head, turning toward the wall. I walked away and left him alone.

8 Accidents

The summer was ending all too soon, and I was flying back to spend more time with Ferrier. New snow clung to the summits of the peaks, and from the air, the yellow leaves of aspen trees covered the mountains' shoulders like smooth and gleaming blankets.

Ferrier had had to drive to the city earlier in the day. He met my plane at the gate, and we rushed to get to his car, parked illegally at the curb of the airport's departure deck—the doctor tempting both fate and the circling tow truck by leaving it unattended. But the Saab had escaped impoundment, and we drove away—two desperadoes galloping ahead of a posse.

Cool air whipped at the car's open windows as Ferrier wove his way through traffic, trying to negotiate the forty miles between the airport and the suburban town where he lived and worked in a breakneck thirty minutes. He had come into the city that Monday to testify at a personal injury trial—one of his patients was suing the insurer of the man who, two years before, had smashed his car into hers, sending the patient's skull crashing into the windshield, her injuries resulting in temporal lobe epilepsy and what now seemed to be a permanent impairment of memory and intellect. Ferrier had been a crucial witness. The patient's lawyers had hoped that he could convince the jury that Barbara Bishop's disabilities were indeed major and that they would limit her throughout her life. But his testimony had taken an hour longer than he had expected it to, my plane was a half hour late, and Ferrier still had four patients to see at his office—the first one due in forty minutes—and he had wanted to make a stop to check on a young woman in County Hospital's intensive care unit who,

216

two nights before, had suffered a massive hemorrhage. I buckled my seat belt and braced my feet against the floor, for some reason reticent to remind Ferrier that it was a speeding automobile that had begun Barbara Bishop's problems.

"Part of me actually enjoys the legal work," he said as he downshifted, boxed in for a moment by two trucks. "It's a huge headache, and I sure as hell would never become one of those forensic-medicine characters, but when it's for my own patients, it can be interesting. Maybe just because it's different. This thing with Barbara Bishop, I bet she actually gets a pretty big award. The attorney for the insurance company seemed like a total dolt—unprepared, seemingly uninterested. You'd think those companies would have some very big guns representing them, but . . ."

"So you tried to make it sound like her life was totally ruined by the accident?"

"Have you met Barbara?"

"A couple of times."

"Well, then you have a sense of what has happened to her. The epilepsy is real, and there's no question that it was caused by the accident, but millions of people have epilepsy and function very normally. Barbara was an incredibly intelligent person, extremely bright, and now she doesn't remember how to get to the grocery store or the fact that she invited a friend over for lunch. It's possible that she could work again someday, but she probably won't. Her kids have begun to have problems, partly because their mother, who used to be terrific with them, now does all these goofy things. And all of it stems from the trauma she suffered when the guy ran the red light."

"But you surely made it sound as grim as you could on the witness stand."

"Well, I didn't lie, if that's what you mean. Everything I said is totally documented in her records. But sure, I was testifying to try to help her get some compensation and I tried to make the best case I could—which was a good one, I think, since the other side's lawyer didn't challenge a word I said. I don't see a doctor's role as being neutral in that kind of situation. She's my patient, so I'm on her side, and I wanted to do the best job I could of explaining just what that accident did to her."

Barbara Bishop, thirty-nine at the time, thin, lithe, and witty, was driving across town on an afternoon two Septembers before when her Japanese station wagon was sideswiped by a drunken man in a pickup truck. She did not remember the accident, nor could she now recall the events that had taken place in the weeks before she was hit or in the first three months following the accident. According to the medical reports made at the time, Barbara was unconscious for only a few minutes, and she was not hospitalized until a week after the accident, complaining of the onset of severe headaches, neck pain, nausea, dizziness, and loss of memory. Her hospital stay was short; the symptoms began to subside, and she had no more medical attention until the following April, when she reported to David Vincent, her family physician, that the headaches seldom bothered her now, and the dizziness was no more than a minor nuisance. But she was, nonetheless, still lethargic, depressed, and her sharp memory had never returned. "I'll walk into the kitchen for something, then I'll have to go back to the living room to ask my husband what it was I was going to get," she told Dr. Vincent. And there was something new: At least once a day she would experience a strange "nauseating sensation" that would soon include an unpleasant taste and smell, which Barbara described as eating melted Styrofoam, followed immediately by a period in which she seemed to "miss time," as though she had suddenly vanished. But it was only the experience of "coming back" at the end of each episode that made her aware of what had just happened. Dr. Vincent subsequently ordered an EEG, which revealed intermittent abnormal "slow" electrical activity in the region of her left temporal lobe. He then prescribed Dilantin, but Barbara took it for only three days before stopping it because, she later said, she was just too depressed to be on medication.

At the urging of the lawyer she had retained in her case against the drunk driver, and with the concurrence of David Vincent, Barbara did agree to begin seeing a psychiatrist. At the close of a series of sessions with Barbara during the summer months, the psychiatrist, Leon Bennett, wrote to Dr. Vincent that his diagnostic findings followed three "axes" or areas of progressive concern": "Axis I: Bereavement, complicated by ongoing loss and by the ongoing demands of litigation. Acute and atypical depression is present and a major depressive episode may at times be diagnosable." In simpler terms, Barbara, he believed, was grieving over the loss of her mental faculties much as someone would grieve over the loss of a loved one, and the grief would be hard to put to rest until the suit was settled. "Axis II: The possibility of a preexisting, nondisabling personality disorder. But it is not diagnosable at this time, given the acute psychopathology present." In other words, Barbara might have been psychologically disturbed before the accident, but he could not be sure because of her current mental disabilities. "Axis III: Postconcussion syndrome. Rule out epilepsy"—meaning he believed she certainly suffered the common posttraumatic symptoms that follow blows to the head—sleeplessness, headache, dizziness, lethargy, depression—and that the possibility of epilepsy had to be investigated. Were the bad tastes and smells and the periods of missing time evidence of temporal lobe epilepsy? It was Leon Bennett who sent Barbara to Ferrier for an evaluation of the question of seizures.

Ferrier first saw Barbara Bishop in September, a year before the trial. I had just begun following Ferrier and I remember that Barbara was lighthearted, animated, seemingly full of energy when she walked into his office, brimming with conversation and intrigued by the objects on his desk and the pictures on his walls. She tucked her feet under her when she sat in the chair opposite his desk and she immediately reached for a wooden letter opener, caressing it in her hands, staring at it, focusing so much attention on it that she had to ask Ferrier to repeat what he had said.

Her story took a long time to tell. She had no personal memory of the accident and it was hard for her to remember what she had been told about it. She remembered her childhood medical history, as well as the births of her children, but each recollection tended to spark a tangential train of thought and her comments would often run far afield before Ferrier, via a subsequent question, would bring her back to the subject she had abandoned. Barbara described herself as once having been very self-confident, certain of her own intellect, boldly dependent on it in her interactions with others. "I knew I could do anything I wanted to," she said. "I had a good head on my shoulders, and I used it. I loved school. I did graduate work in architecture, community development, water resources. I was interested in all kinds of things. I probably kept changing disciplines because it was only the academics that seemed really challenging. I didn't want to have to get a job."

When Ferrier focused on Barbara's mental status during the year since the accident, she grew sullen, suddenly quiet, tearful. She seemed at once to be both ashamed of her current self and sympathetic to her plight. Her voice now devoid of its energy, she listed a catalog of changes. "I get lost going places; I forget what I'm saying half the time. I have this weird tendency to say cruel or tactless things, which was never the case before. I'm irritable, irrational; I can't do simple math—balancing a checkbook is impossible. Socially, I've become a hermit. I can't concentrate. In a roomful of people I can't hear a single conversation; I hear them all, all at once, and it drives me crazy. I was an extrovert; I loved people, but now I'm just afraid."

Barbara began to sob when she described the battery of neuro-psychological tests that Leon Bennett had performed. "I knew the accident had screwed me up, but I had never confronted the extent of the change in me. Those tests were a terrible shock. I finally had to confront the fact that I had become basically stupid."

When the subject shifted to the issue of possible epilepsy, Barbara's descriptions of the strange gastric sensations, the bad tastes and smells, and her sense of "coming back" from an unsettling kind of absence—together with the abnormal EEG report contained in her records—quickly convinced Ferrier that an ongoing seizure disorder was a very strong possibility. When Barbara admitted in response to his further questions that on a few occasions she had fallen to the floor before she "came back"—that she had also bitten her tongue and become incontinent—Ferrier had to assume that a seizure focus in her left temporal lobe was also occasionally prone to generalize into a grand mal attack.

Following his examination of her, Ferrier told Barbara he was certain that the accident had sufficiently damaged her left temporal lobe to have caused an ongoing seizure disorder, one that was probably permanent, but that medication would very likely control. She was still reluctant to begin a regular drug regimen— and the notion of having to take Dilantin or some other seizure medication *forever* sounded hideous—but Ferrier told her she simply had no choice. When he added that successfully interrupting the seizure activity could possibly improve her memory, Barbara acquiesced.

During the succeeding months, four hundred milligrams of Dilantin each day made a marked difference. The periods of "missing time" that had occurred at least once a day now were as infrequent as once a week. The Dilantin seemed to erase what Barbara described as a cloud that had muddled her thinking, and amitriptyline, an antidepressant prescribed by Dr. Bennett, seemed to ease her depression. But through that winter and into the following spring, her memory and mentation did not improve. She still could not stand to be in a group of people, she still could not do simple math, and the realization of her loss still caused a kind of desperation. Barbara had to begin to keep a detailed appointment book, making entries to remind herself when her kids would be home from school, reminding her to check to see if the stove was off and to take her medication, reminding her of the days and times when a deposition was scheduled, or a strategy session with her lawyer was planned, or when she was due for yet another evaluation by a psychologist, a psychiatrist, or a neurologist—the seemingly endless series of examinations supposedly leading toward a settlement or a trial.

But there was no settlement. The drunk driver's insurance company would not agree that the epilepsy was caused by the accident, and it held out the opinion of a forensic psychiatrist that Barbara's disabilities were psychological rather than organic as proof that it should not settle. Richard Arkin, Barbara's lawyer, sent Ferrier a letter late in the summer. He apologized for the inconvenience, but the trial was now scheduled for late September, he said, and Ferrier would have to be subpoenaed.

"When I have to do depositions in the office," Ferrier said as we sped along the freeway, "I charge the same as if it's an evaluation of a new patient, $100 an hour. The lawyer has to wait until there's an opening; I certainly don't go out of my way for them. But when I actually have to go to court—and you either show up or they throw you in jail—I charge the hell out of the insurance companies that the lawyers work for—200 big ones an hour from the time I leave the office—partly because it's such a huge pain in the ass. We have to cancel a half day's or whole day's patients and figure out some way to reschedule them, squeeze them in at lunch, or whatever. And partly because I sort of think it's fair. They *always* ought to figure out a way to settle, for God's sake, or there ought to be other ways to judge what kind of compensation somebody deserves. This system where the insurance companies squeal like hell when they have to pay a claim and where the ambulance chasers live off the misfortunes of people who've been injured, using their dramatic skills to make the jury members cry, seems crazy. Of course, I'm making money from people's injuries, too, aren't I? Maybe there really isn't much difference, but it seems like there is. I can definitely feel guilty for charging what I do, but dammit, it serves them right for taking two whole years to settle this thing."

It was three o'clock. Ferrier's first patient was surely waiting for him, but he pulled into the doctors' parking area at the rear of the hospital instead of turning into his office. "This'll be quick," he said. "I need to keep close tabs on this woman for the next day or two." I followed him through the door and down a dark corridor. "She had a massive intracranial hemorrhage on Friday night— very interesting story—and Burns had to go in and clamp off her right carotid on Saturday, but it doesn't look like she's going to make it. Her EEG is virtually flat-line. No gag reflex. No response to pain since early yesterday. I've already talked a bit with her family about ending the life support. If we don't see any improvement before long, we'll hope they can make a decision. They want to—" He stopped in midsentence as we passed the waiting room near the intensive care unit. A man in his thirties, wearing jeans and a cotton sweater, his face full of the exhaustion that comes from endless waiting, leaned against the jamb of the open door. Beyond him, seated on a couch, were two older people, certainly husband and wife, the husband smoking a cigarette, the wife simply sitting. Ferrier slowed enough to smile and say hello. "I'll stop back after I've seen her," he added before he pushed through the swinging doors.

A few months before, I had watched Ferrier examine a brain-dead three-year-old boy, his fragile cerebrum also destroyed by a spill of blood, the child's face bespeaking the peace and perma-

222

nence of death while his heart still beat and his lungs, assisted by a respirator, still heaved with the ebb and flow of air. And I had seen Ferrier perform the same confirmatory tests on four other people whose ages made their deaths seem less unkind—their skin pale and wrinkled, almost hairless, their eyes fixed and open, as if they were asking when the end could come. In each case, I had watched the patient's final minutes with a sense of being present in the midst of something profound. The deaths seemed to me, spared as I was from the overwhelming sense of loss that a friend or family member would feel, less sad or tragic than transcendent. Something elemental was in process, something that, despite the web of tubes and hoses, seemed simple and direct, and that demanded reverent attention.

But watching Jayne Welty die was very different. She was thirty-three, dark and beautiful. Her hair had been combed recently, her brown eyes were open, and a clear tube was inserted into each nostril and held in place by a strip of white tape. A bandage covered the surgical incision on her neck, the skin at her throat was freckled, her hospital gown hugged her breasts. She reminded me of my wife, Karen; she reminded me of all the women I had ever thrilled to observe in secret, and I was shocked that my first reaction to this woman at the edge of death was to be attracted to her.

My second reaction was to think that she must not die. She was too young, too lovely, somehow her motionless body still suggesting so much life. I saw no resignation in Jayne Welty's face, no final understanding in her open eyes. This was simply sleep, wasn't it? Couldn't Ferrier wake her up and tell her she would be all right? Surely something could be done.

An intensive care nurse named Beverly had walked into the room with us. She stood by the bank of monitors that circled the head of the bed and spoke to Ferrier in a controlled yet compassionate voice that suggested Jayne was a special patient. "I've been checking for a pain response every hour or so. Still nothing. Her urine output has slowed a lot, less than 150 cc's since six this morning. But she's still tripping the respirator on her own. Pulse is steady."

"How much fluid is she getting?"

"Sixty cc's an hour."

223

Ferrier took a pen from his shirt pocket, picked up Jayne's hand, and pressed the shaft of the pen against her thumbnail, its paint scraped away by repeated testing. Ferrier squeezed her nail until he grimaced, but Jayne's arm did not withdraw. She remained motionless; her expression did not change. Next Ferrier lifted the bedcovers and similarly squeezed the nail of her large toe. He sighed when he finally released the pressure, when it was clear he could not elicit a response. "I'm going to need some ice water and a large syringe," he told Beverly.

"Sure," she said, and she left the room.

Bending over the bed, Ferrier tapped Jayne's cheeks, calling her name, telling her who he was, asking her to close her eyes. He blew into each eye, then touched each cornea with the tip of a cotton swab, but still there was no response. He laid his palm across her forehead and briskly turned her head from side to side—a test of the oculocephalic or "doll's eyes" reflex. Instead of moving in the direction opposite of her head rotation, as would have been normal, Jayne's eyes remained fixed and moved with her head. When Beverly returned, Ferrier filled the syringe with water and injected it into Jayne's left ear. A patient with intact brain-stem function would have turned her eyes to the left, toward the cold stimulus, in this test of the caloric reflex, but Jayne's eyes did not move. When he injected water into her right ear, still her eyes were fixed.

Ferrier sat on the edge of the bed, his hand on Jayne's forearm. "Jayne, are you going to come back to us?" he asked, as though she might actually offer him a response, but one was not forthcoming. Ferrier looked down, tapped his feet on the floor, and waited.

"I'm going to push to take her off," he said after a long silence, turning to look at Beverly. "What do you think?"

"There isn't much to pin our hopes to, is there?"

"How often is the family coming in?"

"Her husband's in for a bit every hour. Her parents not quite so often."

"I'll tell them they can stay in as much as they want now, if you don't mind. We'll try to arrange a family conference for this evening, and maybe we can reach a decision," he said as he stood. "Thanks, Bev."

"Sure, Doctor," she said, combing Jayne's hair away from her forehead with her fingers.

I stood outside the waiting room, but I could hear Ferrier explaining to Jayne's husband and parents that he had seen no change for the better. He told them that the slowed output of urine added to Jayne's poor prognosis, and he said he would like to meet with them and the rest of the family later. "We don't have to make any decisions this evening—and any decision will be yours to make—but I'm afraid it's time we all discussed taking her off the life support in a little more detail—what would be best for Jayne and best for you all."

"If she came off the machine, how long would she live?" asked a voice that must have been her mother's.

"Well, if we do decide to take her off, we'll only do so when we're certain that her brain is no longer functioning, that her brain is dead. So my opinion would be that she would already *be* dead at that point. In most situations like this, patient's hearts can keep pumping anywhere from a few minutes to several days. It's hard to be any more definite than that. But—"

"She wouldn't want to live on a machine," said the voice that belonged to her husband. "But you're sure? I mean that . . . that she can't. . . ."

"I want to wait a bit longer—till this evening, or even tomorrow morning. But yes, I'm basically as sure as I ever am." Ferrier's voice was faint from the place where I stood in the empty corridor. "But you need time to think about this, to talk about it. I can come back at about six o'clock and we'll all sit down together, if that's a good time for you."

"Her sisters will be here by then," her mother said.

"Good. I'll see you then."

"Thank you," someone said.

Ferrier caught my eyes as he left the room, pursing his lips as if to say there was nothing that could be said.

Jayne Welty lived outside San Francisco. She was a sales representative for a book publishing company and came to town frequently on business. For almost a year, she had been having an affair with a man who worked in a local bookstore. On Friday evening, they had had dinner together, then had gone to her hotel.

225

According to what Stan Singleton, her lover, later told Ferrier, Jayne had drunk only a glass or two of wine; she seemed to feel fine and was in good spirits. They went to bed sometime after midnight. Then, in the midst of making love, just as Jayne was reaching an orgasm, she suddenly went unconscious. Stan tried to rouse her, but could not. Ten minutes later, Jayne regained a groggy kind of consciousness, moaning, complaining that the light in the room hurt her eyes, vomiting, her limbs convulsing slightly before she became comatose again. Stan was worried, afraid, confused. What on earth could have happened? Could her exertion simply have knocked her out? Had she failed to tell him she had seizures? But by now, Jayne was breathing normally; the convulsing had stopped and she seemed to be in a deep and quiet sleep. Stan watched her sleep and worried for four more hours.

It was beginning to grow light when Stan became convinced that Jayne was not sleeping. He could not wake her, her limbs had begun to shake again, and she had wet the bed. He called for an ambulance. Ferrier got a call from County Hospital's emergency room at a quarter after six.

When Ferrier first examined Jayne, she was responsive to pain stimulus—she successfully pulled her hands and feet away from pressure on her nails—but her eyes were dilated, her neck stiff, reflexes virtually absent, and she had a temperature of 102°. Wanting to rule out the possibility of meningitis and in order to investigate the possibility of stroke, Ferrier performed a lumbar puncture and a CAT scan. The fluid he pulled from the tap needle was dark red, so bloody he almost hoped he had hit a vein, but a second puncture confirmed his fears—he had indeed extracted cerebrospinal fluid, the normally clear fluid now contaminated by a huge bleed in the subarachnoid space surrounding Jayne's brain and possibly in her brain itself. The CAT scan had shown that there likely was bleeding in the right frontal area of her cerebrum, and a subsequent angiogram pinpointed an aneurysm—a saccular weakness in the wall of a blood vessel—in her right internal carotid artery, just beyond the junction of the ophthalmic artery.

The hemorrhage had stopped, at least for the time being, but a second bleed was very possible and had to be prevented. The location of the aneurysm, however, made it impossible for a surgeon to be able to open her skull and directly approach and seal the artery near the source of the bleed. The only surgical option was to open Jayne's right common carotid artery as it rose through her neck, to insert a clamp around it, and to *slowly* close the clamp, maintaining the supply of blood to her right hemisphere primarily through her left carotid system and its network of interconnecting arteries at the so-called circle of Willis at the base of her brain.

Roger Burns was ready to operate by eight o'clock that morning, joined by Dwayne Steidel, the EEG technician, and by Ferrier, who closely monitored the electrical activity in Jayne's right hemisphere as Burns began to close the valve. Closing it too quickly could effectively infarct her whole right hemisphere; waiting too long to plug the artery's flow would allow the aneurysm the opportunity to rehemorrhage and do more damage. As the operation began, Jayne had been hyperventilated to decrease the pressure inside her skull and lessen the possibility of a fatal herniation—the tendency of a swollen brain to press the vital brain stem through the hole at the base of the skull. She had been given massive dosages of mannitol, a chemical that effectively draws fluids into blood vessels, also in hopes of reducing the pressure inside her skull. She had been given steroids to minimize tissue swelling, and she had been put deeper into coma with pentobarbital, a barbiturate that would slow the metabolic action in her brain, producing less lactic acid and other by-products of the oxidation of glucose that tend to retain fluids inside brain tissues.

With the valve in place in Jayne's common carotid artery, and the EEG electrodes in place on her scalp—the machine's needles tracing the frantic, rhythmic squiggle of her brain waves—Roger Burns began the slow process of shutting the artery's flow. Listening to Ferrier call out what evidence of right-sided slowing he saw on the tracing paper, Burns at last completely closed the plastic valve, the blood in her left carotid system successfully circulating into her right hemisphere, the right-side electrodes never indicating a dangerous amount of slowing.

Virtually all that could be done for Jayne had now been done. The hemorrhage was controlled as best it could be, brain fluids lessened, swelling minimized. But her cerebrum had suffered a massive injury, and as well, the huge hemorrhage had caused

227

dangerous, perhaps irreversible damage to other parts of her brain. Five hours after the surgery, Jayne had not regained consciousness, and a new EEG showed serious slowing in both cerebral hemispheres. Jayne's husband and her parents arrived at the hospital at eight o'clock that evening, while Dwayne and Ferrier were performing still another electroencephalogram, this one evidencing more deterioration, signaling a poorer prognosis.

Ferrier met Jayne's family outside the doors of the intensive care unit in a quiet corridor bathed in bright fluorescent light. He had spoken with her husband on the phone early that morning— Stan Singleton had placed the call from the emergency room. Singleton had said he was a friend and, before Ferrier got on the phone, explained that there had been an accident. Singleton had stayed at the hospital throughout the day, imagining, while he waited, the conversation he would surely have to have with the husband he had never met. As he was about to leave that evening, he told Ferrier he would be back early the following day. Thirty minutes after he had gone, Bill Welty and Jayne's parents arrived in a rented car.

Standing with them in the deserted hallway, Ferrier explained to Jayne's family what had transpired during the course of the long day. Ferrier was tired, relaxed now that there was little left for him to do, apprehensive about Jayne's chances, but hopeful as he offered his detailed account.

"What can cause something like this?" Jayne's father wanted to know.

"Well, the hemorrhage was almost certainly caused by an aneurysm, a weakness in the wall of that artery. Aneurysms are very prone to hemorrhage, but beforehand, you don't know they're there and they can rupture very suddenly. When patients are fortunate, the rupture is small and they get what we call a warning bleed, one that is small enough to do minimal damage but still show us that a weak artery has to be clipped. Unfortunately, in Jayne's case, the first bleed was a major one."

Bill Welty hardly spoke during that first meeting with Ferrier. He stood with his hands in the pockets of his pants, his lips parted, his eyes showing more shock than sadness. "Would it have helped if her friend had found her sooner?" he asked at last, his question finally bringing tears.

"Well . . . it, well no. Almost certainly not."

The word *stroke* derives from the Anglo-Saxon word *strican*, meaning to strike. It is synonymous with *apoplexy*, a word all but abandoned nowadays, one derived from the Greek word *apoplexia*, which means to strike down. Both words refer, of course, to the suddenness with which many strokes or apoplexies strike, often doing their foul damage in little more than an instant. In the medical parlance, the several types of stroke are known as *cerebrovascular accidents*—calamities caused not by invading viruses or by mysterious degenerative processes within the brain itself, but by abnormalities of the blood vessels that supply the brain. Brains affected by stroke are not diseased, but rather damaged— injured, sometimes destroyed, by hemorrhage or by occlusion, the blockage of a vessel's blood supply. Most stroke patients do suffer disease—hypertension and atherosclerosis (narrowing of arterial walls) are the diseases that account for the majority of strokes, but they are diseases of the cardiovascular system, not of the brain. The brain is a victim only because it is intricately laced with arteries, veins, and capillaries; because it receives so much of the body's blood supply; and because it is so fragile. Even a minor hemorrhage or a temporary occlusion can result in the permanent loss of function of a limb, of sight, or speech.

Aneurysms, ballooning weaknesses in vascular walls, are the principal causes of hemorrhage. Vessel walls in the brain that are congenitally weak or that have been stressed by disease, and that very often have been pounded from within for decades by high blood pressure, are very prone to rupture. Sudden exertions sometimes precipitate the ruptures, but they can occur at any time, without warning. Ruptured arteries are doubly destructive; the rupture drains much or all of the blood the artery normally carries, cutting off the part of the brain that is dependent on it, as well as creating a hematoma—a clot, an often enlarging pool of effused blood whose pressure destroys or inhibits normal neuronal activity. Whether lodged in the subarachnoid space beneath the layers of meninges, or within the brain itself, pressure from a hematoma can, depending on its size, cause temporary loss of localized function or complete brain failure, resulting in coma, permanent impairment, or death.

Occlusions of veins and arteries, caused either by a "thrombus" or an "embolus," precipitate the destruction of brain tissue by causing the "infarction" or death of neurons that normally receive essential oxygen and glucose via the blocked blood vessel. A thrombus is a blood clot formed at a site where blood flow is slowed by the roughening of a vessel wall or by the narrowing caused by the buildup of fatty deposits and other material. Thrombi can occur in the large carotid arteries that supply the head—causing, when they do, loss of function throughout much of one cerebral hemisphere—as well as in the many thousands of threadlike vessels that supply every fold in the gray-matter cortex, the brain stem, or cerebellum, their effects major or minor, or even asymptomatic, depending on their location.

An embolus, in contrast, is a plug of material—clotted blood, cholesterol, fat, air, bacteria, tumor tissue—circulating in the bloodstream that lodges between the walls of an artery it is too large to pass through, limiting or blocking the flow of blood to the arterial system that lies beyond the blockage. One of the most frequent causes of cerebral emboli are clots formed in the heart, most of them the result of chronic cardiac diseases, and about half of all circulating emboli thrown off by the heart travel to the cerebral arteries. A speck of embolic material that may cause no damage at all if it lodges in an artery that supplies other internal organs or the extremities, can result in severe and permanent neurological deficits if it lodges in a vessel that supplies the brain.

The pathological processes responsible for arterial hemorrhage and occlusion are obviously very different, as are the ways in which they do damage—one destroying areas of the brain or limiting their function by spilling blood, the other by damming the blood supply. And there are more distinctions: Occlusions from emboli tend to be peripheral, causing infarcts of the cerebral cortex. So-called berry aneurysms tend to form on the major arteries at the base of the brain, their hemorrhages flooding over the cortex or within deep brain structures.

Thrombi within blood vessels tend to occur slowly, often when patients are sedentary, relaxing or sleeping, their effects crescendoing over hours or even days. Hemorrhages and emboli, on the other hand, tend to cause sudden symptoms and to strike without warning. Hemorrhages strike during periods of stress or activity.

On first examination, patients who have suffered an infarct—either from a thrombus or an embolus—usually complain of weakness on one side of their bodies; they often suffer "homonymous hemianopsia"—the loss of the left or right field of vision in both eyes—speech is slurred or absent; many are dazed or confused, but few complain of pain. Patients who have just suffered a subarachnoid hemorrhage or a major hemorrhage inside their brains, in contrast, are usually in much more serious condition when they first receive medical attention; they are often comatose or semiconscious, their examinations tend to reveal a generalized neurological deficit more often than a localized loss of function. Those patients who can communicate often complain of head pain.

In most cases of infarct, the maximum degree of impairment is evident within three days following the accident, and most of the recovery that is possible usually will have occurred within three to six months. Infarcts are seldom fatal. As many as 75 percent of all intracranial hemorrhages, however—those that occur in the subarachnoid space and those that spill into or begin in the brain itself—result within hours or days in death.

When Ferrier had seen the last of his office patients on Monday afternoon, when his dictation was finished, his calls completed, and the thick stack of charts initialed, he returned—alone—to the hospital. I waited for him in the empty office, rummaging through the journals that had recently arrived, reading the current cartoons he and Putnam and the secretaries kept posted near the coffee machine. It was the first time in nearly a year of visits that I had declined an opportunity to trail behind him, to watch while he earned his living, observing his successes and embarrassing him with my presence when he occasionally did something dumb. But this was not a quick trip across the street to look at a CAT scan, or to test the strength and reflexes of a patient about to be operated on, or to quiet the seizures of someone who had been brought into the busy arena of the emergency room. This time Ferrier would simply sit in a dimly lit lounge filled with sofas and overstuffed chairs. He would simply talk with Jayne Welty's family about whether she should be allowed to die. I was somehow certain that I should not monitor their conversation.

"Sure, you can come. They've seen you with me before," Ferrier had told me as he hurried out the door. Earlier, it had seemed as if their decision was already almost made, and there had been no indication that Jayne's husband, her parents, or her two sisters would argue she must not be taken off her respirator, that a miracle must be awaited. Nonetheless, their decision, if they were to make one, was a profoundly private matter. So I decided to stay behind.

Ferrier's role in the slow and quiet conversation would be to answer their questions; he would outline the possibilities for organ donation if they were interested; he would presume what Jayne's future would be *on* the respirator, if they asked him to; he would listen as each one spoke. The conversation would be a quiet one and there would be long periods of silence. If Jayne's family had already found the strength to reach a decision, the meeting would be short and Ferrier would simply accede to their wishes. If they disagreed about what they should do, or if they could not bring themselves to speak the words that seemed like a kind of sentence, the meeting would be long and awkward and achingly sad. If the family members seemed divided, or if they simply could not decide what to do, Ferrier would offer no opinion except to suggest that they wait a few more hours, then meet again. If it seemed certain that they believed Jayne should be taken off the respirator but could not bring themselves to say so, Ferrier would likely lend the weight of his position in support of that conclusion. If Jayne's husband pressed him for his own opinion at that point, Ferrier would surely say, "Well, if it were my wife . . . ," as a prelude to saying that Jayne simply had no hope.

During my months with Ferrier, I had known of similar meetings he had had with families facing the same terrible options. I had been surprised to discover that the possibility of taking a patient off a respirator or of forgoing heroic treatment was not a great ethical and legal dilemma for him or for the hospitals that housed his patients. As life-sustaining technology had become increasingly sophisticated in recent decades, both medical and legal practitioners were now aware that horribly traumatized bodies could be kept "alive" virtually indefinitely. Yet there was growing and widespread agreement that there were few ethical, emotional, or economic reasons to use that technology for weeks or months or years simply in the name of the Hippocratic oath. A physician would still be legally accountable if he chose to inject poison into a patient or, perhaps, to withhold intravenous food, but to remove a patient like Jayne from a respirator would not be construed as "mercy killing." It would instead be seen simply as what it was: a decision made by the patient's family, in consultation with a physician, that a particular type of treatment should be stopped because it could no longer improve the patient's condition. Ferrier had never so much as hinted at concern about whether he conceivably could be charged with committing euthanasia, and the people who staffed the intensive care units seemed to treat decisions to end life-support as sadly inevitable occurrences. Death was as common in their wing of the hospital as was birth in the obstetrics ward, and recognizing hopelessness seemed to them to be as critical a part of their jobs as recognizing when and how they could help.

Ferrier now could no longer help Jayne, but he could be a bit of help to her family, speaking to them not so much as a counselor but as someone who had been part of similar situations, who knew what could be expected if her nostril tubes were removed and what could be expected if they were not, someone who had witnessed many others struggle with the same decision in this matter of life and death.

An hour and a half after he had gone to talk with Jayne Welty's family, Ferrier and I sat drinking scotch in the bar of the old Victorian hotel downtown, his whiskey served neat, as had become his habit when he lived in Britain, mine served with the requisite American "rocks." There was nothing left to be done with the day. The teams playing the Monday night game on the big television above the bar didn't interest us, so we simply stuck to the scotch, eating a supper of sandwiches in the big upholstered chairs that flanked a round black cocktail table.

"Things like this are always easier when it's been several days since the accident," Ferrier said. "Not that they are ever easy, but after the family has seen several days of no response, it's easier for them to deal with the possibility that their wife or daughter isn't going to come round."

"Why don't you always, as a policy, leave the patient on life support for a set length of time before you do anything?"

"Because each situation is different. And for practical reasons. I think we all approach it very cautiously. We try to be absolutely honest about a patient's chances, but we don't even bring up the issue of life support until we feel that there is just no hope—until brain death or terrible disabilities are certain. And when we bring it up, when I bring it up, it's because it would be cruel to do otherwise. The patient is dead, his brain is, even though the heart may be pumping away like nothing ever happened. And to get heroic at that point just doesn't make any sense. It's very expensive; it puts enormous strain on the family, and it doesn't serve any purpose. Death is already a fact."

"How can you make a reliable diagnosis of brain death?"

"It's a bedside diagnosis. You do a variety of tests to check for even the subtlest kind of response—response to pain being one of the most critical. If a patient has no response to deep pain, no grimace, no attempt to pull away, if the gag reflex is absent, no caloric response—the ice water in the ears—no doll's eyes, pupils fixed and dilated, no attempt to breathe on his own, off the ventilator, that patient is in pretty grave shape. But someone with all those findings sometimes can still breathe on his own, or can slightly move his eyes if a bit of his brain-stem function is still intact. Jayne is still triggering the respirator on her own, but left on her own, her intake is quite poor. They did another EEG late this afternoon. A flat-line EEG is almost eerie, the tracings just these steady horizontal lines, absent of anything. And they did a nuclear brain scan while I talked to her family. It's a procedure we don't use a lot these days, but it can still be helpful occasionally. It tracks the movement of a radioactive material that's injected into the bloodstream. None of the material got to her head; there's no blood flow to her brain from any vessel. It's so swollen that the pressure is keeping it out."

"And her family knows the results of that?"

"They know everything. They want to spend tonight with her, her husband does. I'm not sure her parents will stay all night. And they decided to donate her corneas and her liver; her kidneys, too, if they don't fail in the next twelve hours."

"What about her heart?"

"I called the transplant team at the university—they'll come up and take the organs—and I'm sure they'll see if there's a recipient for the heart."

"I wonder if her husband knows the whole story."

"Stan Singleton was waiting in the hall when I went back to the hospital. I guess he and Bill talked for an hour or so, and I'm sure Bill suspects something, but . . . I hope Singleton didn't spell out too many details. I don't know what purpose they would serve at the moment. Bill was crying a lot this evening; I'm sure her death has begun to sink in."

"Is she dead? Right now?" I asked.

"She . . . she's brain dead, yes, which, from my perspective means that *Jayne*, Jayne the person, is dead. Parts of her body are still functioning, but. . . . Death can be pretty relative. Muscles can contract for hours after a heart stops beating. They are as functional as ever. Are you still alive because some of your muscle fibers still respond to stimuli?"

"What will the records show as her time of death?"

"Oh, the time when her heart stops beating, I'm sure."

We talked on into the autumn night, staying inside the hotel, sinking deeper into the wing-back chairs, discussing death and infidelity. I confessed to Ferrier that Jayne was the first person I had ever been attracted to who might already have been dead. "With my luck," he said, smiling, "I'm just thankful that I wasn't in Singleton's shoes."

"Would she have made it if he had brought her in right away?"

"Who knows. It was a big rupture and it did a lot of damage immediately, I'm sure. But Stan Singleton's going to have to deal with that for a long time, isn't he? Medically, though, I'm not sure that if we had seen her two or three hours earlier it would have made a lot of difference. With smaller ruptures, you need to clip the artery early to limit the trouble it's going to cause, but with a major rupture, you inevitably get so much pressure from the bleed and so much swelling from damaged tissue that the whole brain is heavily traumatized. If the swelling damages the brain stem, then that's pretty much the end of things. You've got to have a fairly intact brain stem to be conscious; it just controls too many vital functions."

When I asked him about the viable treatments for nonfatal kinds of strokes, Ferrier explained that with the exception of surgically clamping arteries and removing hematomas following rupture—procedures that are only sometimes done, in cases where a bleed is still in progress or where the hematoma is threatening a critical local area like the brain stem—or the administration of anticoagulant and antiplatelet drugs to prevent further thromboses, treatment of stroke victims is largely rehabilitative. "If you infarct most of your left hemisphere, bringing back your speech is pretty problematic. Some function often returns when the edema, the swelling, is reduced; sometimes damaged nerve cells are able to sprout new dendrites, new connections that effectively reprogram certain functions—and speech and physical and occupational therapy play a fundamental role in that process. It's the therapists and the families who really get stroke victims back on their feet."

He asked me if I remembered Eddie Ruiz, the man he had been called away from lunch to see sometime during the previous winter, a man who had suffered a sudden left-sided weakness while he was shoveling to reach a water main. I remembered Eddie Ruiz—jovial, wisecracking despite the fear that must have beset him, his left arm and leg shockingly limp and uncooperative. CAT scans performed that winter afternoon had shown swelling in Eddie's right frontal and parietal lobes—his nondominant hemisphere—and an angiogram had shown a severely occluded right common carotid artery. Sensation and movement in Eddie's left arm and leg had slowly returned over the next few days, his loss of function presumably the result of a "transient ischemic attack," a short-term loss of blood to the brain that is not sustained long enough to cause an infarct. But Ferrier and Dennis Mitchell, a vascular surgeon, had recommended a carotid endarterectomy—a surgical scraping of the artery's internal walls—fearing that, without it, a major infarction was probable. The surgery itself had posed a risk of sending an embolus into his brain, of causing the kind of infarct they were attempting to prevent, but it was a risk that they and Eddie had decided should be taken.

Eddie awoke from the surgery with severe right hemispheric deficits—his left arm and leg nearly immobile, the left half of his face numb and uncontrollable. He spent the following two months in the rehabilitation wing at St. Luke's Hospital, regaining enough use of his left leg to allow him to walk with a cane, trying to relearn the reading and calculating skills the stroke had taken from him, trying, with only limited success, to regain cognizance of the left half of his body.

"Eddie's a good example of how much better we often are at managing stroke with therapy than with surgery. Not that the surgery was a drastic mistake; I think that without it he stood a strong chance of totally occluding his carotid and maybe causing himself even more trouble, but we'll never know about that. Since the infarction from the surgery was in Eddie's nondominant hemisphere, he didn't lose his speech. But, of course, when he spoke, he could use only half his mouth and tongue, so his speech sounded flat and slurred. But what was amazing to observe—and he wasn't unique by any means; you see this with most people who have nondominant strokes; it's a phenomenon called ignoral—was that he totally lost recognition of his left side and of the left half of the world. If you asked him to follow the words he was reading with his finger, the finger would move to the end of one line, then would only go back to the middle of the next line. He had his full field of vision, but he just no longer *knew* about his left. You could touch his right hand and ask him what it was, and he'd tell you it was his right hand. If you asked him what his left hand was, he'd say, 'oh, it's, uh, it's,' and he couldn't tell you. If you moved it over to his right side, he'd say, 'oh, it's a hand.' One time, I asked him to draw a clock with the hands set at four o'clock. He drew the hands correctly, and the right half of the clock was circular, but the left half was flat. When I asked him to draw nine o'clock, he couldn't do it. He just couldn't visualize nine o'clock."

"How do the therapists work with those kinds of problems?"

"With patience. It takes a long time. You repeat things endlessly and you teach the patient little tricks, little habits that help him to notice things, to be aware of them. People will eat from only half the plate, or put on only one shoe, or only comb their hair on one side; women will put makeup on only half their face. But by the time Eddie left the hospital, he had improved a lot. He had enough use of his left side that he could walk with a cane, and he could follow a whole line of print, and he was learning how to avoid leaving food in the left half of his mouth—but that much took two months to learn. I saw him in the office a few weeks ago. He was getting around pretty good, complaining about how in the world they expected his OT to be able to teach him how to cook when she didn't even know what *menudo* was."

"You said something about how critical the brain stem is, or how it's sensitive to stroke."

"It's not particularly prone to stroke, no, except that, remember, hemorrhages are prone to occur in deep brain areas, like the brain stem. The complication is that the brain stem is so vital to basic brain function. It serves as a kind of alerting center, to keep you conscious, to keep you asleep or awake and aware. Also, it's a conduit for motor and sensory tracts, connecting the cerebrum and spinal cord. Sometimes it's called the 'reptilian brain' because all reptiles, and the birds and mammals that are descended from them, have brain stems. That's about all reptiles have—nothing complicated. But, I guess, if you're a lizard out cruising the rocks, you probably don't need much. With people, you need a hell of a lot more than the brain stem, but you also *have to have* the brain stem. Even a big hemorrhage or lots of edema up in the cerebrum, or in the cerebellum that sits behind it, can exert enough pressure to shut down your brain stem and pretty well close out your account. And infarcts or hemorrhages within the brain stem are usually disastrous.

"Putnam's got a patient—who I'm rounding on while Putnam's lecturing at the university this week, by the way—a guy in his fifties who had a brain stem stroke early this summer, June, I think. He infarcted his lower brain stem and was brought in with steadily progressing symptoms—one-sided facial weakness, difficulty swallowing, then difficulty moving his eyes, then no body movement at all, no speech, virtually nothing. It's really a sad situation. He seems to be receptive; he can hear and understand what you say. His eyes stay open, and they're fixed in central gaze, meaning he cannot move them from side to side, but if you ask him to look up or down, he can move his eyes with seeming ease. It's very difficult to know just how intact his intellect, emotions, and other higher functions are. The presumption in this kind of situation is that you become a kind of child, or less than a child—very dependent, living for the moment—but we just don't know—except to know, in his case, that he can follow eye movement commands and can communicate a bit of information with eye movements. I mean, compare him with Jayne. He is definitely *not* brain dead; his brain stem still has enough function for him to survive, but God, he's locked inside himself."

A long computer printout stretched from one end of the wall to the other, its thousands of Xs forming large letters that read GET WELL SOON, SAL. WE MISS YOU. Salvador Maldonado, wearing a hospital gown and pajama bottoms, his dark, handsome face freshly shaved, lay curled on his side when we walked into his room at St. Luke's Hospital on Tuesday morning. An IV line was taped to his forearm; a fatter catheter tube snaked across his mattress, attached to a urine bag that was pinned to the bottom sheet. His eyes were open, unblinking, his lips slightly parted. Except that he had no tubes in his nose, he appeared to be in the same grave condition that Jayne Welty was in—surely this man was not responsive, surely they would decide that his brain, too, was dead. But when Ferrier moved around the end of the bed and crouched a few inches away from his eyes, he said, "Good morning, Mr. Maldonado," as if Sal Maldonado might have been able to say good morning in reply. "It's Dr. Ferrier. Remember me? Remember that Dr. Putnam is down at the university this week? How are you today? Look up high for me so I know you can hear me, Mr. Maldonado."

Sal Maldonado's eyes, his irises so dark they were hard to distinguish from his pupils, rose smoothly up, then down again. "Raise them one more time, Mr. Maldonado," Ferrier urged, and he obliged. "This time," Ferrier said, his words spoken slowly, "I only want you to raise your eyes if your wife has been in to see you this morning. Raise your eyes if your wife has come to see you today." His eyes did not move; Ferrier waited but there was no response.

While Ferrier was checking his muscle reflexes with a hammer—they were brisk, indicative of the damage to the upper motor neuron tracts in his brain stem—a nurse walked into the room, and Ferrier asked her if Mr. Maldonado's wife had been to the hospital yet that day.

"No. She almost never comes till the middle of the afternoon, does she, Sal?" The nurse put her hand on his shoulder and squeezed it before she turned away. "I'll be back after a bit," she told him.

It was astonishing. If he was aware that his wife had not yet come that day, then surely he was aware of everything that transpired within that small room. Surely he could see the photographs of his wife and children that were taped to the wall, surely he could read his huge get-well card, and could hear the conversations of the nurses as they bathed him and changed his sheets. He *was* in there, wasn't he? He was locked in, as Ferrier had said, unable to initiate any kind of communication, unable to say please bring me a radio to help me get through these interminable days, or to say he was cold and needed a blanket—able only to say yes or no by lifting his haunting eyes.

But there was another possibility. Perhaps his eyes remained motionless because Ferrier's question about his wife was too complex, too difficult for him to understand. It was certain that he understood enough to raise his eyes in response to simple commands, but was he really aware of who had been to see him and who had not? Perhaps his response—the absence of one—had only meant that at that moment his wife was not within his field of vision, or even that the word *wife* no longer had any meaning. It was frightening. How could anyone know how much he knew, how much he perceived, how much of him still lived behind his eyes?

Ferrier brushed back Sal Maldonado's hair, then held his hand as he said good-bye, telling him he would see him in the morning. The dark eyes now seemed somehow desperate to me, but they did not move again before we left.

"He's really in there, isn't he?" I asked Ferrier as we walked to the nurses' station.

"Oh, he definitely has some comprehension, there's no question, but—"

"My God. Imagine if his thinking processes are totally intact. What must it be like for him day after day?"

"I'm almost afraid to ask too many questions," Ferrier said. "Do you think he'd raise his eyes if we asked him if he wanted us to kill him?"

I waited while Ferrier scribbled a note into Sal Maldonado's fat chart—page upon page, three months now of pages, each one recording his blood pressure, his temperature and pulse, recording the daily amounts of glucose that were administered intravenously and his output of urine and feces, recording the sad fact that his condition remained essentially stable.

"He's had a small pneumonia or two, a couple of other complications, and I know that Putnam tried to talk with his wife about whether they shouldn't consider those complications kind of fortunate, as a blessing, in effect, something that would allow him to die. But she and the rest of the family, from what Putnam said, wouldn't hear of it. They want absolutely everything treated as aggressively as possible. They're waiting for a fucking miracle."

"Could he come out of it?" I asked. Could his brain stem somehow recover enough to let him move and speak and swallow again? Could this man's mind ever be unlocked?

Ferrier held the heavy door open, waiting for me to reach it. "You mean, do I believe in miracles?"

Yes, Ferrier believed in the miraculous brain itself. But no, he did not believe that Sal Maldonado's brain stem would somehow recover, that he would simply "wake up" one day, say hello to his wife and good-bye to the nurses who now had cared for him for months. Yet Sal was by no means in the same condition that Jayne Welty was. Her brain had entirely ceased to function. With the assistance of an artificial breathing apparatus, her heart continued to beat, but it could not pump blood into the organ that had made it possible for her to move, to think, to speak. Her brain had ceased to be, and her family had decided not to hold her body hostage to their grief.

At least part of Sal Maldonado's brain remained alive, however. Because of the severity of his stroke, Ferrier could not know how much of his higher cortical function remained intact, but Sal certainly could respond to simple commands, and that meant his brain was at least minimally capable of receiving and decoding spoken stimuli and of initiating a muscular response. Sal, in contrast to Jayne, was very much alive. He was breathing without assistance, and neither Ferrier nor Putnam would have argued that for him there was no hope. But both men characterized that hope as only a very small one, a thin theoretical hope that he might one day move his arms or speak.

In asking his family to consider whether they should be unaggressive in treating the pneumonias he had already suffered, and the infections that would inevitably beset him in the future, the two doctors were asking a very difficult and profound question. It seemed extremely unlikely that Sal's condition would ever improve, and if it did not, was his life now enough of a life to warrant heroic measures to sustain it?

At least for now, Sal's family answered that it was. At least for now, Sal could raise his eyes in recognition of his wife; at least he could lift his eyes in greetings to his children, and for them that was miracle enough.

Before Ferrier saw Jayne Welty in the intensive care unit at County Hospital, he saw three other patients on the wards, two of them Putnam's. The third patient he checked on was Wayne Byers, the stoic, nearly silent man with melanoma, who had been admitted to the hospital ten days before. Wayne had begun to take his Dilantin regularly again since I had last seen him—racked by seizures in the emergency room. The seizures had abated for two weeks, but then they had begun again, a normally therapeutic level of Dilantin in his blood now unable to quell the chaotic firing of nerve cells irritated by his swollen tumors. In addition, Wayne had begun to become confused for short periods of time, not knowing where he was, or even who he was, ignoring the friends that now seemed to be strangers. Ferrier and the oncologist had agreed that Wayne now needed to be hospitalized, and Ferrier was currently trying, with some limited success, to raise his dosages of Dilantin, and now Tegretol as well, to levels that would again stop the seizures, high levels that inevitably made him very drowsy and even more lethargic than before. There would be no more surgery, Wayne's doctors had decided; and the chemotherapy, apparently unsuccessful, would not be tried again.

Wayne was asleep when we walked into his room. Small bandages still covered his surgical scars; his scalp was still bald, his face gaunt, his skin pale and chalky. A copy of the newspaper he no longer worked for lay on the tray beside his bed.

"I won't wake him up," Ferrier said in a whisper. "We'll come back after lunch. Chart says he hasn't had a seizure for, well, not since the night before last. Thirty hours or so. Maybe we're getting—" Ferrier's beeper suddenly sounded; he reached for it and silenced it. Wayne stirred but did not wake up, and we made our way out of the room.

It was Bonnie, a secretary at the office, who was trying to reach him, and Ferrier called her from the nurses' station. She told him Barbara Bishop had just telephoned, saying she urgently needed to talk to him. Bonnie gave him the number and he placed the call, listening briefly, saying little before I heard him say, "good, I'll see you then." He hung up the phone and turned to me, looking a little shocked, astounded, his querulous expression suggesting that the news was not good. "Barbara Bishop. She said the jury was back by eight-thirty this morning with a verdict. It took them just thirty minutes and they awarded her *two . . . million . . . dollars.*"

"You won," I said.

"They didn't award me anything."

"But you helped her get it."

"Two million bucks. That's outrageous. That's *obscene*, for God's sake. I mean, yes, she's disabled, but Jesus!"

"Maybe you did too good a job."

Ferrier shook his head, mumbling something as he stepped away to make a note in Wayne Byers's chart. We walked to the stairwell when he was finished. "That verdict, what in the hell . . . I just can't believe it," he said, sounding genuinely disturbed.

"Oh, you know, they'll appeal. She probably won't end up getting that much."

"I feel like a whore," he said.

Two million dollars did seem like a lot of money, but surely Barbara Bishop deserved compensation for her injuries. Except for her misfortune of having been in the drunken driver's path, her brain would not have been damaged—her memory would not have faltered, her intellect would not have lost its once-sharp edge, her temporal lobe, scraped by her skull when she hit the windshield, would not have become prone to sparking seizures. Her accident was not her fault, the deficits it left her with were not of her own doing, so didn't the jury's award represent a certain justice? It seemed to me that it did.

In contrast, was anyone at fault when Sal Maldonado's brain stem suffered its terrible infarct? Did Eddie Ruiz deserve compensation for the surgery that caused him to abandon the left side of his world? Who was culpable when Jayne Welty's hemorrhage destroyed her brain? None of their three strokes, each one a cerebrovascular *accident*, was caused by another's negligence, so it was fair that none of them would receive compensation, was it not? None of the three of them were *victims* like Barbara Bishop, were they? Well, yes, it seemed to me that they were—victims of nothing more than the capricious risks of living, perhaps, but victims nonetheless. Jayne Welty was the victim of a congenitally weak cerebral arterial wall. Eddie Ruiz, like millions of people, was the victim of atherosclerosis, and a victim, too, because he lived in a time when occluded arteries could not be surgically cleared without running a horrible risk. Sal Maldonado, surely a victim, surely proof that justice has no meaning in matters of health, suffered enormously simply because a primitive part of his brain, robbed of its blood supply, had forgotten how to function. Their three profound misfortunes did not seem so different from Barbara Bishop's, after all. Crossing the wrong intersection at the wrong time, Barbara was a victim of chance. But Sal, Eddie, and Jayne were injured by chance as well.

During my visits I had met many patients whose brains had been injured, their deficits caused by trauma instead of by infectious agents, tumors, compromised immune systems, or mysterious degenerative processes. Stroke, too, was a kind of trauma, and I tried to consider whether trauma was fundamentally different from disease, and it didn't seem that it was.

I had met, for instance, one of Ferrier's fellow physicians, a general practitioner whose spinal cord had been severed when his motorcycle roared off the edge of a mountain highway, a man who was now a paraplegic, able to practice medicine but embittered by his disability, embittered by the phantom pain in his groin and his legs that constantly beset him.

I had met an eighteen-year-old boy who, during the course of an operation to remove a subdural hematoma, had been a victim of a surgical drill that malfunctioned and bore too deeply, tearing his middle cerebral artery and infarcting much of his left hemisphere, leaving him wheelchair-bound, epileptic, and asphasic, his chances for an independent adulthood very slim.

244

I had met an oilfield roustabout whose facial bones had been shattered by a flying wrench and whose brain had been so severely concussed that he had not worked for a year, still suffering constant dizziness, loss of appetite and libido, sleeping sixteen hours a day, unable to do the most menial chores without first finding a way to get angry, his rage temporarily giving him the energy to mow his lawn or to do the breakfast dishes.

I had met a twenty-three-year-old woman with severe cerebral palsy—fixed and permanent brain injury caused by trauma at birth—who always wore a helmet to protect her head from the falls that accompanied her constant seizures, who could walk but could not speak, making herself understood only by grunting and pointing with her finger at objects that intrigued her, who received good care, and even affection, in a state-supported group home, and who might live in a kind of suspended infancy for many more years to come.

These four and many others whose brains and spinal cords had been traumatized in accidents, most of whom saw Ferrier only once or twice a year, their chronic but stable conditions not requiring the constant attention of a neurologist, seemed little different from his patients who suffered disease—those who were made numb and ungainly by multiple sclerosis, or tremulous by Parkinson's disease, or immobile by ALS, or whose clogged and corroded arteries resulted in sudden strokes. All illness was accidental, wasn't it?—whether injury or disease, whether caused by a car wreck, an invading virus, or by some cellular twist of fate— all illness occurring for no purpose, arriving uninvited, enduring with no justice.

In the lounge near the ICU, Jayne Welty's family waited. Her parents, holding hands, sat on a small couch across from a television set that was turned off. Her sisters, both younger than Jayne, one of them still a teenager, sat in straight-backed chairs, both wearing skirts and makeup as though they had dressed up to say good-bye to their sister. "I'll see you in just a minute," Ferrier said to them, momentarily leaning into the room.

Ferrier looked at Jayne's most recent EEG—performed at seven that morning, the fourth EEG since she had been admitted—and he studied her chart at the nurses' station before we walked into her room. Bill Welty sat in a folding chair at Jayne's bedside, holding her limp hand, his face looking worn and weary, his expression almost vacant, his tears long since exhausted. "Bill," Ferrier said, "good morning. Were you here all night?"

Bill nodded. "Morning."

Ferrier walked to the opposite side of the bed. He peered into Jayne's eyes, but did not take his ophthalmoscope out of his briefcase. He, too, took her hand. "The EEG that they did early this morning doesn't show any change. It's flat-line, like the last one was. I'll do some final tests here in a minute as well, but everything we discussed last evening still seems to hold. Her urine output is slowing down a lot, which is something we would expect to happen at this point, but if her kidneys are going to be intact enough for transplant, they have to be taken soon—and, of course, that decision doesn't have to be final. You all may certainly change your minds. But assuming you don't, the transplant team is due here at about nine-thirty."

"I think everybody feels the same way they did last night," Bill said. "I'll go check with them again though. Jayne and I talked one time about transplants. I'm sure she'd want to try to help somebody else. It's the one thing that. . . ." Bill couldn't speak for a moment. "It . . . I'll be in the lounge," he said, his voice quaking with a sadness that seemed to envelop him and Jayne and Ferrier and me as well. For the first time ever, in that instant, I had an inkling of what that kind of loss must mean, a glimpse of grief's bleak and consuming blanket. Bill delicately laid Jayne's hand and forearm on the bed, as though he might injure her if he were not careful, then he stood and walked out of the room.

I had not wanted to intrude on Jayne's family the night before, yet there I stood at her deathbed, surely intruding now, observing as her family ended their vigil, not needing to be there, but wanting to be there for reasons I could not explain. I had never seen a patient whose heart had stopped, and in the years before, the bodies I had seen after death were only bizarre embalmed mannequins, waxy facsimiles of the people they had recently belonged to. At death, a body would be different, I presumed. The transition from life to death would be sudden, definite, dramatic in its clear finality. Life—glorious, incomprehensible life—would simply stop, and the silence of death would be unmistakable. A body at death would be the one thing in the world that would be truly straightforward, cold, and utterly uncomplicated.

But Ferrier claimed that Jayne was already dead, that death had taken hold of her a day or so ago. If he were right, then even death had no simplicity. Jayne's skin was still warm and supple, her heart still pumped, her breasts still heaved with each intake of breath. Yet her open eyes suggested nothing; they were devoid of expression, offering no hint of ever having glittered with delight, of having mirrored understanding, of ever having seen.

Ferrier held Jayne's forehead and quickly turned it from side to side, watching the eyes, observing that they remained totally fixed. He did not inject cold water into her ears again, but he did press his pen against the nails of a finger and toe, again getting no response, seeing no trace of movement, no grimace, nothing but the open, empty eyes. Ferrier turned off the respirator and left it off for a couple of minutes, confirming that Jayne herself was not breathing, before he turned it back on. He pressed Jayne's hand between his palms before we walked out of the room.

In the lounge, everyone in the family was standing, each person's face looking apprehensive, uncertain about what was about to happen, unsure of what was expected. Ferrier shook Jayne's father's hand, and the hands of her sisters, then asked them if Bill had explained that the transplant team would arrive in about twenty minutes. They nodded. "We feel good about it," Jayne's mother said.

"What will happen," Ferrier explained, "is that they'll arrive—and you all might want to spend some time with Jayne before they do—then we'll ask you to come back here while they briefly take her into surgery. They won't be taking her heart; there wasn't a matched recipient, but she'll stay on the respirator while they remove her corneas, and the kidneys, and the liver. When they've finished, we'll take her off the respirator. She isn't breathing on her own anymore, so when it's gone, she probably will stop breathing rather quickly. And, of course, just as soon as all that's done, you can go back in again. I'll be here, so let me know if there's anything you need, okay?"

"Mother," Jayne's father said to his wife, "let's go see Jayney for a minute." His eyes were wet; his wife had begun to cry and he took her by the arm. Bill and Jayne's sisters stayed behind.

"Thanks," Bill said to Ferrier, shaking his hand, unable to say anything else. Jayne's sisters were tearful now, too, and Ferrier hugged them both before we left them alone.

We spotted Stan Singleton, standing alone, near the door into Medical Records at the opposite end of the corridor and we walked to meet him. "Doctor," he said, "I don't want to get in their way. I won't bother them, but I . . . wanted to be here, at least. When I called in last evening, Bill said they were going to take her off the respirator this morning. Is she still—?"

"Right now we're waiting for the transplant team from the university. The family decided to donate her organs. When they're finished, then we'll take away the life support."

"And she'll die?"

"She'll be on her own. She isn't breathing on her own now. Off the respirator, she probably won't breathe at all, but—"

Stan Singleton started to cry. "She was such a wonderful. . . ." His tears made it hard for him to speak. "She. . . ." We stood beside him, saying nothing, offering him nothing but our silent presence until the three men who made up the transplant team turned the corner into the corridor—the three of them wearing scrubs and carrying two red and white coolers, looking as they walked toward us like surgeons planning a picnic. Ferrier reached for Stan Singleton's arm, saying, "Listen. This wasn't your fault. Call me in a couple of days, will you?" Stan nodded, and Ferrier escorted the three men down the hall and through the doors into the ICU.

At the door of Jayne's room, Ferrier briefly outlined for them Jayne's accident, the surgery, and her deteriorating status since. Beverly, Jayne's nurse, followed them into her room to help them transfer her onto the cart that would roll her into surgery.

Jayne's family waited in the lounge again, all of them still standing, embracing one another, saying little except to assure themselves that she would have wanted it this way. Ferrier told them he would come back for them in just a few minutes before he went to the nurses' station to begin dictating a death summary.

The three surgeons spoke briefly with Ferrier when they returned from the operating room, then left, their coolers containing Jayne's gifts. I followed Ferrier and Beverly into the room where Jayne had been returned. The bedcovers were pulled up over Jayne's shoulders now; her hair was mussed from her short journey; her eyes, missing their corneas, looked strangely flat and opaque. There were sucking, gurgling sounds when Ferrier and Beverly, working together, pulled the tube that had reached to her stomach, and she gasped—or seemed to gasp—as the second nostril tube came up from her lungs. Jayne's strong heart beat for four minutes after Ferrier closed her eyes.

9 Concerning Minds in Tangles

In November 1906 German neurologist Alois Alzheimer delivered a landmark paper to the South West German Society of Alienists, a regional group of physicians who specialized in the field that would one day be known as psychiatry. The paper, entitled "Concerning a Unique Illness of the Brain Cortex," recounted his clinical and pathological findings in a fifty-one-year-old female patient whose neurological symptoms had begun with disorientation and a disquieting loss of memory. The patient later became severely depressed and began to suffer hallucinations. In less than five years, her memory and her abilities to converse, to reason, and to act had disappeared. She was unable to feed herself, or to walk, or, finally, to speak. At death at age fifty-six, she had become a kind of infant.

Alzheimer was intrigued by how his patient's "dementia"—the progressive loss of her mental functions—resembled the dementia that was common in the elderly, one characterized first by loss of memory and then by the gradual, irreversible loss of related functions—planning, calculating, reasoning, and self-care. When he performed an autopsy on his patient's brain, Alzheimer found that her cerebral hemispheres had severely atrophied; they had shriveled to a size that would certainly not have been expected in a woman her age. With the aid of a microscope and a recently developed staining technique, Alzheimer was also able to observe that large numbers of neurons in the patient's temporal and frontal lobes had been destroyed by the clumping and twisting together of filaments within the nerve cell bodies, abnormalities that he labeled "neurofibrillary tangles." Alzheimer knew that

250

aging brains almost always lost some of their mature size and weight, and it was widely understood that neurons increasingly "dropped out" or died as brains grew older. But neurofibrillary tangles were certainly not present in every aging brain, and he speculated that it was the tangles—whose cause he did not guess at—that were responsible for his patient's early dementia and death.

For decades following Alzheimer's first description of the disorder, it was considered by most researchers and clinicians to be a rare, middle-age form of the dementia that, to varying degrees, beset so many elderly people—believed to be as common and natural a companion of old age as minor arthritis or the diminution of hearing. Some brains, the scientists presumed, simply wore out at an early age, a condition that became known as "presenile dementia."

As research continued over the years into the variety of degenerative processes to which the brain can fall prey, fewer and fewer neuroscientists were willing to consider severe dementia at any age a "natural" phenomenon. People did not lose their minds at the end of their lives simply as a matter of course. And those who did suffer progressive dementias often shared similar pathological conditions—their cerebral hemispheres were shrunken; numerous neurons showed evidence of Alzheimer's "tangles"; and "senile plaques," waxy proteins that cluster in nodules, appeared profusely throughout the cortical tissue. None of these four pathological finds was unique to progressive dementia, but the four occurring in concert, and in great number throughout the cerebral cortex, did appear to be evidence of a specific, if mysterious, disease process—one that most often attacked its victims in their eighth or ninth decade, but that could also begin its insidious course in patients still in their fifties. In an effort to help obliterate the notion that old brains inevitably become demented, the terms "senile" or "presenile" dementia gradually fell out of favor, and the disease that puts minds in tangles ultimately took on its discoverer's name.

Alzheimer's disease has no known cause, no prevention, no treatment, no cure. It begins so subtly—showing no more sign than the benign forgetfulness we all exhibit from time to time—that many patients have significant mental deficits by the time their families realize something is wrong. Simple forgetfulness slowly gives way to strange lapses of memory. Patients forget to pay bills, to go to church services that they have attended weekly for years; ovens are left on overnight, grandchildren's names cannot be recalled, questions and answers no longer connect. Eventually, Alzheimer's patients fail to recognize old friends, clocks become meaningless, shoes cannot be tied. Patients forget to dress themselves; they get lost inside their living rooms; they urinate in flower pots; they see spoons and forks as strange, unmanageable tools. Finally, Alzheimer's disease is fatal, usually six to eight years after memory begins to fail. Patients who are no longer able to walk or speak or attend to themselves in any way gradually sink into coma and die.

Like heart disease, cancer, and stroke—the only three more common causes of death of people over sixty-five—Alzheimer's disease is ubiquitous. It spares neither sex, nor any race or ethnic group. Because the median age of the general population is increasing, the incidence of Alzheimer's disease is growing correspondingly. It currently afflicts about three million people in the United States—roughly 7 percent of the population over sixty-five. By the end of the century, an estimated five million people will suffer Alzheimer's, meaning that one in every ten people over sixty-five will be a victim, as will thousands of people whom the disease will attack in middle age. The statistics pose an intriguing question: If each of us lived long enough, would each of us eventually succumb to this slow atrophy of the mind?

The answer is, probably not. There remains no evidence to indicate that something about the aging process itself triggers the pathological changes that produce Alzheimer's dementia. Yet aging brains do inevitably tend to slow down. Like bones that grow brittle and eyes that lose their acuity, most brains suffer minor lapses of function at the end of their long lives. Remote memory—the remembrance of things long past—remains remarkably sharp in most people, but short-term forgetfulness is common. Calculating skills occasionally suffer; fine movements lose some of the coordination that for decades has been second-nature; and learning is a much slower process than it once was. These benign losses of brain function, however, these reminders of mortality that each of us now knows or will someday discover, are by no means dementia. In this era in which Alzheimer's disease receives such notoriety, perhaps it is important to point that out. Most aging brains do *not* become demented, and also—not all dementia is the product of Alzheimer's disease.

Current estimates are that Alzheimer's accounts for a little more than half of all dementias. So-called multi-infarct dementias, spawned by a succession of minor strokes, are the next most common cause, followed by mixed dementias (which exhibit pathological evidence of both Alzheimer's and cortical infarcts), tumors, the late-stage effects of Parkinson's disease, rare brain viruses, and chronic psychiatric disorders. Dementialike symptoms, often reversible, can also be produced by a variety of acute illnesses, including drug toxicity, syphilis, depression, thyroid disorders, alcoholism, and vitamin B_{12} deficiency.

One of the cruelties of Alzheimer's disease is that it is not only the most common form of dementia, it is also the least understood. Why do filaments within some aging nerve cells become fatally entangled? Why do amyloid plaques encrust nerve axons? Why does the transmission of impulses become difficult, then impossible? Why do some brains shrink inside their skulls?

It was November now. The sky was gray, steely, presaging snow. An icy wind had begun to blow before dawn that Tuesday, and in Ferrier's office at midmorning it rattled the decorative bars outside his window. Across the desk from Ferrier, Harold Culver held his wool coat in his lap. In the chair next to his, Frances Culver still wore her quilted coat. Her short gray hair was matted and uncombed; her red lipstick spread beyond her lips. She sat silently, inattentively, watching the windblown shimmy of the bars while Ferrier and her husband spoke.

"I really didn't know what ought to be done," said Harold Culver. "I mean, if there was anything that could be done." He spoke slowly, his words wrapped in a farmer's drawl. "Got to the point finally where I knew we needed to see somebody. I talked to Doctor Blasier—I suppose you know him, he's doctored our family for probably twenty years. After I told him how Frances was doing, he said he thought we probably ought to come see you. So here we are. He said you're the guy who sees this sort of thing pretty regular."

Frances was sixty-five, the mother of two children, Mr. Culver told Ferrier. She had had a hysterectomy and an appendectomy, both surgeries done many years before, but other than that, her health had always been good. A year and a half ago, however, Frances began to get forgetful. She would repeatedly ask what day it was; pots would boil dry on the stove; and her hair, which she had always worn long, braided, and wrapped in a bun, now seemed of little interest to her; sometimes it would hang uncombed all day. "Then a few months after I started to notice stuff like that, she kind of took a turn for the worse. I'd come in at nine-thirty or so and find her cooking breakfast all over again, like we hadn't had it yet. Or, here's an example. We've fed squirrels out behind our place for I don't know how long. Frances has always enjoyed them. But for some reason, she decided they was rabbits. I would ask her if she'd ever seen a rabbit climb a tree, and she'd say, 'Well, I guess not.' But then five minutes later, they'd be rabbits again."

When Ferrier asked how his wife was doing currently, Mr. Culver said he was now afraid to leave her alone, even for short periods of time, for fear she might hurt herself. "She could real easy stick her hand in some boiling water or something like that," he said. "She just completely loses track of what's going on. The simplest things are just all out of whack for her. And she does crazy stuff. One afternoon I walked into the house and there she sat at the kitchen table, stark naked, playing solitaire, just like that was the way you was supposed to do it. Then she took a pair of sewing scissors to her hair; chopped it all down to an inch long. I don't know. . . ." His words trailed off, dragging his frustration with them. "You know those diapers they make for old folks? Have to keep her in those day and night now."

Ferrier tried to get Mrs. Culver's attention, calling her name. Her husband reached for her arm. "Mrs. Culver. Can we talk to you for a minute?" Ferrier asked. She turned away from the window and seemed surprised to find him sitting across the desk from her. "I'm Doctor Ferrier, Mrs. Culver. How are you today?"

"Well, I'm fine. And you?" she said, her response smooth and automatic.

254

"Do you know why you're here, Mrs. Culver? Do you know why your husband brought you here today?"

She appeared confused for a moment. "Well, I guess we wanted to get some lunch, didn't we?"

"No. Not lunch. This is a doctor's office. I'm a doctor. Your husband wanted you to see me because he thinks you might have a problem with your memory. Has your memory been slipping a little?"

Again she waited before she spoke, and she turned to her husband, as if for help. "Well, I . . . I still look after the kids don't I?"

"Do you know what day this is, Mrs. Culver?"

She said nothing this time, and her husband shook his head.

"What did you have for breakfast this morning?"

"We . . . well, I guess . . . well, chicken and dumplings, I suppose."

"Try real hard for me, Mrs. Culver. I want you to add two numbers for me. How much is six plus six?"

Mrs. Culver silently mouthed Ferrier's question. She was trying hard. She raised her eyes, as if the answer would be visible if she looked up, but she did not find it. "Frances?" said her husband, prompting her with his impatience.

"I'm thinking before I say the answer," she said, her tone of voice a little cross. But still the answer would not come. "Let's see. It was six, wasn't it?, plus . . . I'm not very good at numbers, am I Harold?"

Ferrier let his question drop. "Tell me about your children," he asked. "How old are they?"

"Well, they're pretty big anymore."

"Boys or girls?"

"One boy and one girl."

"What's the boy's name?"

"Robert."

"How old is Robert?"

"Well, he must . . . well, about forty, isn't he?"

"And how old is your daughter?"

"She . . . I guess she just turned thirteen, didn't she, Dad?" Harold Culver shook his head again.

Mrs. Culver's physical exam was basically normal. Her reflexes and strength were symmetric; her coordination was average for

255

someone her age; her gait was slow but balanced. When Ferrier asked her to tie her shoe, she tried repeatedly, but she could not make a bow. "Have you been having trouble tying your shoes lately?" Ferrier asked.

"Kind of," she said. "Guess it's a little arthritis."

Still in the small examining room, Ferrier turned his questions to Mr. Culver. Had she ever had a head injury? Had she ever complained of weakness on one side or blindness in one eye? Had she ever been anemic? Did she ever do work that could have exposed her to lead or other toxins? The answer to each of the questions was no. What about her family history—did anyone in her family have memory problems?

"Her daddy was killed when she was real little. Tractor turned over on him. Her mother lived to be eighty-five. Sharp as a tack till the day she died."

When we returned to Ferrier's office, Mr. Culver was ready with a question. "What I wanted to find out was whether Frances's trouble might be this Alzheimer's disease that you hear about. Some friends of ours at church was saying that that could be the problem. I asked Doctor Blasier, but he said you were the guy to answer that question. You'd think it might just be old age, but shoot, I'm seven years older than her and, at least as far as I can tell, I'm doing fine."

"I think you're doing fine, too," Ferrier said with a smile. "But yes, I think Mrs. Culver has Alzheimer's disease. There are some tests we'll do to make sure that her confusion and memory loss aren't caused by a lot of little strokes or a vitamin B_{12} deficiency or something, but frankly, I'm afraid they'll be normal. After everything you tell me, and in talking with her and examining her—well, I think it's very unlikely that the problem is something else. And the difficult thing about telling you that is—and you probably already know this—that her mental processes will get worse and worse. At this point, there isn't anything we can do to slow down or stop the deterioration in the brains of Alzheimer's patients. Some people report that lecithin, a kind of fatty substance that's found in milk and egg yolks and other foods as well as in human nerve tissue, and which you can buy in powdered form at a health-food store, sometimes seems to slow the loss of memory, but people really can't pin too much hope on it. Families, of course, can be and need to be loving and supportive, but later on, there's very little that even they can do. Eventually, almost everyone with this disease needs some sort of institutional care."

"How long till then for Frances, do you suppose?"

"I can't really say. She has lost quite a bit in a year and half, though, so . . . well, it wouldn't be too early even now to begin looking into the various nursing home possibilities."

"I guess there's some places where we could get a kind of apartment for us both, aren't there?"

"Yes. That would be a definite option for you." Ferrier reached into his desk drawer for a card. "There's a support group for Alzheimer's families here in town. They have meetings and put out a monthly newsletter, and, if you're interested in getting in touch with them, they would be a very good source of information on lots of different care options."

Harold Culver took the card. Frances was looking out the window again.

Ferrier pushed the drawer closed, then folded his hands. "I hate not being able to do any more for people like you and Mrs. Culver than to give you a card and mention things like lecithin, but at least I do know that the people in that group would be very helpful. I really do encourage you to get in touch. You're going to need to be able to talk to some people who know what it's like to be in your situation."

Harold Culver scraped his teeth across his upper lip. He was quiet for a moment, but he was not near tears. He did not seem to be the kind of man who could have cried if he had wanted to. "Well," he said, "it's a sad situation because you love your wife, and pretty soon she doesn't even know who you are, and you can't do nothing for her."

We sat in the Saab, waiting in the drive-up lane at Jack-in-the-Box, having another hamburger lunch in the twenty minutes before Ferrier was due at the health clinic at the university. Ferrier was quiet, preoccupied by two patients in intensive care since early that morning, and I was bothered about what little he had been able to say to Harold Culver an hour before, bothered about how Harold could seek out some support and commiseration, but that nothing could be done for Frances. Weren't there better drugs to use than lecithin, more tests that ought to be performed? Like those who attempt to mobilize the frozen fingers and arms of stroke patients, shouldn't someone try to rehabilitate Frances Culver's fleeting mind? Would Ferrier simply see her once, doing nothing more for his money than to confirm her husband's fears?

"I only see most of my Alzheimer's patients twice. I do the evaluation and have a talk with the spouse or the children. I encourage them to get hold of those support groups, then I write a letter to the referring physician. Most of the time the GPs feel pretty certain that it's Alzheimer's, but at least *they* can do something by referring the patients to a neurologist. But the neurologist is the end of the line. I could make myself feel better, I suppose, if I always ordered a big battery of tests, but Jesus, would it help people like Mr. Culver if it cost them a thousand dollars instead of a hundred to get a diagnosis?"

"I'm not sure I've ever seen you offer anybody so little before. No hopeful tests, no pills with much of a chance of doing anything, no therapy, nothing."

"There are cases, especially when the dementia symptoms have come on rather suddenly, when you work up the patient as exhaustively as you can—looking for toxins, or thyroid troubles, vitamin deficiencies, stroke, or obviously for something growing inside the brain. Well, an example is Mrs. Bridgewater. Her doctor first suspected Alzheimer's when she began to behave strangely. And, at her age, that made a certain amount of sense until her short-term memory proved to be rather good. That was enough to send us looking, and, of course, we found the meningioma. But with people like Mrs. Culver—and there are a lot of them—there aren't any red flags to find. All there is symptomatically is the slow, progressive deterioration that begins with the loss of recent memory."

It was our turn at the window. Ferrier paid for the hamburgers, then handed me two white paper bags, and we drove away. "Sure, I could order a magnet scan and complete blood work, maybe a neuropsychological battery and an EEG, but we wouldn't learn anything more than I learned in that hour with her," Ferrier said, pulling into the noon-hour traffic. "I mean, part of the business of being a clinician is knowing when you need every diagnostic test in the book and when you don't. And with Alzheimer's, nothing is absolutely confirmatory anyway. CAT scans obviously show brain atrophy and the enlarged ventricles that are a sign of a lot of cell death, but you only see the plaques and the neurofibrillary tangles at autopsy. Once PET scanners are in common use—scanners that look at how brain tissue metabolizes—we may be able to observe some of the pathology while the patient is still alive, and in a year or two we may be able to test for a specific protein in the cerebrospinal fluid, but for now, the diagnosis is always just 'probable Alzheimer's.' "

For now, the diagnosis of probable Alzheimer's disease is a statement that says something very specific about what is transpiring in a patient's brain and about how that brain inevitably will be destroyed. But it tells nearly nothing about what causes this terrible collapse of memory, this destruction of intellect and the meat of human consciousness. Yet there are glimpses into the genesis of the disease; the clinicians still have no means of slowing its course—they can do little more than to explain what its course likely will be—but they and the neuroscientists now have scattered clues about the cause, compelling shards of information.

Following the presentation of Alois Alzheimer's seminal findings at the beginning of the century, little new was learned about the disease until the mid-1970s, when British neuroscientist Peter Davies made a discovery that gave a dramatic focus and impetus to Alzheimer's disease research. Davies and his colleagues at the Institute of Neurology in London were able to demonstrate that the brains of Alzheimer's patients have drastically reduced levels of an enzyme called choline acetyltransferase, the chemical responsible for the synthesis of the essential neurotransmitter acetylcholine. The Alzheimer's patients in Davies's study produced from 60 to 90 percent less acetyltransferase than did age-matched control subjects.

Later experimentation seemed to confirm the role acetylcholine plays in the normal function of the brain's two principal memory centers—the temporal lobes of the cerebral cortex and the hippocampi, "sea horses," two small structures that curl around the egg-shaped thalami deep within the brain. When David Drachman at the University of Massachusetts Medical Center administered scopolamine, a drug known to block acetylcholine receptors in the brain, to healthy young-adult volunteers, each

259

one suffered temporary memory loss and confusion that appeared similar to the symptoms of Alzheimer's disease.

In the early 1980s, Donald Price, Joseph T. Coyle, and Mahlon DeLong at the Johns Hopkins University School of Medicine added to the emerging link between acetylcholine and normal memory function. The three researchers reported that their autopsies of Alzheimer's patients revealed the profound destruction of cells in the "nucleus basalis of Meynert," a small deep-brain region where, intriguingly, most of the brain's acetylcholine is normally produced. The depletion of acetylcholine in the cortex and the hippocampi, and the resultant pathological changes, they theorized, were actually triggered by the mysterious death of cells in the nucleus basalis.

The course of Alzheimer's disease began to appear to numerous researchers to be analogous to the process of Parkinson's disease, whose symptoms of tremor and rigidity are believed to be caused by the depletion of the neurotransmitter dopamine that results from the destruction of the tiny substantia nigra in the basal ganglia. The drugs now used to treat Parkinson's disease successfully increase dopamine levels in the brain, but they do not slow or reverse the deterioration of the substantia nigra. Perhaps, researchers hoped, Alzheimer's disease could be treated with similar limited success by administering drugs to patients that would mimic acetylcholine or spur its production.

Disappointingly, however, experiments to date with drugs designed to boost levels of the neurotransmitter have produced no impressive decrease in Alzheimer's symptoms, perhaps because they do not increase acetylcholine activity enough, perhaps because other neurotransmitter deficits are also involved in the disease process.

The possibility that an as-yet-unrecognized virus might trigger the Alzheimer's process has been under investigation for more than two decades now, even before Nobel laureate Carlton Gajdusek of the National Institutes of Health was able to prove in the mid-1960s that a fatal degenerative brain disease called "kuru," suffered only by members of the isolated Fore tribe in New Guinea, is caused by a specific "slow virus"—one that remains dormant within its victims for decades before initiating its destruction. Kuru, Gajdusek discovered, principally infects the women of the tribe because it is they who handle the infected brains of deceased family members as part of the tribe's mourning rituals.

Gajdusek's findings paralleled what was already known about another rare but worldwide disorder called Creutzfeldt-Jakob disease, named after the German neurologists who discovered it in the 1920s, a dementia whose pathology is different from Alzheimer's and that strikes people who are younger than typical Alzheimer's sufferers, a disease that is often fatal within as little as six months. The demonstrations that kuru, Creutzfeldt-Jakob, and similar diseases that occur only in animals—such as scrapie, a fatal brain disease of sheep—are caused by slow viruses have spawned studies into whether Alzheimer's, too, begins when a dormant virus becomes active. As yet, that possibility can only be theorized; despite intensively focused efforts, no Alzheimer's virus, "slow" or otherwise, has been identified.

Those scientists who are directing their attention to the possibility of a genetic cause are inevitably intrigued by the unexplained connection between Alzheimer's disease and Down's syndrome, the mental retardation and physical abnormalities caused by an extra chromosome twenty-one in the body's cells. For reasons that are as yet completely mysterious, virtually all Down's people who reach age thirty-five or forty begin to develop memory loss and related intellectual deficits. Their brains, correspondingly, show signs of cerebral atrophy and the presence of neurofibrillary tangles and senile plaques. People with Down's syndrome seldom live much beyond their fourth decade; in general, their bodies age very rapidly. Yet unlike the 7 percent of the aging population with normal chromosomes who acquire Alzheimer's disease, 100 percent of the people with Down's syndrome acquire a condition that is indistinguishable from it. Genetic researchers are now grappling with this compelling question: Does something within the twenty-first pair of chromosomes contain the secret to Alzheimer's genesis?

Mind was a word I seldom heard during the time I spent with Ferrier, one that he disliked. Every examination he performed included an evaluation of the patient's "mental status" or "higher

261

cortical functions"—memory, language, attention, and the variety of cognitive (knowledge-related) processes, but they were of interest to him as aspects of *brain* function. They had nothing to do with something called *mind*—a word he did not know the meaning of, he would claim a bit facetiously.

Many of the rest of us assume that we know what we mean by *mind*, of course. Mind is the aspect of each of us that is real but intangible, essential but imperceptible, the wondrously complex amalgam of what we perceive and know, believe and fantasize, what we remember and what we hope. The English word derives from the Anglo-Saxon *mynd*, which first meant memory, its meaning expanding over the centuries to include myriad conscious and subconscious cortical processes. An individual mind, the special mix of those processes that distinguishes each of us, certainly exists in concert with a three-pound brain—it exists only *because of* a brain—yet it is surely something more, an ineffable object, born out of gray and white matter, that has no weight, no size, no bounds.

"I just don't buy that," Ferrier said. We sat in his living room at the end of that Tuesday, ten hours after Ferrier had examined Frances Culver's failing mind. The hard wind continued to whip through the dark sky, but still there was no snow. I had made a fire thirty minutes before while Ferrier, his saxophone in hand, had gone into his bedroom to play along with an old Ben Webster record—his shy musicianship an increasingly regular method of relaxation. But now his solitaire's concert was over. Ferrier's sax lay on the couch beside him, and he was taking exception to my tentative efforts to distinguish mind from brain. "What you're trying to say is that if I reach out and pick up this sax, the movement is initiated by a brain function. But if I remember the first girl I ever kissed or how the streets of Edinburgh smell, it's my mind at work. Why do you have to call one 'brain' and the other 'mind'?"

"Mind is sort of a poetic term, I suppose. I'm not trying to make a big case for separating the two, but neither do I think there's anything wrong with talking about the mind—meaning what the brain does, as opposed to the anatomical thing inside the skull."

"The problem is that the brain has so many functions. There's just no reason to consider motor and sensory functions as aspects of the brain, and memory and intellect, et cetera, as the mind. Compare it with other organs. The liver performs a variety of functions, but we don't call some of them liver functions and others 'hepatic-wonderfulness' or something. They're all just *liver function*. Nice and simple."

"Maybe the term *mind* is valuable because it implies creativity and potential. I think you could make a case that some of the brain's functions, some of its capabilities, are so extraordinary that we need more than just an anatomical word to describe them."

"Why is that valuable? Does Einstein seem less amazing if you talk about his brain instead of his mind? Or is Picasso diminished if you have to think that his art is simply the product of a brain? I know what you mean, but from my perspective—that of somebody whose job it is to try to pay attention to the brain—the use of such a wildly nonspecific word like *mind* is just a bad idea. Because frankly, I've never seen evidence that any activity—whether you're talking about studying quantum physics or composing a symphony or experiencing some sort of mystical revelation—is anything other than the product of a series of electrochemical reactions in the brain. I know that puts a lot of people off, but I guess I don't understand why."

"Well, it's because looking at it that way doesn't allow any room for wonder."

"Not so. See, to me it's just the opposite. The *wonder* is what the purely physical brain is capable of. It is simply and precisely this wrinkled piece of tissue that is so incredible. But don't get me wrong about this. I really don't think I'm being ridiculously literal about it. I completely agree with Chomsky's theory that we are all somehow preprogrammed for language, for instance. And you know how important I think Jung's work was. His ideas that humans share, that they are born with, this rich foundation of archetypes, of symbols that have a universal resonance, are very valid. He also claimed that each of us is born with specific personality traits, and I agree. And they are passed along to each of us through genetic inheritance. I mean, I would argue that Jung's collective unconscious is very specifically coded into our genes. The understanding of universal symbols is an organic process. I really am convinced that we literally inherit many of the qualities of what you call mind, probably more than any of us would dream of."

"Okay. But that still doesn't explain why you can't live with using *mind* as a term to deal with these, well, more ethereal aspects of brain function that have to do with the unconscious, with dreaming, with these universal symbols and personalities."

"Because it's just a semantic game. It doesn't do us any good to use it. It's like the concept of God. If God is love, fine. I believe in love—I can't get enough of that stuff. If God is truth, fine, I'm a big fan of truth; and if you want to say God is light, that's okay, too. But if that's what God is, then let's just talk about love or truth or light. The extra terms like *God* or *mind* don't do anything but muddy the waters. They add a semantic layer that just causes trouble." Ferrier stood, his saxophone in his hand. "Enough of this. This brain's got to go play some more sax." He turned toward his bedroom.

Ferrier made his rounds at seven on Wednesday morning. The sky had blown clear, but the storm had dropped an inch of snow. We parked in the doctors' lot at St. Luke's Hospital and walked up the service stairs, then through a medical ward to the intensive care unit, where Ferrier would look in on Bernie Fries.

Ferrier had been asked to do a consultation on Bernie Fries forty-eight hours before, soon after he had been brought to the hospital in a coma. A thirty-five-year-old man with Down's syndrome, Bernie lived in a group home and had been found at dawn lying unconscious on the floor of his room. He had been incontinent; his tongue was swollen; his eyes were dilated and fixed, his breathing erratic. Aides at the home had suspected that Bernie might have overdosed on a street drug; he had no history of drug abuse, and they had found nothing in his room, but occasional problems with opiates and barbiturates were not uncommon at the home. On his arrival at the ICU, Bernie was given Narcan, a drug that blocks opiate receptors in the brain, and he briefly responded, but soon slipped back into coma. An hour after he arrived at the hospital, Bernie suffered a grand mal seizure, and Ferrier was given a call.

In consultation with Bernie's internist, and also suspecting an overdose, Ferrier ordered a Dilantin load—the intravenous administration of enough of the drug to bring it quickly to an optimum level in the bloodstream—and an EEG. Bernie responded to pain, albeit sluggishly, and the two doctors agreed to continue the Narcan.

By Monday evening, Bernie had suffered two more seizures. The EEG had shown slow-wave activity throughout his cortex, and a CAT scan revealed massive swelling, suggesting that his whole brain had gone without oxygen for a time. Bernie had not overdosed, but now the doctors' knowledge of the cerebral damage did nothing to improve his prognosis. His coma had deepened, his response to pain was minimal now, and his urine output had begun to slow.

Twenty-four hours later, kidney failure, also presumably the result of the lack of oxygen, seemed apparent—there had been no urine for fifteen hours. Bernie showed little sign of brain activity, and Ferrier and Scott Hayes, the internist, agreed that the treatment that followed would not be too aggressive; at thirty-five, Bernie was near the end of his life span.

On Wednesday morning, five staff members from Bernie's home waited in the corridor, aware that their friend probably would not pull through. Ferrier stopped to talk with them, explaining that the absence of urine and the lack of response to pain were both bad signs. Bernie had not had another seizure, but he was no longer triggering the respirator on his own, Ferrier told them. The one woman in the group asked him why they could not operate to reduce the pressure from the swelling, and he explained that damage to the brain following such massive edema is never reversed by surgery. When Ferrier asked how Bernie's recent health had been, they explained that he had had few problems, other than high blood pressure and chronically poor vision. "He's a great guy," said one man. "His memory is getting pretty bad, but, of course, that's real common."

Bernie's friends had brought his cowboy hat and sailor's cap to the hospital and had laid them at the foot of his bed. His Special Olympics ribbons were taped to the wall to his left, along with photographs of him and his many friends. The room looked as if the home's staff had wanted Bernie's important possessions to be with him when he died.

Ferrier tested Bernie's fingers and toes for response to pain; there was none. Then I watched as he examined his eyes, Bernie's boyish face sallow and surprisingly wrinkled. The extra chromosome that he possessed had flattened the bridge of his nose and caused a vertical fold of skin at the edge of his eyes; it had shortened his fingers and shortened his height and shortened the length of his life. He was only thirty-five, joyful and very loving, we were told, but because of his extra chromosome, his mind had begun to go.

After Ferrier wrote a note in Bernie's chart, we stopped in the corridor and chatted briefly with the staff people from the home, Ferrier telling them that he had seen no change, all of them agreeing that perhaps they should consider Bernie lucky—fortunate that he would not live long enough to forget his friends or how to feed himself, fortunate that he would not be debilitated at the end of his days by what would otherwise be known as Alzheimer's disease.

In the intensive care unit at County Hospital, Phillip Davis, two years older than aging Bernie Fries, was dying before his time. A Methodist minister, Phillip had moved back to his hometown to live with friends ten months earlier, after he was diagnosed with AIDS. He had been given the AIDS diagnosis in Portland, Oregon, soon after he acquired Kaposi's sarcoma, the otherwise rare form of skin cancer that is very often seen in AIDS patients. Following Phillip's move, Ferrier had first treated him for herpes zoster, shingles, then for postherpetic neuralgia, the excruciating pain that often follows shingles. Then, three weeks prior to today, Phillip was hospitalized with pneumocystis, a rare, often fatal, form of pneumonia that is common in AIDS patients.

While he was in County Hospital, Phillip began to suffer terrible headaches. A CAT scan revealed several large lesions at the gray matter—white matter junction in both cerebral hemispheres. It was possible that the lesions were tumors, but Ferrier guessed it was more likely that they were abscesses caused by infectious bacteria—that possibility increased by his immunosuppressed condition. A surgical biopsy had confirmed that streptococcus, a bacteria common to the mouth, had infected his brain. Phillip had

had an impacted wisdom tooth extracted a week before he was hospitalized, and it seemed likely that that procedure had precipitated the infection.

On large dosages of antibiotics, the abscesses had shrunk; two had disappeared, and Phillip's headaches were nearly gone. But the pneumocystis had never abated. His lungs were racked by infection, his weight had dropped to ninety-seven pounds, and in recent days he had been beset by a growing delirium. His speech seemed nonsensical now; he no longer knew where he was, and he often thrashed violently on his bed. His friends, who had spent most of each day with him when he was first hospitalized, now only stopped by briefly, each of them taking turns and staying only minutes.

In his isolation room in the ICU on Wednesday morning, Phillip moved in a restless stupor. An oxygen mask was strapped to his thin, whiskered face; cloth straps held his hands at his sides. The nurse who was attending to him wore a mask and surgical gloves as she cleaned saliva from his mouth with a suction device, but Ferrier put nothing on before he examined Phillip's hollow, helpless eyes and tested his heightened reflexes. "How febrile is he?" he asked the nurse.

"A hundred and one. Briefly up to a hundred and four during the night."

"Does he come out of this at all?"

"He hasn't really been with it since you saw him yesterday morning. His friends know he's getting bad. I think one of them is going to be here all the time from now on. Do you think this is it?"

"It? Oh, yeah, before long," Ferrier said. "Let's hope so anyway." He straightened the sheet that crossed Phillip's shrunken chest.

Wendy Stetham was standing at the reception counter in Ferrier's office, talking to Bonnie, when we walked in the back door. Wendy, Ferrier's complex seizure patient, the one I first had met when she was pregnant and suffering uncontrolled seizures, was on her way to an epilepsy center in California in an attempt finally, decisively, to determine whether her seizures had an organic cause, whether they were pseudoseizures caused by a very perplexing personality disorder, or whether, in fact, as Ferrier suspected, they were a complicated combination of both.

Wendy's son, Timothy, now nearly ten months old, still lived with a foster family, but Wendy was able to take him to her apartment two days a week. Her seizures had never abated. She still averaged three or four of them each week, despite Ferrier's long efforts to find the proper combination of anticonvulsants. And she continued to injure herself in the midst of her seizures. She had broken a wrist, burned an arm, cut her scalp, and she had dislocated her right shoulder so often that recently she had to have surgery to repair it.

Ferrier was not entirely sure what he hoped the epilepsy center would determine. During her stay in California, Wendy would be taken off all her anticonvulsants and would be monitored around the clock by an EEG machine and by video cameras. Each seizure, assuming she had any while she was there, would be definitively examined. If any seizure was organic—evidence of true epilepsy—the EEG would reveal it, and it would once again be Ferrier's job to try to find some chemical means of keeping Wendy seizure-free, something he had so far been unable to do. If all of Wendy's seizures turned out to be pseudoseizures—caused by a disturbed psyche instead of a damaged brain—then Ferrier effectively would be off the hook, and anticonvulsants could be stopped. But Wendy's own path to recovery would appear to be much more complex, and she would doubtless require psychotherapy for some time.

"Hey. You have to sign this," Wendy said to Ferrier as he set down his briefcase, addressing him as if he were a high school teacher with whom she had some special rapport, handing him a one-page authorization form. "It's so the insurance will pay for the center." Ferrier scanned it quickly and scribbled his signature.

"So. What's it going to be out there, kiddo?" he asked her, handing it back. "Is this going to settle it?"

"You're the one with the questions. Not me. I know I'm not faking these things. So this will prove it."

"I hope it will. And I never said you were consciously faking them. But I'm telling you," Ferrier said with a smile, "if you go two whole weeks out there without a single seizure, there's going to be hell to pay." Then he was serious. "Besides, if that were to happen, that in itself would tell us quite a lot, wouldn't it?"

"You worry too much," Wendy said. "You want me to send you a postcard? I can. I'm not going to be doing anything else."

"Please," Ferrier said. "We're going to miss you."

"Sure you are," said Wendy, turning away from the counter with a coquettish whirl.

Ferrier saw two new patients during the morning—one a woman who was afraid her classic migraines were something decidedly more sinister, the other a charming seventy-two-year-old man who complained of a recent loss of libido. He took two phone requests for consultations: a pediatrician hoped he could quickly do a developmental screen on an eleven-month-old boy at St. Luke's who had been set back by a congenital liver disorder, yet who might also be showing the first signs of retardation; and the director of a nursing home hoped Ferrier could stop by briefly to see Elizabeth Yeats, an Alzheimer's patient whose condition lately had deteriorated. Ferrier told both callers he could come before his afternoon appointments began, so, as often happened, lunch had to be sacrificed and we assured ourselves we would have an early supper.

The pediatrics unit at St. Luke's was painted an astonishingly ugly color of orange and, since it was mid-November and because it was difficult to be very festive about Thanksgiving, Christmas decorations already lined the corridor. Roger McShan, the cherubic pediatrician, waited for us at the nurses' station. He explained to Ferrier that young Jason Whitmore had been born with a so-called black liver, and in the months since his birth he had suffered severe eczema. Dr. McShan had admitted Jason to the hospital the day before for a series of liver tests, which had shown his liver function was nearing normal, but before he released him, Dr. McShan had hoped to answer his concerns about Jason's developmental progress. At eleven months, Jason's head circumference was forty-four centimeters, the median size for a six-month-old. He had only begun to crawl within the last week, but he had been able to pull himself onto his feet for nearly a month. Suspiciously, he had not yet begun to be shy of strangers. He was quick to smile and liked to play peekaboo, but he had not spoken his first word.

Dr. McShan and I stood near the doorway in Jason's room while Ferrier spoke with his mother. Jason's development was slower than her daughter's had been, she said, but she assumed that it was due to his ongoing liver troubles. She bounced her son on her knee while she spoke. He was a very good baby, she said, telling Ferrier that she honestly wasn't worried about his developmental delays. "I mean, I would be if he wasn't making progress, but you ought to see him tear around and get into mischief now that he can crawl."

Ferrier took a set of faded wooden blocks, two dried raisins, and a red tin wind-up toad out of his briefcase and sat down on the carpeted floor to play with Jason. Jason was happy to play and Ferrier seemed delighted by this exam. Pediatric cases certainly were not the mainstay of his practice, but he was entranced by children and he relished his encounters with them, each one reigniting his own unfinished debate about whether one day he would like to be a father.

In the midst of Ferrier's apparently casual play with Jason, he was attempting to gauge Jason's developmental milestones—his language and social development, as well as his range of motor skills. He wanted to determine whether Jason would turn toward his voice, whether he could imitate speech sounds or indicate his wants with vocalizations other than crying. He wanted to know whether Jason would resist when a toy was taken from him, whether he would move toward a toy held out of reach, whether he could play pat-a-cake, sit upright without support, crawl symmetrically, or steadily bear weight on his legs.

Ferrier's red toad quickly captured Jason's attention. He resisted Ferrier's attempts to take it away, then crawled to get it when Ferrier placed it a few feet away from him. He laughed easily, his laughter a loud squeal, but otherwise he was silent. He could not pick up a raisin between his thumb and index finger, and although he sat comfortably without support, he seemed to drag his left leg slightly when he crawled. When Ferrier took his hands and lifted him to stand, Jason's legs tended to buckle as the soles of his feet touched the carpet. When he pulled himself up with the aid of a chair, however, he could stand steadily upright.

Ferrier told Jason what a good boy he was when he returned him to his mother, then told her and Dr. McShan that he would be back in a minute. At the nurses' station, he plotted each of Jason's milestones on a graph that showed the median developmental curve for infant boys. In comparison with it, Jason's own curve was unmistakably slow, yet it paralleled the median curve. Had Jason been nine months old instead of eleven, he would have appeared perfectly normal; no developmental aspect seemed slower than the others and the curve showed steady progress.

"Well," said Ferrier, back in Jason's room, "I sure don't see anything that alarms me. There's no question that he's behind, and I would guess that he might not catch up for quite a while." He showed Dr. McShan and Mrs. Whitmore the graph. "But the thing that is more significant to me is that his progress curve basically looks the way we want it to. I would be more worried if he was markedly slow in one or two specific areas, but he doesn't seem to be."

"What about that asymmetric crawl?" asked Dr. McShan, still a bit concerned.

Ferrier smiled. "Well, he's obviously just a creative crawler." He turned to Mrs. Whitmore. "No. If that leg dragging continues, or if he seems to have a weak left leg or arm as he learns how to walk, you should let us know. But his reflexes are symmetric on both sides, and he seems strong, so I really don't think the crawl represents any kind of trouble." He took Jason in his arms. "Since we can't find anything wrong with you, I guess we'll just have to let you go home, won't we?"

This time Jason wasn't so sure about Ferrier. He started to cry and reached out for his mother, gaining another milestone.

This nursing home was an enormous place, its forty-bed "nursing unit," where people in poor health could receive constant care, attached by a breezeway to a ten-story retirement complex. We found our way to the nursing unit and walked down an administrative corridor to the brightly lit nurses' station. Two dozen people in chairs and wheelchairs, most of them women, most of them silent, their faces pale and patient, sat against the walls of the room, watching the activity of the nurses and aides, some of the old people dozing, a few holding quiet conversations, one woman shouting about how she had to get home at once, everyone else blithely ignoring her. At the counter, Ferrier asked for the director, and while we waited, a short woman with wild gray hair walked up to us. She took me by the arm and spoke conspiratorially. "I've got to get some help," she said. "When I came here, they assured me I would have a room. Well, I've been here six months and they haven't given me a bedroom yet."

"Where do you sleep?" I asked.

"Well, out here, don't I? But it's so busy I don't think I can."

"What is it, Margaret?" the director, Joyce Burleson, asked the woman as she walked up to us.

"I've got to get a room. I need a place to sleep," said Margaret.

"Don't you remember where your room is, honey?" She turned to a teenaged girl behind the counter. "Beth, Margaret wants to go to her room. Would you show her where it is?" Beth and Margaret walked away, Margaret shuffling her small feet, and Joyce Burleson introduced herself to us. She thanked Ferrier for making the visit and explained that Elizabeth Yeats, whom Ferrier had diagnosed with Alzheimer's disease only a year before, seemed to be deteriorating much more rapidly than most of the other Alzheimer's patients in the unit. "She's a lovely lady, she really is, and I hate to see it. She doesn't know her sons or daughter anymore, and I can't help but be embarrassed for her. She was really just the most proper and modest person, you know, but lately she seems to constantly be pulling at her skirt, hiking it up clear around her waist. I know that it doesn't bother her in the least now, but, well, just knowing the kind of woman she was, I hate to think it has to come to this. And she isn't like some of the men who want to show themselves all the time, like little boys—I don't think that's why she does it. But really, the main reason I hoped you could see her was because the disease seems to be taking her so much more rapidly than it is the others. I can't help but be concerned that maybe something else, like a tumor or something, is involved."

"Sure," Ferrier said, and we followed Joyce Burleson to the examining room where Elizabeth Yeats waited.

I had met Mrs. Yeats a year before, when her daughter brought her to Ferrier's office. Mrs. Yeats, sixty-eight, thought her daughter's insistence on the evaluation was silly, but she agreed to it to prove to her daughter that her mind was just fine. She might be a little forgetful, she said, but weren't most people her age?

In the office that day, Mrs. Yeats wore a wool skirt and a choker of pearls under the collar of a silk blouse. Her gray hair had just been set; she obviously cared about her appearance, and she looked attractive and apparently healthy. She listened while Caroline, her daughter, expressed her concerns, but was disbelieving when Caroline began to list a catalog of times her mother had gotten lost and the details of family history she had forgotten. "Now, that's just not true," Mrs. Yeats said, sounding hurt rather than angry when Caroline said she could not remember what business her deceased husband had been in.

"Well, what did he do then?" asked Caroline, posing a sudden challenge.

"Well, of course I know, but you've made me nervous," said Mrs. Yeats. "He, well . . . he did several things, of course, but mostly, well, it was office work, but I . . ."

Caroline let the subject drop.

When Ferrier began to ask a series of questions, Mrs. Yeats grew more nervous, and she was embarrassed by her memory loss. She was able to tell Ferrier the names of her four children, but she did not know the cities in which they lived. She said her husband had been dead for two years, but Caroline said it was seven. She knew she had been born in Nebraska, but she did not know how long ago she had moved away. She knew the day and the date and gave Ferrier her correct address. She named the president but could not name the governor. She could not add sixteen plus seven nor subtract twelve from twenty. She explained Ferrier's favorite exam proverb by saying it meant that people who live in glass houses shouldn't throw stones "because they'll destroy their houses."

Caroline told Ferrier she was afraid her mother could no longer live alone. She said her mother recently wrote a two-thousand-dollar check to someone who knocked on her door, offering to replace her roof before he vanished, and she said that three days before, her mother had burned a pot holder and an apron she had left on her stove and might have burned down the house had Caroline not stopped by to visit.

Mrs. Yeats staunchly refused to consider moving out of her home, Caroline told him, but before she left Ferrier's office that day, she said she might agree to take in a boarder, just to appease Caroline, not because she was some sort of crazy lady.

Three months later, after Mrs. Yeats had to be assisted by security guards who found her walking aimlessly through the corridors of a shopping mall at closing time, Caroline and her brothers moved their mother into the nursing home.

A year after Ferrier and I had first met Mrs. Yeats, she seemed to be a different person, sitting absently in a narrow chair in the white-walled examining room. She wore no makeup now; her face looked wan and weary; her hair had been brushed severely back, and she had lost a lot of weight. Her forearms, lying in her lap, looked so thin that they might snap. Her fingers busily kneaded the fabric of her skirt.

"Elizabeth," Joyce Burleson said in a loud voice as we walked into the room, "this is the guest I was telling you about. Do you remember who this is?"

Mrs. Yeats stood up awkwardly and Joyce took her arm. She looked intently at Ferrier for a moment, but nothing seemed to register. "Well, you're the boy who was taking us to town, aren't you?" she asked, her voice a dry whisper.

"No, I'm Dr. Ferrier. I met you a year ago in my office. But that was a long time ago, wasn't it? Do you remember why your daughter brought you to see me back then?"

"Well, by six or so. That'll be cats, I think," she said.

"Would you like to sit down, honey?" Joyce asked. Mrs. Yeats nodded, seeming to understand, but she could not initiate the movements that would allow her to sit. With Joyce assisting her from one side and Ferrier from the other, Mrs. Yeats at last bent her knees and they lowered her to the chair. Her fingers clutched at her skirt and she began to knead again.

"Mrs. Yeats. Who did I just say I was? Who am I?"

"You . . . well . . . by six or so, I guess."

"What is this place we're in. Where are we?"

"By six or . . ." Her voice trailed away.

Ferrier turned to me. "This repetition of a phrase is called perseveration. It's very common with late-stage patients. It's as if the phrase gets stuck somehow, isn't it?"

"That's what I was referring to," Joyce said, gesturing toward Mrs. Yeats's hands, her fingers clawing at the skirt now bunched in her lap above her white and bony thighs. "Is it sort of a tick or something?"

274

"No. But it's very common with bifrontal or diffuse brain disease. It's like the grasp reflex that an infant has, the same kind of thing you see babies do with a blanket. Here." He slid his index fingers beneath her clenched fists and Mrs. Yeats locked her fingers around them. He tried to pull them away, but her grip was strong. "Let go. Let go of my fingers, Mrs. Yeats," he said.

"Yes. After a fashion," said Mrs. Yeats, holding tight. Joyce pried her fists open enough to release his fingers.

"An infant loses his primitive reflexes as his cortex develops," Ferrier explained. "It's the development of the frontal lobes that causes the suppression of those reflexes. You suppress your grasp reflex so you can learn how to manipulate your fingers. You suppress your Babinski reflex so you can learn how to walk. But now, with Mrs. Yeats, it's the atrophy of her cortex that is bringing back those reflexes. Let me show you something." Ferrier extended his index finger and held it near Mrs. Yeats's right ear. As he moved it toward her mouth, she turned toward it, opening her mouth as if to take it in. "I've always thought this is a pretty profound thing to see. It's called the rooting reflex, the newborn's instinctive response to a nipple, and even it returns as the higher centers in the brain are destroyed. You know, there are all the literary and poetic discussions of old age being related to childhood, and here is a kind of proof of it. I'll never forget the first time I saw it—an eighty-some-year-old Scottish crofter, also with Alzheimer's, going for a tongue depressor as if it was his mother's nipple."

Earlier in the afternoon, Ferrier had tried to gauge what milestones young Jason Whitmore had gained, his primary reflexes disappearing as he learned how to reach for a toy toad and how to stand on his feet. Now here Ferrier was with Elizabeth Yeats, measuring what milestones she had lost because of her disease, those same reflexes as Jason's dormant since her infancy, returning in advance of her death. Yes, there were ways in which the old came round again to youth, at least these unfortunate elderly people whose brains were beset by dementia. Like infants, they were uncoordinated and sometimes incontinent, their bodies no longer under their brains' control. Like infants, their speech was virtually nothing but sounds, its meaning lost in the destruction of their temporal lobes. Like infants, they were dependent on

275

others for survival, their once-agile and once—wondrously creative brains now a haywire of compromised neurons.

Ferrier reviewed Mrs. Yeats's chart, then assured Joyce Burleson before we left that she was unlikely to be suffering anything more than the ravages of Alzheimer's dementia. He could not explain why she had grown so infantile so much faster than the other Alzheimer's patients in the home, other than to say that this disease, like every other, is unpredictable, its course as capricious as its selection of victims.

"You take good care of yourself," he said to Mrs. Yeats before we left, pressing his hand against her fragile arm.

"Oh, the boys will finish," she said in reply, her eyes growing misty. "Always by the end of the day."

At the close of the twentieth century, medical science possesses no antidote to aging. The human body remains prone to multisystem failure by the eighth or ninth decade of life. Hearts weaken and pump less blood and the circulation slows. Lungs lose their pliability; less oxygen is inhaled than in middle age, less carbon dioxide is blown off with each breath. Metabolism slows; food is converted to energy less efficiently and activity decreases. Joints calcify and are prone to decay; bones grow brittle and are prone to break.

The three-pound brain loses about three ounces in weight by age seventy, the result of the death of millions of neurons and their supportive cells. Healthy brains shrink slightly as they age; the fissures of the cortex grow broader and deeper, and the ventricles, the fluid-filled cavities deep inside the brain, continually increase in size. The arteries that supply the brain and the veins that drain it tend to narrow.

As the brain inevitably atrophies, its functions perceptibly suffer. Coordination lapses and muscles tend to waste. Nerve velocities slow; balance can become precarious. Vision, hearing, tasting, smelling lose their sharp acuity. Appetites for food diminish, and sexual activity often abates. Intellectual processes also decline. Short-term memory grows less acute and the retention of recent information becomes more difficult. Facility with calculations and dexterity with language suffer only a little, even in extreme old age, but logical reasoning becomes a slower process.

Yet unlike other organs in the body, the healthy aging brain can compensate for its own decline, countering diminished motor, sensory, and intellectual function with a remarkable fund of experience. Old brains inevitably lose the speed and precision they once possessed, but they gain a kind of sagacity, the collected learning and understanding called wisdom.

"You know, you tend to think of it just as a particularly clear perception of personal relationships, or of whatever truths life has to offer, but the brain's experience also plays an important physical role. It definitely hit home to me a couple of weekends ago when I was up visiting my folks. My dad and I were out for a hike and we had to come down a rocky hillside to get back to the house. We both took it kind of easy—I sure wasn't rushing or anything—but I fell down three goddamn times before I got to the bottom. Dad didn't fall once. I'm almost four decades younger than he is, and I ought to be a little more agile, a little more coordinated. You'd think he'd be the one more likely to fall. But he wasn't. His explanation was just that he has climbed down more hillsides than I have. And that's probably it. His brain is better than mine at knowing what rocks are going to topple, at recognizing safe footholds, and even though his fine coordination is probably not as good as mine, he probably has a better understanding of what his abilities and his limits are. He's a wise guy." Ferrier turned to me and smiled. We were driving from the nursing home back to his office. "He's wise about a lot of things, but it's interesting that one of them turns out to be how the hell to get down off a mountainside.

"The sixties, the seventies, even eighties, ought to be great years for people. Their kids are out of their hair, and they don't have to work like crazy, and they know a thing or two at last. Who cares if they move a little slower or don't see quite as well or if they have to ask three times when they're due for dinner. It's stupid of people our age to let little, inconsequential things like that get in the way of realizing what they understand, what they have to offer."

"But people like Mrs. Yeats . . . whatever wisdom she accumulated has vanished, hasn't it?"

"That's the challenge, medicine's challenge. In some ways, it's the diseases of old age that we ought to be pressing hardest to get rid of, so that the end of life is as healthy and as good as possible for everybody. Of course, it's absolutely critical that we come to grips with young people's diseases like MS. And think of Phillip Davis. From my perspective, the AIDS research so far really is evidence of medical science at its best. In just about three years— no time at all by medical standards—the HTLV virus has been isolated and the possibilities for a vaccine or for a viable treatment look very real. It can't come too soon—it won't be soon enough for people like him—but it will come."

"You can't be nearly as optimistic about diseases like Alzheimer's," I said, my statement a kind of question.

"The three principal degenerative diseases—Alzheimer's, Parkinson's, and ALS—are very complex, and we don't know nearly enough, and no, we probably won't solve them very soon. But what I meant to say was that they have to be addressed with the same kind of ethical imperative as the diseases that strike people in their early years. I mean, what kind of society would we be if we said, 'yes, well, Alzheimer's is a bad disease, but at least it only happens to old people.' "

Bernie Fries, already old but still a young man, died at six o'clock on Wednesday evening. His body had been taken to the morgue when Ferrier and I walked into his room half an hour later. The staff people from the home, saying little, some of them tearful, but their spirits now somehow lighter than they had been while they kept their vigil, were taking down the photographs from the walls. They took down the ribbons and awards and put Bernie's hats inside a box.

Phillip Davis, who might have lived for many more years, died before dawn on Friday morning. A friend from childhood was with him at the end. She told Ferrier that he seemed extraordinarily at ease in his final minutes. As the sun came up, a custodial crew in rubber gowns and gloves was scouring his room, and Phillip's body, which he had offered for research, was en route to the university in a private van.

Elizabeth Yeats, who did not know it and who could not mark the days, lived through the long winter and into the nascent spring.

Epilogue

This time the brain belonged to someone I had met. As Ferrier, Putnam, and I watched the pathologist slice through the cerebrum with a long serrated knife, I tried to imagine how this delicate gray tissue had animated Suzanne just three weeks before, given her movement and language and intellect, but there still seemed to be magic, some kind of sorcery, in the certainty that it had.

During the past year, I had made a beginner's inquiry into the brain, its exquisite and intricate physiology, its phenomenal control of the body, its mysteries and its miseries. At the flank of Ferrier's desk, I had heard the complaints of hundreds of patients whose brains seemed to be betraying them. I had seen dozens of CAT scan images of brains beset by trauma and disease. From the side of a surgical table, I had observed the red and supple tissue that was part of a living brain, and on an autopsy table, I now had touched two brains preserved in formalin. Yet despite my familiarity, there still seemed to be something wondrous about this three-pound mass of tissue whose incessant synaptic pulse had sparked the life that was Suzanne.

Ferrier had diagnosed Suzanne Forester with probable multiple sclerosis nine weeks before. Suzanne, a twenty-nine-year-old buyer for a clothing store, had first come to his office in October, complaining of blurring and difficulty focusing in her left eye, which had begun about two weeks before. Soon after the problem began, it was joined by a low and steady hum in her left ear and a strange sensation in the skin on the left half of her face. Then her right ear began to hum, sometimes steadily, intermittently at other times, and her right eye also began to blur. Two days before her first appointment with Ferrier, food began to get stuck in her throat.

Ferrier's impression, following the examination, was that Suzanne's presentation of symptoms most likely represented the first episode of multiple sclerosis. In both eyes, he noted pronounced nystagmus—a rapid and involuntary oscillating movement. Her left eye saw the color red less intensely than her right, but her hearing and facial sensation seemed normal on that day. The fact that these two symptoms had improved by the time he saw her made MS seem likely, its symptoms normally tending to remit following exacerbations that last a week or two. The other likelihood, especially in light of her difficulty swallowing, was some sort of brain stem pathology—a tumor, hemorrhage, or infection.

Ferrier was frank with Suzanne, discussing the three most probable culprits with her, assuring her that there was nothing to be panicked about, but agreeing that her problems needed to be taken seriously. Suzanne, short, blonde, and engaging, was obviously battered by the news, but she told Ferrier she wasn't terrified. "Let's just get it figured out," she said. "It would help just to know what's going on." The two of them agreed that she would have an MRI, if her insurance would cover its cost, a CAT scan if it would not, and Ferrier began her on a short course of prednisone that he hoped would reduce her current symptoms.

When Suzanne returned in two weeks, the nystagmus had improved, but her swallowing had not. Ferrier tried a second course of steroids and ordered a series of evoked potential tests to determine whether there was evidence of slowed transmissions in her brain stem or optic nerves, as well as an MRI—regardless of whether the balking insurance company would agree to pay for it—in hopes it would answer the question of the type of brainstem lesion and to see if there was evidence of MS elsewhere in her brain.

Ten days later, Suzanne told him the problem with swallowing was becoming very worrisome; she said she was able to consume only about a quarter of the food and liquid she normally did, and she often choked. The results of the evoked potentials were normal except for bilateral abnormalities in her visual responses, which might have been caused by her continuing minor nystagmus. The MRI also was normal; Suzanne's brain stem appeared clear, but Ferrier still suspected that microscopic MS plaques within it were the roots of her problems.

Four days later, while Ferrier was spending a week in Texas, Suzanne frantically phoned Putnam, telling him she could not make herself swallow, even when her mouth and throat were empty. Putnam immediately hospitalized her and ordered a sine-esophagram, during which she was asked to try to swallow an X-ray opaque barium solution as X-ray films were made. During the procedure, much of the barium solution was held up in her esophagus; she had no cough reflex and some of the solution was aspirated into her lungs.

A few hours later on that November Tuesday, Putnam performed a lumbar puncture to determine whether laboratory examination of Suzanne's cerebrospinal fluid would reveal the oligoclonal banding that is common with multiple sclerosis. At dinnertime, Suzanne was able to swallow well enough to eat a little. At seven o'clock, she received the steroid Decadron intramuscularly and Halcion, a sedative, by mouth. At eight-thirty, a nurse noted that she was sleeping quietly. At ten minutes past nine, the nurse found Suzanne in complete cardiac arrest, with fixed and dilated pupils, no pulse, and no respirations. The staff was able to resuscitate her, although they had some difficulty in clearing her airway, but she did not regain consciousness.

By morning, it was apparent that Suzanne had gone without breathing long enough the night before that oxygen deprivation had destroyed her brain. Putnam found no evidence of any brain function, and her mother and sister decided that they did not want to begin heroic measures to keep her alive. Suzanne's ventilator was stopped ten minutes before noon.

At autopsy early in the afternoon, the pathologist found nothing that appeared to cause the catastrophe. Her pharynx, epiglottis, and esophagus were normal. Her lungs were clear; her pulmonary and carotid arteries were open and elastic, and her heart, too, seemed normal. The surface of Suzanne's brain appeared flattened from massive swelling. He noted that Suzanne's cerebellum, brain stem, and spinal cord appeared unremarkable, but, on Putnam's request, the pathologist waited until Ferrier returned from Texas so that he and Putnam could observe the sectioning of the brain. Perhaps one of the three of them would note some small telltale pathology, a minute bit of evidence that might explain her sudden death.

Following each careful cut of the cerebrum, the pathologist laid the thin oval section at the edge of the cutting board for Ferrier and Putnam to examine. They did not expect to find anything abnormal in Suzanne's cerebral hemispheres, but nonetheless, the two bearded neurologists, their sleeves rolled up to their elbows, determinedly scoured the sections for clues, feeling the texture of the white matter with their gloved fingers, cutting into the cortex and the corpus callosum with small scalpels to peer still further.

The slices of the cerebellum and brain stem were even thinner, and the three men examined each section at length before the next one was cut, the pathologist lifting away pieces for microscopic study at every spot where there seemed to be some mild discoloration. By the time they had studied every slice, a microscopic discovery of the cause of Suzanne's symptoms and her death seemed to be the only possibility that remained. They had not found visible MS plaques, no evidence of infarct or hemorrhage, no tiny neoplasm, no infection. Like the cerebrum, the cerebellum and brain stem also had been swollen, so enlarged with edema that the brain stem had herniated and pushed through the hole through which the spinal cord passes at the base of the skull. But what had triggered her cardiac arrest, the subsequent hypoxia— lack of oxygen—to her brain and its attendant fatal swelling? Laboratory examination of Suzanne's cerebrospinal fluid had revealed two oligoclonal bands, making it appear even more likely that she had acquired multiple sclerosis, but given her pronounced symptoms, why was there no visible evidence of demyelination anywhere in her brain? Suzanne's progressive swallowing disorder almost certainly represented an abnormality in her brain stem, yet why did her brain stem appear unscathed?

Ferrier and Putnam pulled off their gloves and Ferrier slowly rolled down his sleeves. They had hoped that the autopsy would provide an answer, or at least point toward where one might be found, but it had not. They had wanted to be able to tell Suzanne's mother and sister what ultimately had befallen her; they wanted to tell themselves. But unless the pathologist discovered something in the tissue he would smear on a slide and observe beneath his microscope, there might never be anything to say.

The sections of brain still lay on the cutting board as Ferrier, Putnam, and I put on our coats and left the pathologist alone. The November night had already descended when we walked out of the hospital. It was clear and cold and we stood for only a minute.

"Well, frankly, I'm glad she wasn't my patient," Putnam said with a subtle smile.

"Listen," said Ferrier, taking up the joke. "She didn't die while I was looking after her, did she?"

Then Putnam was serious. "I really thought we'd find something in the brain stem. But . . . well, let's cross our fingers that something shows up on micro."

"Yeah. I don't know. . . ." said Ferrier before we walked away.

In two days' time I would at last leave Ferrier alone. There would be no more silly questions from me, no more need to explain to nurses why I followed him like a shadow, like a cloying chaperone, like some sort of silent apprentice. No longer would he have to wait for me to catch up with him at the end of every corridor. Our discussions of neurotransmitters, synaptic clefts, and seizure foci, at least for now, were finished. On that wintry night of Suzanne's autopsy, somehow it seemed fitting that I was leaving in the midst of a mystery, fitting that one of the last things I would observe would be Ferrier and Putnam and the cheerful pathologist struggling together to find an answer that was not apparent, an answer to a question that ceaselessly had to be asked: How does the brain work, and why does it go awry?

I had begun to watch Ferrier at work a year before, hoping to learn something about science, but what I had observed instead was medicine. Only in recent decades has medicine been akin to science at all, I had discovered. Only in the twentieth century has medicine begun to employ the scientific process, abandoning superstition and liberal guesswork in favor of the systematic ordering of questions and observations, experiments and conclusions. Medicine is an *applied* science, if it is a science at all; it is science set to work, science with a cause. Unlike pure scientific inquiry, undertaken for its own sake, medicine seeks specific ends; it audaciously tries to treat disease, to cure it, to lengthen and improve human lives. And perhaps it is this bold attempt, constrained by the methodical requirements of science, that has allowed medicine to gain so much in this century, yet that also continually disappoints us because its goals are not yet met.

There was no possibility when I began to observe Ferrier and his profession that my assessments of either of them could be objective. Ferrier was a friend, a remarkably genial and generous friend, and I knew from the beginning that I would not come away from my time with him possessing an unbiased opinion of his professional life. It would be easier to judge other doctors and the practice of medicine in general, but only a little easier. My exposure to them, my perceptions of them, inevitably would be bent by Ferrier's own partisan perspective. Surely in part for that reason, I came away from my year as a medical spectator believing that despite its enormous costs and its sometimes cumbersome organization, despite doctors' eccentricities and insensitivities and their occasionally scurrilous demands on their patients, medicine is indeed a decent profession. It is probably inevitable that its practitioners are perceived by those of us on the cold end of the stethoscope with a mixture of adoration and repulsion, if only because their stock in trade is so desperately dear to us. Our health, and the certainty that health will lapse and one day utterly leave us, are of elemental importance. Is it surprising that we have ambivalent attitudes about these custodians of health who are all too often the messengers of disease?

Yes, it seemed to me, Ferrier sometimes put unrealistic demands on his frantic schedule. His attentions could become so scattered on occasion that none of the several patients he was managing would receive the best measure of his talents. He would sometimes expect patients, and particularly their families, to be able to understand a complex stream of information far more quickly than they could, and his impatience would spill over on occasion when they were slow to make decisions based on that information. He expected nurses, technicians, therapists, and secretaries to be as quick-witted and exertive as he was, and few of them ever were. Without ever saying so, he expected his patients to treat their infirmities as challenges, as opportunities, in effect, but only some of them did so.

Yet one of the most intriguing things to me about Ferrier the physician was that this extremely self-confident man, who had known little adversity and who had no personal knowledge of defeat, could so readily be caring and empathetic. People whom he would be put off by if he encountered them on the street would immediately capture his attention and his concern when they sat across the desk from him and began to tell their stories. He would scream that he could not stand it anymore when hypochondriac patients would make their regular phone calls with their regular complaints, then would dutifully and politely return their calls, sometimes spending fifteen minutes or more engrossed in conversation, as if nothing in the world mattered more at that moment than their chronic arm pains or their persistent headaches. He would make the sickest possible jokes about patients as we rushed through the corridors of the hospitals to see them, then at their bedsides, he would clutch their arms and hug them, sometimes becoming tearful, as he discussed the likelihood of multiple sclerosis or the certainty of a tumor.

If the range of Ferrier's compassion was a surprise to me, his curiosity was not. Nothing, with the possible exception of contemporary art or classical jazz, could capture his attention like a newly published monograph on the use of Tegretol in the treatment of multifocal seizures or on the possibility that fetal testosterone levels play a decisive role in cerebral hemispheric dominance. Unexplained symptoms were engaging riddles; the endless adjustments of drug levels were elaborate kinds of contests; and the cryptic and chaotic squiggles of an EEG tracing, perhaps his greatest enticement, were codes that demanded to be broken. But despite his delight in solving puzzles and coming at last to an answer, he was seldom defeated when solutions were absent, answers unobtainable.

Ferrier seemed to know the limits of what he knew, and what he could know. The fact that his discipline could not yet cure or treat a number of the diseases and dysfunctions it confronted was not proof of its failing, from his perspective, but rather evidence of its integrity. Ferrier was outraged by the vitamin pushers and the bone-crunching chiropractors, the all-American kids in the robes of Eastern mystics, and the enlightened earth mothers who touted exotic grains and cathartic enemas—each of them laying claim to quick fixes and unfailing health. He was fundamentally suspicious of catchall preventions and miracle cures. He responded to the claims that *his* profession failed to treat the whole person by countering that it seemed silly to assume that it was always the *whole person* who was sick, rather than only that person's liver, or small bowel, or brain.

Ferrier had been a doctor for only a decade, but he had observed enough suffering, he had witnessed the progression of enough disease that he was certain that its cause could not be relegated simply to being out of cosmic balance. Disease was not a punishment and not a test. It befell those whose health was robust and those who were chronically weak. It was acquired by those people who understood and liked themselves as well as by people who were racked by doubt and delusion. Capricious disease descended on people who were enlivened by its presence and on those to whom it brought the cruelest kind of defeat. Some illness was unquestionably the product of diet, toxins, stress; other illness was clearly caused by invading bacteria, by elusive, constantly mutating strains of virus; some bodies strangely destroyed themselves. And much illness, it had to be admitted, remained a mystery.

On the day before my final visit ended, Ferrier took a call from the pathologist, who had done his best, he said, to find any microscopic abnormalities in the specimens he had taken from Suzanne Forester's brain. He had found no hard evidence of any culprit, and every test had returned negative, yet he had sent off tissue from four suspicious-looking areas of the brain stem for further examination at the National Institutes of Health. It would be a month or so before he would receive that final report. Ferrier thanked him for his efforts; he buzzed Putnam and gave him the news, then returned his attention to the patient who sat across from him.

Jean Martin Charcot, the French neurologist who is revered as the founder of his discipline, had this to say at the close of the nineteenth century:

> *Disease is from old and nothing about it has changed. It is we who change as we learn to recognize what was formerly imperceptible.*

Charcot was speaking to his colleagues, and the recognition he spoke of was their growing, shared understanding of the etiology of disease, its pathology, and its clinical manifestations. He was not entirely correct about disease being unchanged—some viral diseases, in particular, are utterly new—but his point, nonetheless, seems important. Disease is as old as the biosphere; human disease is as integral to our species as reproduction. It is the catalyst of decay and death, and in a very real sense, the struggle against disease is a confrontation with the only indisputable verity of living. The physicians who battle disease are changed not only because they learn something about the nature of disease but also because they are continually reminded of the outcome of life itself.

It seemed to me that Charcot's words as readily could have been directed to his patients, to the people who suffer disease. There was no question that Ferrier's patients were changed, whether for good or bad, by their encounters with serious illness. And it seemed certain that most of them did recognize something—something about themselves, about the business of being alive, and about what, in the end, they could pledge to be of importance—that they would not have known before their diseases took their grisly holds. I did not envy them; I did not want to learn intimately and brutally what some of them had learned. Disease extracted an awful price before it taught you anything, it seemed, and surely no one would ever willingly choose to pay it. Yet from my safe and privileged vantage point, observing the patients' misfortunes but neither suffering alongside them nor being charged with trying to help, fragments of the lessons that they learned somehow seemed transmissible to me. In the end, I felt very fortunate to have been able to observe their struggles, their conquests and defeats.

Ferrier had told me that he measured his success by the numbers of patients he lost track of—those who canceled appointments because they were so improved, those for whom he planned no follow-ups because none were needed. Sometimes, of course, Ferrier lost touch with his patients because they sought out other physicians. Some patients simply grew out of their petit mal seizures; others grew tired of ineffective treatments. Some patients moved away; others died while they were under his care.

I would have guessed when I began the year that most of

Ferrier's patients would see him merely two or three times in hopes of getting symptoms stopped, some nagging problem fixed—and perhaps half of his patients did see him for only a short time. But the other half, whose chronic maladies had become integral parts of their lives, effectively became his business associates, his long-term clients in the enterprise of illness. He was in very regular contact with them; their acquaintances grew warm and mutually reassuring. He would attend a favorite patient's piano recital, take riding lessons from another, and several patients would send him birthday cards. Once a year or so, he would attend a patient's funeral.

During my final visit, I tried to check on many of the patients I had met, those whose illnesses I had inquired into, those who, for many different reasons, had captured my concern. Some were well, their once-consuming maladies already receding into memory. Others, of course, still continued to struggle.

Mark Sanders, Mark the Mime, had been denied disability compensation, his multiple sclerosis deemed mild enough by the case workers at Medicaid that he could continue to work. Mark had found a new part-time janitorial job, and for the most part, he said, he was able to do what was required of him as long as he did not tax himself. The disease continued to exacerbate periodically—he would suffer blurring in one or both eyes, his right side would become numb, his arms horribly weak. Short courses of prednisone continued to lessen his symptoms during the exacerbations, and he would phone Ferrier for a prescription at the periodic onset of new symptoms. We continued to see Mark on occasion, walking home with an armload of groceries. Ferrier would honk the car horn and Mark would strut for a few steps to show him how well he was doing.

Richard Randolph's experiment with smoking less marijuana was short-lived. As far as Richard was concerned, it did not aggravate his tremor or lack of coordination, and he believed it had an important therapeutic effect on how he coped with MS. Ferrier had told Richard he would leave the administration of that particular medication to him, and his wife, Julie, at last had acquiesced to his heavy use. At least when Richard was stoned, his depression seemed to lift a bit. Julie's own, still-untreated psychological trauma—spawned by having to care for a husband who could not walk or feed himself, who could not manage his own wastes or make his speech intelligible—remained untreated. Each time she rolled Richard into Ferrier's office, her anger and frustration were more indelibly etched on her face.

Joan Billitson, the MS patient whose sons Ferrier had spoken to a year before, had recently had surgery. In a last-ditch effort to relieve the severe spasticity and pain in her legs, Ferrier had referred Joan to a neurosurgeon down in the city who had surgically transsected seven pairs of sensory nerve roots in her spinal cord. The procedure was a remarkable success. Joan's legs, always absent of sensation, were now malleable and relaxed. Their terrible frozen contortions were gone and she was out of pain. On their first return visit to Ferrier following the surgery, Joan's husband, Ted, said, "As far as we're concerned, it's a medical miracle." Joan smiled; she was not quite as exuberant. "Well, it's a wonderful relief, at least," she said. Ferrier asked about the boys. "Doing fine," said Ted. "Typical teenagers. Everything's got to be way-out or they're not interested in it, but they're good kids." Joan amended what Ted had said. "They're *very* good kids," she said, her spirits bright.

I did not see Mrs. Pembroke again, though I had hoped to. I had often meant to phone her, to inquire about how she was doing and to thank her again for her hospitality on the day she served us tea, but I never did. Ferrier continued to see her once a month or so, each time making minor adjustments in her levels of medication to try to quiet her constant tremor. Ferrier told me that she always looked splendid when she came to his office. She was invariably charming and witty, and she always told him how terrible her life had become.

Yoshi Kurumata returned briefly from Japan at the end of September to visit friends. He made an appointment with Ferrier and came to the office accompanied by Dr. Fukuda. He brought with him a CAT scan from Japan, which revealed the infarct in his left temporal and parietal lobes, its size diminished in the six months since his stroke. Yoshi's arms and legs virtually had returned to full strength, but he said his right hand still seemed clumsy. Dr. Fukuda told Ferrier that Yoshi seemed to comprehend 100 percent of the Japanese he heard; his ability to express himself was perhaps 75 percent of what it once had been. What little English

Yoshi had retained following the accident had further waned during his months at home. Yoshi was now working for his father's company, but in a year or two he hoped to return to the United States to study English again. He told Ferrier, through Dr. Fukuda's translation, that he no longer planned to be a politician. Because of his disabilities, which he still perceived to be significant, he said, he thought it would be more advisable to go into business.

Marilyn Roybal, the patient from the pain control center who had had to be detoxified, completed a four-week program at the center following her release from the hospital. In their discharge summary, the center staff wrote that Marilyn had been highly motivated for treatment and was very cooperative. They reported dramatic improvements in her posture, gait, strength, mobility, and endurance, and her pain seemed to vanish as she gained self-confidence. A week before her program ended, however, Marilyn became agitated and very unhappy, expressing her fears about what she would encounter when she returned home. She asked repeatedly if somehow she could stay at the center, telling the staff that because of her husband's lack of support, she was sure she would lose what she had gained. Marilyn could not stay at the center indefinitely, but she was encouraged to return one night each week for an outpatient support group meeting. She attended one meeting following her discharge at the end of June, then never returned to the center again.

Lisa Benedict, the migraine patient who lived in the mountains, missed an appointment in September—perhaps her headaches were much improved, and I hoped her home life was better as well. She made another appointment in early November, but for a second time she did not arrive on the day when she was due.

Wendy Stetham had returned from the epilepsy center in California in partial vindication—she had had one seizure while she was there, off all medication, that was unmistakably epileptic. But four other seizures were accompanied by absolutely no abnormal brain-wave activity, despite the disturbing and unusual fact that during one of the pseudoseizures she had again dislocated her shoulder. Ferrier would continue to treat Wendy for a true seizure disorder, one that probably was already fairly well controlled, and, with the concurrence of Katherine Braverman, Wendy's social worker, he referred Wendy to a psychiatrist who would begin the long process of discerning why her psyche was so prone to produce imitative seizures at times when her brain had clearly not caught fire.

Mrs. Bridgewater remained in glorious good health following the removal of her meningioma, she told Ferrier when she returned for a checkup. She would remain on a low, postoperative dosage of Tegretol for a year, but Ferrier told her the likelihood of her having a seizure now seemed very small. Her daughter, who accompanied her, said her mother was her old self again. "Sorry to say," said Mrs. Bridgewater with a wink.

Wayne Byers, his tumors still inside his skull, died on October 12. He had not left the hospital again. The newspaper he had worked for ran a photograph of him at his desk, smiling, his tie loosened and his sleeves rolled up. The obituary said he had passed away following a short illness.

Sal Maldonado, now in a nursing home, his brain stem destroyed by hemorrhage, remained unchanged. He could still raise and lower his eyes, but nothing more. He was still locked inside himself.

And what of this Doctor Ferrier? What had become of him by the time my visits stopped? At the end of the year, he still survived on little sleep. He still astounded me with his maniac energy; he still screamed about how his schedule wore him down. At the end of the year, Ferrier still drove his car like a madman; he would still forget by five o'clock the dinner plans he had made at three. He could still be exuberantly chauvinistic about his native mountains, yet he seldom found time to get out of town. He continued to savor sudden infatuations and long, anguished affairs, yet he still yearned to be completely and permanently in love. And he still swore that he would not be a neurologist forever.

He was serious, I knew. He said he could not imagine that clinical medicine could hold his interest until he was an old man. For now, he still enjoyed the challenges of diagnosis and the satisfactions of occasional cures. He still enjoyed his comradeship with physicians and his intense emotional ties with patients in crisis. He loved, he said, to walk into hushed, low-lit hospitals in the middle of the night. But there would be a time, he continued to claim, when he would choose to give it up.

I had no particular reason to doubt him, yet it was hard for me to imagine that in ten years or so, Ferrier would be painting canvases in seclusion or playing saxophone in smoky clubs. No, he agreed, neither possibility was likely. But he might be tempted to return to school, he said, to study architecture or art history again, perhaps astronomy. Or, he would say, his eyes full of mischief, he might simply retire for a year or two, then at last get an honest job.

My best guess was that in a decade's time—or perhaps a little longer, say, at the turn of the century—Ferrier would still be reading EEGs, the tracings now on high-resolution video screens. By then, he would routinely be examining MRI films, finding tumors and infarcts that were nearly microscopic. He would be prescribing remarkably sensitive drugs that controlled Parkinson's disease with only the most mild side effects, countering pain with site-specific analgesics, checking the growth of tumors with drugs that spared healthy tissues, perhaps even administering the first drugs that effectively slowed the onslaught of Alzheimer's disease.

It was only a hunch, but I suspected that by then Ferrier would still be choosing the fat, small-print neurology journals for his bedside reading matter. His schedule would still send him into frenzies, but he would still be entranced by his patients' stories. When the calls came in the middle of the night, he would still make trips to the hospitals without begrudging them, and he would be strangely happy as he stole through the quiet corridors.

On the afternoon that Ferrier drove me to the airport, my final visit finished, we stopped en route at the nursing home where Peter Koppel lived. He had called Ferrier the day before, hoping he could chat with him soon, and I was glad to be able to see him once again.

This time we met him in his room, the curtains open to the snow on the sloping lawn, his bed tidily made, Mr. Koppel sitting in a wheelchair beside it. He still wore his turquoise choker, which hung over the collar of a white T-shirt. His hair was shorter than it had been four months before, and his hands, now completely motionless, had been laid across his lap. His voice had become very nasal, his words now heavily slurred and hard to understand. He greeted us with a smile, then quickly proceeded to tell Ferrier what had been concerning him.

His disease seemed to be progressing very rapidly, he said. He had hoped the ALS would take him before Christmas, but that now seemed unlikely. Yet his death seemed imminent enough that he had begun to think about it, to wonder whether he could communicate if he lost his speech entirely, to wonder whether pain or delirium would accompany the pneumonia he was likely to acquire. He still did not want his life to be prolonged in any way, but he said he hoped he could be conscious and comfortable at the end.

"I'm not a doctor," Mr. Koppel said to Ferrier, his words slow and awkward. "I don't know what to expect. I guess I'm actually a little afraid, not of what will follow death, but you know, of those few minutes when it happens."

Ferrier sat on Peter Koppel's bed, his elbows on his knees. He explained to him that his disease was indeed taking a quick course and said it was very unlikely that he would lose all his speech before he died of infection. "You know, most people actually expire because of lung infections—people who die of cancer or old age or whatever. And it's a good, calm way to go. There is little, if any, pain, I promise you that, and if you do have some pain, I'll take care of it. What will happen is that with pneumonia, one day a fever will put you into a slight coma, and after a while you'll just slip away."

"Okay," said Mr. Koppel after he had been silent for a moment. "This isn't much, being stuck here, not able to move a damn muscle, but I'd . . . I'd like to actually *live*, you know, as long as I'm alive, if I can. Right up to the end."

"And you will," Ferrier said, reaching out to touch his forearm.

As I listened, I thought about what a remarkable business my friend was in, this practice of medicine, this craft of caring in which he sometimes simply helped his patients prepare to die. I had watched him for a year, yet I could still be moved by what he and his patients sometimes had to do and say. And at that moment, listening to this solemn conversation, I was surprised that I somehow seemed to have more in common with a dying man forty years my senior than with the young physician who sat across from him and held his hand. Like Peter Koppel, I was not a doctor; like him, I wanted to be alive as long as I lived, and I, too, sometimes was afraid.

Index